# Consciousness

# Consciousness

*Essays from a Higher-Order Perspective*

PETER CARRUTHERS

*Professor and Chair, Department of Philosophy,*
*University of Maryland*

CLARENDON PRESS · OXFORD

# OXFORD

UNIVERSITY PRESS

Great Clarendon Street, Oxford OX2 6DP

Oxford University Press is a department of the University of Oxford.
It furthers the University's objective of excellence in research, scholarship,
and education by publishing worldwide in

Oxford New York

Auckland Cape Town Dar es Salaam Hong Kong Karachi
Kuala Lumpur Madrid Melbourne Mexico City Nairobi
New Delhi Shanghai Taipei Toronto

With offices in

Argentina Austria Brazil Chile Czech Republic France Greece
Guatemala Hungary Italy Japan Poland Portugal Singapore
South Korea Switzerland Thailand Turkey Ukraine Vietnam

Oxford is a registered trade mark of Oxford University Press
in the UK and in certain other countries

Published in the United States
by Oxford University Press Inc., New York

British Library Cataloguing in Publication Data

Data available

Library of Congress Cataloging in Publication Data

Data available

Typeset by Newgen Imaging Systems (P) Ltd., Chennai, India
Printed in Great Britain
on acid-free paper by
Biddles Ltd., King's Lynn, Norfolk

ISBN 0-19-927735-4    978-0-19-927735-3
ISBN 0-19-927736-2 (Pbk.)    978-0-19-927736-0 (Pbk.)

1 3 5 7 9 10 8 6 4 2

*For my brother Ian*

*without whose example I would never have thought to become a thinker*

# PREFACE AND ACKNOWLEDGEMENTS

The present book collects together and revises ten of my previously published essays on consciousness, preceded by a newly written introduction, and containing a newly written chapter on the explanatory advantages of my approach. Most of the essays are quite recent. Three, however, pre-date my 2000 book, *Phenomenal Consciousness: A Naturalistic Theory*. (These are Chapters 3, 7, and 9.) They are reproduced here, both for their intrinsic interest, and because there isn't really much overlap with the writing in that earlier book. Taken together, the essays in the present volume significantly extend, modify, elaborate, and discuss the implications of the theory of consciousness expounded in my 2000 book.

Since the essays in the present volume were originally intended to stand alone, and to be read independently, there is sometimes some overlap in content amongst them. (Many of them contain a couple-of-pages sketch of the dispositional higher-order thought theory that I espouse, for example.) I have made no attempt to eradicate these overlaps, since some readers may wish just to read a chapter here and there, rather than to work through the book from cover to cover. But readers who *do* adopt the latter strategy may want to do a little judicious skimming whenever it seems to them to be appropriate.

Each of the previously published essays has been revised for style. I have also corrected minor errors, and minor clarifications, elaborations, and cross-references have been inserted. Some of the essays have been revised more significantly for content. Wherever this is so, I draw the reader's attention to it in a footnote.

I have stripped out my acknowledgements of help and criticism received from all of the previously published papers. Since help received on one essay may often have ramified through others, but in a way that didn't call for explicit thanks, it seems more appropriate to list all of my acknowledgements here. I am therefore grateful for the advice and/or penetrating criticisms of the following colleagues: Colin Allen, David Archard, Murat Aydede, George Botterill, Marc Bracke, Jeffrey Bub, David Chalmers, Ken Cheng, Lindley Darden, Daniel Dennett, Anthony Dickinson, Zoltan Dienes, Fred Dretske, Susan Dwyer, Keith Frankish, Mathias Frisch, Rocco Gennaro, Susan Granger, Robert Heeger, Christopher Hookway, Frank Jackson, David Jehle, Richard Joyce, Rosanna Keefe, Simon Kirchin, Robert Kirk, Uriah Kriegel, Stephen Laurence, Robert Lurz, Bill Lycan, Jessica Pfeifer, Paul Pietroski, Georges Rey, Mark Sacks, Adam Shriver, Robert Stern, Scott Sturgeon, Mike Tetzlaff, Michael Tye, Carol Voeller, Leif Wenar, Tim Williamson, and Jo Wolff.

I am also grateful to the following for commenting publicly on my work, either in the symposium targeted on Chapter 3 of the present volume that was published in *Psyche*, volumes 4–6; or in the on-line book symposium on my 2000 book, published at www.swif.uniba.it/lei/mind/; or in the 'Author meets critics' symposium held at the Central Division meeting of the American Philosophical Association in Chicago in April 2004: Colin Allen, José Bermúdez, Derek Browne, Gordon Burghardt, Paola Cavalieri, Fred Dretske, Mark Krause, Joseph Levine, Robert Lurz, William Lycan, Michael Lyvers, Brian McLaughlin, Harlan Miller, William Robinson, Eric Saidel, William Seager, Larry Shapiro, and Josh Weisberg.

Finally, I am grateful to the editors and publishers of the volumes listed below for permission to reproduce the articles/chapters that they first published.

Chapter 2: 'Reductive Explanation and the "Explanatory Gap" ' *Canadian Journal of Philosophy*, 34 (2004), 153–73. University of Calgary Press.

Chapter 3: 'Natural Theories of Consciousness' *European Journal of Philosophy*, 6 (1998), 203–22. London: Blackwell. (Some of the material in the new concluding section of this chapter is drawn from: Replies to critics: explaining subjectivity. *Psyche* 6 (2000). <http://psyche.cs.monash. edu.au/v6/>)

Chapter 4: 'HOP over FOR, HOT Theory', in R. Gennaro (ed.), *Higher Order Theories of Consciousness*. Philadelphia: John Benjamins, 2004, 115–35.

Chapter 5: 'Phenomenal Concepts and Higher-Order Experiences' *Philosophy and Phenomenological Research*, 67 (2004), 316–36. International Phenomenological Society.

Chapter 7: 'Conscious Thinking: Language or Elimination?' *Mind and Language*, 13 (1998), 323–42. London: Blackwell.

Chapter 8: 'Conscious Experience versus Conscious Thought', in U. Kriegel and K. Williford (eds.), *Consciousness and Self-Reference*. Cambridge, Mass.: MIT Press, 2005.

Chapter 9: 'Sympathy and Subjectivity' *Australasian Journal of Philosophy*, 77 (1999), 465–82. Oxford: Oxford University Press.

Chapter 10: 'Suffering without Subjectivity' *Philosophical Studies*, 121 (2004), 99–125. London: Springer-Verlag.

Chapter 11: 'Why the Question of Animal Consciousness Might not Matter Very Much', *Philosophical Psychology*, 18 (2005). London: Routledge.

Chapter 12: 'On Being Simple Minded' *American Philosophical Quarterly*, 41 (2004), 205–20. University of Illinois Press.

# CONTENTS

# LIST OF FIGURES

# CHAPTER 1

# Introduction

This book is a collection of essays about consciousness (focusing mostly on a particular sort of reductive explanation of phenomenal consciousness and its implications), together with surrounding issues. Amongst the latter are included the nature of reductive explanation in general; the nature of conscious thought and the plausibility of some form of eliminativism about conscious thought (while retaining realism about phenomenal consciousness); the appropriateness of sympathy for creatures whose mental states aren't phenomenally conscious ones; and the psychological continuities and similarities that exist between minds that lack phenomenally conscious mental states and minds that possess them. I shall conclude this chapter by saying just a few words about each of the remaining eleven essays, drawing out connections between them. But first I shall elaborate some background assumptions, and situate the theory that I espouse within a wider context and range of alternatives.

## 1. KINDS OF CONSCIOUSNESS: THE EXPLANATORY OPTIONS

A number of different kinds of consciousness can be distinguished. These are discussed in the opening pages of Chapter 3. Here I shall introduce them very briskly, in order to say something about the explanatory relations that might be thought to exist amongst them. This will help to locate the project of this book, as well as that of Carruthers (2000).

The three distinctions I want briefly to focus on are between *creature* consciousness and two different forms of *state* consciousness—namely, *phenomenal* consciousness and *access* consciousness. On the one hand we can say that a *creature* is conscious, either *simpliciter* (awake as opposed to asleep), or conscious *of* some object or property in its environment (or body). On the other hand we can say that a *mental state* of a creature is a conscious one—the creature is undergoing a conscious experience, or entertaining a conscious thought, for example.

Which, if either, of these two kinds of consciousness is explanatorily prior? Dretske (1995) maintains that state-consciousness is to be explained in terms of creature-consciousness. To say that a mental *state* is conscious is just to say that it is a state by virtue of which *the creature* is conscious of something. So to say that my perception of a rose is conscious, is just to say that *I* am conscious of the rose by virtue of perceiving it. But this order of explanation is problematic, given that there is a real distinction between conscious and *non*-conscious mental states. This distinction is elaborated in a number of the chapters that follow (most fully in Chapters 4 and 11). Here I propose just to assume, and to work with, the 'two visual systems' hypothesis of Milner and Goodale (1995).

According to this hypothesis, humans (and other mammals) possess one visual system in the parietal lobes concerned with the on-line guidance of movement, and a distinct visual system in the temporal lobes concerned with conceptualization, memory formation, and action planning. The parietal system is fast, has a memory window of just two seconds, uses body and limb-centered spatial coordinates, and has outputs that aren't conscious ones. In contrast, the temporal system is slower, gives rise to medium and long-term memories, uses allocentric spatial coordinates, and has outputs that are characteristically conscious (at least in humans).

Now consider the blindsighted chimpanzee Helen (Humphrey, 1986), who had the whole of her primary visual cortical area V1 surgically removed, and so who had no inputs to the temporal lobe system (while retaining inputs, via an alternate subcortical route, to the parietal system). When she bent down to neatly pick up a seed from the floor between thumb and forefinger, or when she was able to pluck a fly out of the air with her hand as it flew past her, was she *creature*-conscious of the objects in question? There is no non-question-begging reason to deny it. Before we knew of the existence of the two visual systems, we would have taken the smooth and directed character of her behavior as conclusive warrant for saying that she *saw* the seed, and the fly, and hence that she was creature-conscious of her environment.[1] In which case, by Dretske's (1995) account, we would have to say that the perceptual states in virtue of which she is creature conscious of these things are conscious ones. But of course they aren't. And the natural way of *explaining* why they aren't is in terms of some sort of *access*-consciousness (see below). We might say, for example, that Helen's visual percepts aren't conscious because they don't underpin recognition of objects, nor guide her practical reasoning.

I therefore think that we shouldn't seek to explain state consciousness in terms of creature consciousness. But what about the converse? Should we explain creature consciousness in terms of state consciousness? We could certainly carve out and explain *a* notion of creature consciousness in terms of state consciousness. We could say, for example, that a creature is conscious of some

---

[1] Even when we learn that Helen was incapable of identifying the seed *as* a seed or the fly *as* a fly until she put them into her mouth, we would still be inclined to say that she saw *something* small on the floor, or moving past through the air in front of her.

object or event if and only if the creature enjoys a conscious mental state concerning that object or event. But this doesn't correspond very well to our pre-theoretic notion of creature consciousness. For as we have just seen, we would find it entirely natural to say of Helen that she is conscious of the fly as it moves through the air (at least, *qua* small moving object, if not *qua* fly). And nor is it clear that the notion thus defined would serve any interesting theoretical or explanatory role.

My own view, then, is that creature consciousness and state consciousness are explanatorily independent of one another. Neither should be explained directly in terms of the other. Since creatures can perceive things without the perceptual states in virtue of which they perceive them being conscious, we can't reduce state consciousness to creature consciousness. But then nor, by the same token, should we want to reduce creature consciousness to state consciousness—we certainly shouldn't say that a creature is conscious of (i.e. perceives) something just in case it undergoes an appropriate mental state that is conscious, for example.

It ought to be plain that the theoretically challenging and interesting notion is that of *state* consciousness. Here we can distinguish two basic varieties—*phenomenal* consciousness, and *access* consciousness. Mental states are phenomenally conscious when it is *like* something to undergo them, when they have a distinctive subjective aspect, or when they have *feel*. In contrast, mental states are access conscious when they are accessible to, or are having an impact upon, other systems within the agent (e.g. belief-forming systems, or planning systems, or higher-order thought systems, or linguistic reporting systems—it is obvious that access consciousness comes in a wide range of different varieties depending on which 'other systems' are specified).

Some people think that some forms of access consciousness are to be explained in terms of phenomenal consciousness. They think that it is *because* a state is phenomenally conscious that the subject is able to form immediate higher-order thoughts about it, for example. And many such people believe that phenomenal consciousness is either irreducible, or at any rate can't be reductively explained in terms of any sort of access consciousness.[2] Such people will be believers in *qualia* in the strong sense. (Some writers use 'qualia' as just a notational equivalent of 'phenomenal consciousness'.) That is, they will think that phenomenally conscious states possess intrinsic, non-relational, non-intentional properties that constitute the *feels* of those states. And these properties can't be reduced to any form of *access*. One option, then, is that they won't be reductively explicable at all, and will have to

---

[2] I say just 'many such people' here (rather than 'all') because it is possible to combine a belief that the relevant higher-order thoughts are caused *because* the subject is undergoing an experience that is phenomenally conscious, with a reductive account of phenomenal consciousness in terms of higher-order thought. This point will become clear in the final section of Ch. 3.

remain as a scientific mystery.[3] Or they will have to be explicable in physical or neurological terms, rather than in functional/intentional ones (Block, 1995).

Other people think that phenomenal consciousness can be reduced to some or other form of access consciousness. There are a wide variety of views here, depending on the form of 'access' that gets chosen. Thus for Tye (1995) and Baars (1997) it is accessibility to belief-forming and/or practical reasoning systems that renders a state phenomenally conscious. For Armstrong (1984) and Lycan (1996) it is accessibility to a faculty of 'inner sense', yielding a perception of that state as such. For Rosenthal (1997) and Carruthers (2000) it is accessibility (in different ways) to higher-order thought. And for Dennett (1991) it is accessibility to higher-order linguistic report.

I shall make some remarks about my own view in section 3 below. But first I want to say something about the main contrast noted here, between physicalist approaches to phenomenal consciousness, on the one hand, and functionalist/ representationalist ones, on the other.

## 2. REPRESENTATIONALISM VERSUS PHYSICALISM

One background assumption made in this book (and defended briefly in passing in Chapter 2) is that the right place to look for a reductive theory of phenomenal consciousness lies in some combination of the distinctive functional role and/or the distinctive sort of intentional content possessed by the experiential states in question. Broadly speaking, then, I assume that some sort of *functionalism* will deliver the correct explanation of phenomenal consciousness.

Many philosophers and cognitive scientists think, in contrast, that the right place to look for an explanation of phenomenal consciousness lies in some kind of physical identity, and that we ought to focus primarily on searching for the neural correlates of consciousness (Crick and Koch, 1990; Block, 1995). Some think this because they believe that the main contrast is with ontological dualism about consciousness, and think that the explanatory problem is to establish the truth of physicalism. (I suspect that something like this lies behind the position of Crick and Koch, for example; see Crick, 1994.) Others believe it because they think that there are knock-down arguments against functionalism (Block, 1978). Let me comment briefly on each of these motivations in turn.

We need to distinguish between physicalism as an ontological thesis (the denial of dualism), and physicalism as a purported reductive explanation of

---

[3] In consequence I (like a number of other writers) call those who adopt such a position 'mysterians'. Mysterian philosophers include McGinn (1991) and Chalmers (1996).

phenomenal consciousness. These aren't the same. Just about everyone now working in this area is an ontological physicalist, with the exception of Chalmers (1996) and perhaps a few others. But some of these physicalists don't believe that phenomenal consciousness admits of reductive *explanation* at all (McGinn, 1991; Levine, 2000). And many others of us think that the right terms in which to proffer such an explanation are functional and/or intentional, rather than physical or neurological (Armstrong, 1968, 1984; Dennett, 1978a, 1991; Rosenthal, 1986, 1993; Lycan, 1987, 1996; Baars, 1988, 1997; Flanagan, 1992; Kirk, 1994; Dretske, 1995; Tye, 1995, 2000; Carruthers, 1996, 2000; Gennaro, 1996; Nelkin, 1996; Papineau, 2002).

Supposing that we knew of an identity between a certain type of neural event in the brain and a particular type of phenomenally conscious experience: would the former really *explain* the latter? It looks as if the most that would be explained would be the distinctive time-course of the experience. (And even this is doubtful when we remember that time, like everything else, is likely to be *represented* in the brain, rather than given by time of represent*ing*; see Dennett and Kinsbourne, 1992.) But it would remain mysterious why that event should have the subjective feel of an experience of green rather than the feel of an experience of blue, for example, or rather than no feel at all. Nor would it have been explained why people should be tempted to say that the experience possesses intrinsic non-relational properties that are directly available to introspection (*qualia*, in the strong sense). And so on. (The various *desiderata* for a successful theory of phenomenal consciousness are sketched in Chapters 2, 4, and 8, and discussed at greater length in Chapter 6.)

Block and Stalnaker (1999) reply that these sorts of objections are inappropriate, because identities neither are, nor admit of, explanation. (See also Papineau, 2002, for a similar argument.) Rather, they are epistemically *brute*. Consider the identity of water with $H_2O$. It makes no sense to ask: *why* is water $H_2O$? For all we can really say in reply—vacuously—is that that's what water *is*. (Of course we can ask: why do we *believe* that water is $H_2O$? This *will* admit of a substantive answer. But then it is another sort of question entirely.) Nor can $H_2O$ explain *water*. Indeed, it is unclear what it would mean to 'explain water'. Likewise, then, with phenomenal consciousness. If an experience of red is identical with a neural event of type $N$, then it will make no sense to ask: *why* does $N$ have the phenomenal feel of an experience of red? And nor will we be able to *explain* the phenomenal feel of an experience of red in terms of the occurrence of $N$.

What these points overlook, however, is that we generally *can* use facts about the reducing property in an identity in order to explain facts about the reduced property, even if the identity itself doesn't admit of, nor count as, an explanation. We can use facts about $H_2O$ and its properties, for example, in explaining why water boils at 100 °C, why it is such an effective solvent, and so on. Indeed, if we *couldn't* give explanations of this general sort, then it is hard to imagine that we would continue to accept the reduction of water to $H_2O$.[4] Likewise, then, with phenomenal consciousness: if physicalist theories of phenomenal consciousness were correct, then we ought to be able to use properties of the reducing event-type (neural event $N$, say) in order to explain some of the distinctive properties of the phenomenally conscious event. But it is hard to get any sort of handle on how this might go.

My own view is that in seeking to explain phenomenal consciousness in terms of properties of neural events in the brain we would be trying to leap over too many explanatory levels at once. (It would be rather as if we tried to seek an explanation of cell metabolism in terms of quantum mechanics.) It is now a familiar idea in the philosophy of science that there are *levels* of phenomena in nature, with each level being realized in the one below it, and with each level having its characteristic properties and processes explicable in terms of the one below it. (So the laws of cell metabolism are explained by those of organic chemistry, which are in turn explained by molecular chemistry, which is explained by atomic physics, and so on.) Seen in this light, then what we should expect is that phenomenal consciousness will be reductively explicable in terms of intentional contents and causal-role psychology, if it is explicable at all. For almost everyone accepts that some forms of the latter can exist in the absence of phenomenal consciousness, as well as being explanatorily more fundamental than phenomenal consciousness.

In endorsing some sort of functional/intentional account of consciousness, of course I have to give up on the claim that consciousness might somehow be necessarily biological in nature. For most people accept that causal roles and intentional contents are multiply realizable, and might in principle be realized in a non-biological computer. So I will have to allow—to put it bluntly—that phenomenal consciousness needn't be *squishy*. But I don't see this as any sort of problem. Although in popular culture it is often assumed that androids and other

---

[4] Might the role-filling model of reduction provided by Jackson (1998) provide a counter-example to this claim? According to Jackson, reduction of a property like *being water* proceeds like this: first we build an account of the *water role*, constructed by listing all the various platitudes about water (that it is a clear colorless liquid, that it boils at 100 °C, that it is a good solvent, that it is found in lakes and rivers, and so on); then we discover that it is actually $H_2O$ that fills those roles; and hence we come to accept that water is $H_2O$. If such a model is correct, then we can accept the identity of water and $H_2O$ without yet reductively explaining any of the properties of the former in terms of the latter. But we are, surely, nevertheless committed to the *possibility* of such explanations. If we think that it *is* $H_2O$ that fills the water role, then don't we think that it must be possible to explain the various properties constitutive of that role in terms of properties of $H_2O$? Aren't we committed to the idea that it must be possible to explain why water boils at 100 °C, for example, in terms of properties of $H_2O$? If the answer to these questions is positive, as I believe, then the point made in the text stands: postulating an identity between phenomenal consciousness and some set of neurological properties wouldn't absolve us from providing a reductive explanation of the distinctive properties of the former in terms of properties of the latter. But it is very hard to see how any such explanation would go.

non-biological agents would have to lack *feelings*, there is no reason to believe that this is anything other than a prejudice.

Let me turn, now, to the question whether there are any knock-down arguments *against* functional/intentional accounts of phenomenal consciousness. Two sorts of example are often adduced. One involves causal-role isomorphs of ourselves, where we have a powerful intuition that phenomenal consciousness would be absent. (Block's 1978 example comes to mind, in which the people who form the population of China simulate the causal interactions of the neurons in a human brain, creating a causal isomorph of a person.) Another involves causal *and* intentional isomorphs of a normal person, where we have the powerful intuition that phenomenal consciousness *could* be absent. (Think here of the zombies discussed at length by Chalmers, 1996.)

The first sort of counter-example can be handled in one of two ways. One option would be to say that it is far from clear that the system in question even enjoys mental states with intentional content; in which case it is no threat to a theory that seeks to reduce phenomenal consciousness to some suitable combination of causal roles and intentional contents. For many of those who have the intuition that the population of China would (as a collective, of course) lack feelings, are also apt to think that it would lack beliefs and goals as well. The other option would be to adopt the strategy made famous by Dennett (1991), denying that we can really imagine the details of the example in full enough detail to generate a reliable intuition. Perhaps our problem is just that of adequately envisaging what more than a thousand million people interacting in a set of highly complex, as-yet-to-be-specified ways, would be like.

The zombie-style counter-examples should be handled differently. For here the intuition is just that zombies are *possible*. And we should allow that they are, indeed, *conceptually* possible. Consistently with this, we can deny that they are metaphysically possible, on the grounds that having the right combination of causal roles and intentional contents is just what it *is* to be phenomenally conscious. (None of those who put forward a causal/intentional account of phenomenal consciousness intend that it should be construed as a *conceptual* truth, of course.) And we can appeal to the distinctive nature of our concepts for our own phenomenally conscious states in explaining how the zombie thought-experiments are always possible. (See Chapters 2 and 5.)

I have been painting with a very broad brush throughout this section, of course; and it is unlikely that these sketchy considerations would convince any of my opponents.[5] But that has not been my intention. Rather, my goal has been to say just enough to explain and motivate what will hereafter be taken as an

---

[5] For a somewhat more detailed discussion than I have had space to provide in this section, see my 2000, ch. 4.

*assumption* in the remaining chapters of this book: namely, that if a successful reductive explanation of phenomenal consciousness is to be found anywhere, it will be found in the broad area of functional/intentional accounts of experience.

## 3. CHARACTERIZING THE THEORY

My own reductive view about phenomenal consciousness is a form of representationalist, or intentionalist, one. I think that phenomenal consciousness consists in a certain sort of intentional content ('analog' or fine-grained) that is held in special-purpose functionally individuated memory store in such a way as to be available to a faculty of higher-order thought (HOT). And by virtue of such availability (combined with the truth of some or other form of consumer-semantic account of intentional content, according to which the content of a state depends partly on what the systems that 'consume' or make use of that state can do with it or infer from it), the states in question acquire *dual* intentional contents (both first-order and higher-order).

This account gets sketched, and has its virtues displayed, in a number of the chapters that follow (see especially Chapters 3, 4, 5, and 6). It also gets contrasted at some length with the various competing forms of representationalist theory, whether these be first-order (Dretske, 1995; Tye, 1995) or higher-order (e.g. the inner-sense theory of Lycan, 1996, or the actualist form of HOT theory proposed by Rosenthal, 1997). So here I shall confine myself to making a few elucidatory remarks.

One way of presenting my account is to see it as building on, but rendering higher-order, the 'global broadcasting' theory of Baars (1988, 1997). According to Baars, some of the perceptual and emotional states that are produced by our sensory faculties and body-monitoring systems are 'globally broadcast' to a wide range of other systems, giving rise to new beliefs and to new long-term memories, as well as informing various kinds of inferential process, including practical reasoning about what to do in the context of the perceived environment. And by virtue of being so broadcast, according to Baars, the states in question are phenomenally conscious ones. Other perceptual and emotional states, in contrast, may have other sorts of cognitive effect, such as the on-line guidance of movement (Milner and Goodale, 1995). My own view accepts this basic architecture of cognition, but claims that it is only because the consumer systems for the globally broadcast states include a 'mind-reading' faculty capable of higher-order thought about those very states, that they acquire their phenomenally conscious status. For it is by virtue of such (and only such) availability that those states acquire a dual analog content. The whole arrangement can be seen depicted in Figure 1.1, where 'C' is for 'Conscious' and 'N' is for 'Non-conscious'.

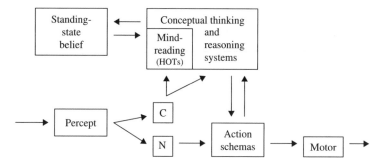

FIG 1.1 Dispositional higher-order thought theory.

It is the dual analog content that carries the main burden in reductively explaining the various distinguishing features of phenomenal consciousness, as we shall see.[6] So it is worth noting that the endorsement and modification of global broadcast theory is, strictly speaking, an optional extra. I opt for it because I think that it is true. But someone could in principle combine my dual-content theory with the belief that the states in question are available *only* to higher-order thought, not being globally available to other systems (perhaps believing that there is no such thing as global broadcasting of perceptual information). I think that the resulting architecture would be implausible, and that the evidence counts against it (see my 2000, ch. 11, and Chapters 11 and 12). But it remains a theoretical possibility.

In the same spirit, it is worth noting that even the element of availability to higher-order thought is, strictly speaking, an optional extra. My account purports to *explain* the existence of dual-analog-content states in terms of the availability of first-order analog states to a faculty of higher-order thought, combined with the truth of some form of consumer semantics. But someone could, in principle, endorse the dual-content element of the theory while rejecting this explanation. I have no idea, myself, how such an account might go, nor how one might otherwise render the existence of these dual-content states unmysterious. But again it is, I suppose, some sort of theoretical possibility.[7]

Not only do I endorse the cognitive architecture depicted in Figure 1.1, in fact, but I believe that it should be construed *realistically*. Specifically, the short-term

---

[6] It is for this reason that I am now inclined to use the term 'dual-content theory' to designate my own approach, rather than the term 'dispositional higher-order thought theory' which I have used in most of my previous publications. But this isn't, I should stress, a very substantial change of mind.

[7] A number of people have proposed that conscious states are states that possess both first-order and higher-order content, presenting *themselves* to us as well as presenting some aspect of the world or of the subject's own body. See, e.g. Kriegel, 2003. Indeed, Caston, 2002, argues that Aristotle, too, held such a view. My distinctive contribution has been to advance a naturalistic explanation of *how* one and the same state can come to possess both a first-order and a higher-order (self-referential) content.

memory store C is postulated to be a real system, with an internal structure and causal effects of its own. So my account doesn't just amount to saying that a phenomenally conscious state is one that *would* give rise to a higher-order thought in suitable circumstances. This is because there are problems with the latter, merely counterfactual, analysis. For intuitively it would seem that a percept might be such that it *would* give rise to a higher-order thought (if the subject were suitably prompted, for example) without being phenomenally conscious. So the non-conscious percepts that guide the activity of the absent-minded truck-driver (Armstrong, 1968) might be such that they *would* have given rise to higher-order thoughts if the driver had been paying the right sorts of attention. In my terms, this can be explained: there are percepts that aren't presently in the C-box (and so that aren't phenomenally conscious), but that nevertheless might have been *transferred to* the C-box if certain other things had been different.

In fact it is important to realize that the dual-content theory of phenomenal consciousness, as I develop it, is really just one of a much wider class of similar theories. For there are various choices to be made in the course of constructing a detailed version of the account, where making one of the alternative choices might still leave one with *a* form of dual-content theory. The reason why this point is important is that critics need to take care that their criticisms target dual-content theory as such, and not just one of the optional ways in which such an account might be developed.[8] Let me now run through a few of the possible alternatives.

Most of these alternatives (in addition to those already mentioned above) would result from different choices concerning the nature of intentional content. Thus I actually develop the theory by deploying a notion of *analog* (fine-grained) intentional content, which may nevertheless be partially conceptual (see my 2000, ch. 5). But one could, instead, deploy a notion of *non-conceptual* content, with subtle differences in the resulting theory. Indeed, one could even reject altogether the existence of a principled distinction between the contents of perception and the contents of belief (perhaps endorsing a belief-theory of perception; Armstrong, 1968; Dennett, 1991), while still maintaining that perceptual states acquire a *dual* intentional content by virtue of their availability to higher-order thought. And at least some of the benefits of dual-content theory would no doubt be preserved.

Likewise, although I don't make much play with this in the chapters that follow, I actually defend the viability of *narrow* intentional content, and argue that this is the appropriate notion to employ for purposes of psychological explanation generally (Botterill and Carruthers, 1999). And it is therefore a

---

[8] In effect, I am urging that dual-content theory should be accorded the same care and respect that I give to first-order representational (FOR) theories, which can similarly come in a wide variety of somewhat different forms (more than are currently endorsed in the literature, anyway). See my 2000, ch. 5, and Chapter 3 below.

notion of narrowly individuated analog content that gets put to work in my preferred development of the dual-content theory of consciousness (Carruthers, 2000). But obviously the theory could be worked out differently, deploying a properly-semantic, widely individuated account of the intentional contents of perception and thought.

Moreover, although I actually tend to explain the consumer-semantic aspect of dual-content theory using a form of inferential-role semantics (e.g. Peacocke, 1992), one could instead use some kind of teleosemantics (e.g. Millikan, 1984). I use the former because I think that it is intrinsically more plausible (Botterill and Carruthers, 1999), but it should be admitted that the choice of the latter might bring certain advantages. (I owe this point to Clegg, 2002.) Let me briefly elaborate.

As I have often acknowledged (and as will loom large in Chapters 9, 10, and 11 below), if dual-content theory is developed in tandem with a consumer-semantic story involving inferential-role semantics, then it is unlikely that the perceptual states of animals, infants, or severely autistic people will have the requisite dual contents. And they will fail to be phenomenally conscious as a result. For it is unlikely that members of any of these groups are capable of making the kinds of higher-order judgments required. But on a teleosemantic account, the experiences of infants and autistic people, at any rate, may be different. For their perceptual states will have, *inter alia*, the *function* of making their contents available to higher-order thought (even if the individuals in question aren't capable of such thought). So if content is individuated by function (as teleosemantics would have it) rather than by existing capacities to draw inferences (as inferential-role semantics would have it), then the perceptual states of infants and autistic people may turn out to have the dual contents required for phenomenal consciousness after all.

Another choice-point concerns the question of *which* inferences contribute to the content of a perceptual state. As is familiar, inferential-role semantics can be developed in a 'holistic' form, in which *all* inferences (no matter how remote) contribute to the content of a state (Fodor and Lepore, 1992; Block, 1993). I myself think that such views are implausible. And they would have counter-intuitive consequences when deployed in the context of dual-content theory. For not only would my perceptual state on looking at a red tomato have the contents *analog-red* and *analog-seeming-red,* as dual-content theory postulates, but it would also have the analog content *the-color-of-Aunt-Anne's-favorite-vegetable,* and many other such contents besides. I prefer, myself, to follow Peacocke (1992) in thinking that it is only the *immediate* inferences in which a state is apt to figure that contribute to its content. So it is the fact that we have *recognitional* (non-inferential or immediately inferential) concepts of experiences of red, and of others of our own perceptual states, that is crucial in conferring on them their dual content.

There is one final point that may be worth developing in some detail. This is that there are likely to remain a number of indeterminacies in dual-content theory, resulting from open questions in the underlying theory of intentional content. In a way, this point ought already to be obvious from the preceding paragraphs. But let me now expand on it somewhat differently, via consideration of one of a range of alleged counter-examples to my dispositional higher-order thought account.[9]

The counter-example is best developed in stages. First, we can envisage what we might call a 'neural meddler', which would interfere in someone's brain-processes in such a way as to block the availability of first-order perceptual contents to higher-order thought. Second, we can imagine that our understanding of neural processing in the brain has advanced to such an extent that it is possible to predict in advance which first-order perceptual contents will actually become targeted by higher-order thought, and which will not. Then third, we can suppose that the neural meddler might be so arranged that it only blocks the availability to higher-order thought of those perceptual contents that aren't actually going to give rise to such thoughts anyway.

The upshot is that we can envisage two people—Bill and Peter, say—one of whom has such a modified neural meddler in his brain and the other of whom doesn't. They can be neurological 'twins' and enjoy identical neural histories, as well as undergoing identical sequences of first-order perceptual contents and of actual higher-order thoughts. But because many of Bill's first-order percepts are unavailable to higher-order thought (blocked by the neural meddler, which actually remains inoperative, remember), whereas the corresponding percepts in Peter's case remain so available, there will then be large differences between them in respect of phenomenal consciousness. Or so, at least, dual-content theory is supposed to entail. And this looks to be highly counter-intuitive.

What should an inferential-role semanticist say about this example? Does a device that blocks the normal inferential role of a state thereby deprive that state of its intentional content? The answer to this question isn't clear. Consider a propositional variant of the example: we invent a 'conjunctive-inference neural meddler'. This device can disable a subject's capacity to draw basic inferences from a conjunctive belief. Subjects in whom this device is operative will no longer be disposed to deduce either 'P' or 'Q' from beliefs of the form 'P & Q'— those inferences will be blocked. Even more elaborately, in line with the above example, we can imagine that the device only becomes operative in those cases where it can be predicted that neither the inference to 'P' nor the inference to 'Q' will actually be drawn anyway.

Supposing, then, that there is some sort of 'language of thought' (Fodor, 1978), we can ask: are the belief-like states that have the syntactic form 'P & Q' in these cases conjunctive ones or not? Do they still possess conjunctive intentional contents? I don't know the answer to this question. And I suspect that inferential-role

---

[9] The particular counter-example that I shall discuss I owe to Seager (2001).

semantics isn't yet well enough developed to fix a determinate answer. What the alleged counter-example we have been discussing provides, from this perspective, is an intriguing question whose answer will have to wait on future developments in semantic theory. But it isn't a question that raises any direct problem for dual-content theory, as such.

As is familiar from the history of science, it is possible for one property to be successfully reductively explained in terms of others, even though those others are, as yet, imperfectly understood. Heat in gasses was successfully reductively explained by statistical mechanics, even though in the early stages of the development of the latter, molecules of gas were assumed to be like little bouncing billiard balls, with no relevant differences in shape, elasticity, or internal structure. That, I claim, is the kind of position we are in now with respect to phenomenal consciousness. We have a successful reductive explanation of such consciousness in terms of form of intentional content (provided by dual-content theory), while much scientific work remains to be done to elucidate and explain the nature of intentional content in turn.

Some have claimed that phenomenal consciousness is the ultimate mystery, the 'final frontier' for science to conquer (Chalmers, 1996). I think, myself, that intentional content is the bigger mystery. The successes of a content-based scientific psychology provide us with good reasons for thinking that intentional contents really do form a part of the natural world, somehow. But while we have some inkling of how intentional contents can be realized in the physical structures of the human brain, and inklings of how intentional contents should be individuated, we are very far indeed from having a complete theory. In the case of phenomenal consciousness, in contrast, we may be pretty close to just that if the approach defended by Carruthers (2000) and within these pages is on the right lines.

## 4. THE ESSAYS IN THIS VOLUME

I shall now say just a few words about each of the chapters to come. I shall emphasize how the different chapters relate to one another, as well as to the main theory of phenomenal consciousness that I espouse (dual-content theory/dispositional higher-order thought theory).

Chapter 2, 'Reductive Explanation and the "Explanatory Gap" ', is about what it would take for phenomenal consciousness to be successfully reductively explained. 'Mysterian' philosophers like McGinn (1991), Chalmers (1996), and Levine (2000) have claimed that phenomenal consciousness *cannot* be explained, and that the existence of phenomenal consciousness in the natural world is, and must remain, a mystery. The chapter surveys a variety of models of reductive explanation in science generally, and points out that successful explanation can often include an element of *explaining away*. So we can admit that there are certain true judgments about phenomenal consciousness that cannot be directly explained (*viz.* those that involve purely recognitional judgements of experience, of the form, 'Here is one of *those* again'). But if at the same time we *can* explain many *other* true judgments about phenomenal consciousness, while also *explaining why* truths expressed using recognitional concepts don't admit of direct explanation, then in the end we can claim complete success. For we will have provided answers—direct or indirect—to all of the questions that puzzle us.

Chapter 3, 'Natural Theories of Consciousness', is the longest essay in the book, and the most heavily rewritten. It works its way through a variety of different accounts of phenomenal consciousness, looking at the strengths and weaknesses of each. At the heart of the chapter is an extended critical examination of first-order representational (FOR) theories, of the sort espoused by Dretske (1995) and Tye (1995, 2000), arguing that they are inferior to higher-order representational (HOR) accounts. The chapter acknowledges as a problem for HOR theories that they might withhold phenomenal consciousness from most other species of animal, but claims that this problem shouldn't be regarded as a serious obstacle to the acceptance of some such theory. (This issue is then treated extensively in Chapters 9 through 11.) Different versions of HOR theory are discussed, and my own account (dual-content theory, here called dispositional higher-order thought theory) is briefly elaborated and defended.

Chapter 4, 'HOP over FOR, HOT Theory', continues with some of the themes introduced in Chapter 3. It presents arguments against both first-order (FOR) theories and actualist higher-order thought (HOT) theory (of the sort espoused by Rosenthal, 1997), and argues for the superiority of higher-order perception (HOP) theories over each of them. But HOP theories come in two very different varieties. One is 'inner sense' theory (Armstrong, 1968; Lycan, 1996), according to which we have a set of inner sense-organs charged with scanning the outputs of our first-order senses to produce higher-order perceptions of our own experiential states. The other is my own dispositional form of HOT theory, according to which the availability of our first-order perceptions to a faculty of higher-order thought confers on those perceptual states a dual higher-order content (see section 3 above). I argue that this latter form of HOP theory is superior to inner-sense theory, and also defend it against the charge that it is vulnerable to the very same arguments that sink FOR theories and actualist HOT theory.

Chapter 5, 'Phenomenal Concepts and Higher-Order Experiences', again argues for the need to recognize higher-order perceptual experiences, and again briefly argues for the superiority of my own dispositional HOT version of higher-order perception (HOP) theory (now described as 'dual-content theory'). But this time the focus is different. There is an emerging consensus amongst naturalistically minded philosophers that the existence of purely recognitional concepts of experience (often called 'phenomenal concepts') is the key to blocking the zombie-style arguments of both dualist mysterians like Chalmers (1996) and physicalist mysterians like McGinn (1991) and Levine (2000). But I argue in Chapter 5 that a successful account of the possibility of such concepts requires acceptance of one or another form of higher-order perception theory.

Chapter 6 is entitled, 'Dual-Content Theory: the Explanatory Advantages'. From the welter of different arguments given over the previous three chapters, and also in Carruthers (2000), this chapter presents and develops the *main* argument, both against the most plausible version of first-order theory, and in support of my own dual-content account. The primary goal of the chapter is, in effect, to lay out the case for saying that dual-content theory (but not first-order theory) provides us with a successful reductive explanation of the various puzzling features of phenomenal consciousness.

Chapter 7, 'Conscious Thinking: Language or Elimination?', shifts the focus from conscious experience to conscious thought.[10] It develops a dilemma. Either the use of natural language sentences in 'inner speech' is constitutive of (certain kinds of) thinking, as opposed to being merely *expressive of* it. Or there may really be no such thing as conscious propositional thinking at all. While I make clear my preference for the first horn of this dilemma, and explain how such a claim could possibly be true, this isn't really defended in any depth, and the final choice is left to the reader. Nor does the chapter commit itself to any particular theory of conscious thinking, beyond defending the claim that, in order to count as conscious, a thought must give rise to the knowledge that we are entertaining it in a way that is neither inferential nor interpretative.

Chapter 8, 'Conscious Experience versus Conscious Thought', is also—but more directly—about conscious propositional thinking. It argues that the *desiderata* for theories of conscious experience and theories of conscious thought are distinct, and that conscious thoughts aren't intrinsically and necessarily *phenomenal* in the same way that conscious experiences are. The chapter shows how dispositional higher-order thought theory can be extended to account for conscious thinking.[11] And like the previous chapter, it explores how

---

[10] I should stress that although the positions argued for in this chapter and the one following *cohere* with my account of phenomenally conscious experience in various ways, they are strictly independent of it. So it would be possible for someone to accept my dual-content account of conscious experience while rejecting all that I say about conscious thinking, or vice versa.

[11] Since the explanatory demands are different, my account should probably be cast somewhat differently in the two domains. On the nature of phenomenal consciousness my view is best characterized as a form of *dual-analog-content theory*, distinguished by a particular account of how the higher-order analog contents come to exist. (Namely, because of the availability of the first-order analog contents to higher-order thought (HOT).) For it is the dual content that carries the main burden in explaining the various puzzling features of phenomenal consciousness. But on the nature of conscious thinking, it is better to emphasize the dispositional HOT aspect of the account. The claim is that conscious acts of thinking are just those that we immediately and non-inferentially know ourselves to be engaged in. (Here 'know' is to be read in its dispositional sense, according to which I may be said to know that 64,000,001 is larger than 64,000,000, even though I have never explicitly considered the question, on the grounds that I *would* immediately judge that the former number is larger if I *were* to consider the question.)

natural language might be both constitutive of, and necessary to the existence of, conscious propositional thought-contents. But at the same time a form of eliminativism about thought *modes* (believing versus desiring versus supposing, etc.) is endorsed, on the grounds that self-knowledge of such modes is always interpretative, and never immediate.

Chapter 9, 'Sympathy and Subjectivity', is the first of four chapters to focus on the mental lives of non-human animals. It argues that even if the mental states of most non-human animals are lacking in phenomenal consciousness (as my dispositional HOT theory probably implies), they can still be appropriate objects of sympathy and moral concern. The chapter makes the case for this conclusion by arguing that the most fundamental form of harm (of a sort that might warrant sympathy) is the first-order (non-phenomenal) frustration of desire. In which case, provided that animals are capable of desire (see Chapter 12) and of sometimes believing, of the objects desired, that they haven't been achieved, then sympathy for their situation can be entirely appropriate.

Chapter 10, 'Suffering without Subjectivity', takes up the same topic again— the appropriateness of sympathy for non-human animals—but argues for a similar conclusion in a very different way. The focus of the chapter is on forms of *suffering*, such as pain, grief, and emotional disappointment. It argues that these phenomena can be made perfectly good sense of in purely first-order (and hence, for me, non-phenomenal) terms. And it argues that the primary forms of suffering in the human case are first-order also. So although our pains and disappointments *are* phenomenally conscious, it isn't (or isn't primarily) by virtue of *being* phenomenally conscious that they cause us to suffer, I claim.

Chapter 11, 'Why the Question of Animal Consciousness Might not Matter Very Much', picks up the latter point—dubbing it 'the *in virtue of* illusion'—and extends it more broadly. The chapter argues that the behavior that we share with non-human animals can, and should, be explained in terms of the first-order, non-phenomenal, contents of our experiences. So although we do *have* phenomenally conscious experiences when we act, most of the time it isn't by virtue of their being phenomenally conscious that they have their role in causing our actions. In consequence, the fact that my dispositional higher-order thought theory of phenomenal consciousness might withhold such consciousness from most non-human animals should have a minimal impact on comparative psychology. The explanations for the behaviors that we have in common with animals can remain shared also, despite the differences in phenomenally conscious status.

Finally, Chapter 12, 'On Being Simple-Minded', argues that belief/desire psychology—and with it a form of first-order access consciousness—are very widely distributed in the animal kingdom, being shared even by navigating insects. Although the main topic of this chapter (unlike the others) isn't mental-state consciousness (of which phenomenal consciousness is one variety), it serves both to underscore the argument of the previous chapter, and to emphasize how wide is the phylogenetic distance separating mentality *per se* from phenomenally conscious mentality. On some views, these things are intimately connected. (Searle, 1992, for example, claims that there is no mental life without the possibility of phenomenal consciousness.) But on my view, they couldn't be further apart. We share the basic forms of our mental lives even with bees and ants. But we may be unique in the animal kingdom in possessing mental states that are phenomenally conscious.[12]

[12] I am grateful to Keith Frankish for critical comments on an early version of this chapter.

# CHAPTER 2

# Reductive Explanation and the 'Explanatory Gap'

Can phenomenal consciousness be given a reductive natural explanation? Exponents of an 'explanatory gap' between physical, functional and intentional facts, on the one hand, and the facts of phenomenal consciousness, on the other, argue that there are reasons of principle why phenomenal consciousness cannot be reductively explained (Jackson, 1982, 1986; Levine, 1983, 1993, 2001; McGinn, 1991; Sturgeon, 1994, 2000; Chalmers, 1996, 1999). Some of these writers claim that the existence of such a gap would warrant a belief in some form of ontological dualism (Jackson, 1982; Chalmers, 1996), whereas others argue that no such entailment holds (Levine, 1983; McGinn, 1991; Sturgeon, 1994). In the other main camp, there are people who argue that a reductive explanation of phenomenal consciousness is possible in principle (Block and Stalnaker, 1999), and yet others who claim, moreover, to have provided such an explanation in practice (Dennett, 1991; Dretske, 1995; Tye, 1995, 2000; Lycan, 1996; Carruthers, 2000.)

I shall have nothing to say about the ontological issue here (see Balog, 1999, for a recent critique of dualist arguments); nor shall I have a great deal to say about the success or otherwise of the various proposed reductive explanations. My focus will be on the explanatory gap itself—more specifically, on the question whether any such principled gap exists. I shall argue that it does not. The debate will revolve around the nature and demands of reductive explanation in general. And our focus will be on Chalmers and Jackson (2001) in particular— hereafter 'C&J'—as the clearest, best-articulated, case for an explanatory gap. While I shall not attempt to demonstrate this here, my view is that if the C&J argument can be undermined, then it will be a relatively straightforward matter to show that the other versions of the argument must fall similarly.

## 1. INTRODUCTION: THE EXPLANATORY GAP

C&J argue as follows:

1. In the case of all macroscopic phenomena $M$ not implicating phenomenal consciousness (and more generally, for all macroscopic phenomena $M$ with

the phenomenally conscious elements of $M$ bracketed off), there will be an a priori conditional of the form $(P \& T \& I) \supset M$—where $P$ is a complete description of all microphysical facts in the universe, $T$ is a 'That's all' clause intended to exclude the existence of anything not entailed by the physical facts, such as angels and non-physical ectoplasm, and $I$ specifies indexically where $I$ am in the world and when *now* is.

2. The existence of such a priori conditionals is required, if there are to be reductive explanations of the phenomena described on the right-hand sides of those conditionals.

3. So, if there are no a priori conditionals of the form $(P \& T \& I) \supset C$, where $C$ describes some phenomenally conscious fact or event, then it follows that phenomenal consciousness isn't reductively explicable.[1]

C&J indicate that Chalmers, although not now Jackson, would make the further categorical claim that:

4. There are no a priori conditionals of the form $(P \& T \& I) \supset C$.

Hence Chalmers, but not Jackson, would draw the further conclusion that phenomenal consciousness *isn't* reductively explicable.

I agree with Chalmers that premise (4) is true (or at least, true under one particular interpretation). I think we can see a priori that there is no a priori reducing conditional for phenomenal consciousness to be had, in the following sense. No matter how detailed a description we are given in physical, functional, and/or intentional terms, it will always be conceivable that those facts should be as they are, while the facts of phenomenal consciousness are different or absent, so long as those facts are represented using purely recognitional concepts of experience. We shall be able to think, 'There might be a creature of whom all *that* is true, but in whom *these* properties are absent', where the indexical 'these' expresses a recognitional concept for some of the distinctive properties of a phenomenally conscious experience. So I accept that it will always be possible to conjoin any proposed reductive story with the absence of phenomenal consciousness, to form an epistemic/conceptual possibility. And I therefore also allow that some of the relevant conditionals, here, are never a priori—those conditionals taking the form $(P \& T \& I) \supset C$ (where $C$ states the presence of some phenomenally conscious property, deploying a recognitional concept for it).

I shall be taking for granted, then, that we can possess purely recognitional concepts for aspects of our phenomenally conscious experience. (Arguments to

---

[1] C&J actually present their case somewhat differently. They first argue that there is an a priori conditional of the form $(P \& T \& I \& C) \supset M$, where $C$ is a description of all facts of phenomenal consciousness, and $M$ includes *all* macroscopic facts. And they next argue subtractively, that if there is no a priori conditional of the form $(P \& T \& I) \supset C$, then this must be because phenomenal consciousness isn't reductively explicable. Nothing significant is lost, and no questions are begged, by re-presenting the argument in the form that I have adopted in the text.

the contrary from writers as diverse as Wittgenstein, 1953, and Fodor, 1998, are hereby set to one side.) This isn't really controversial in the present context. Most of those who are engaged in the disputes we are considering think that there are purely recognitional concepts of experience of the sort mentioned above—sometimes called 'phenomenal concepts'—no matter which side they occupy in the debate.[2] These will be concepts that lack any conceptual connections with concepts of other kinds, whether physical, functional, or intentional.

Block and Stalnaker (1999) respond to earlier presentations of the C&J argument—as it appeared in Chalmers (1996) and Jackson (1998)—by denying the truth of premise (1). They claim that, while conditionals of the sort envisaged might sometimes be knowable from the armchair, this isn't enough to show that they are a priori. For it may be that background a posteriori assumptions of ours always play a role in our acceptance of those conditionals. While I am sympathetic to this claim (see also Laurence and Margolis, 2003), in what follows I propose to grant the truth of the first premise. In section 2 below I shall discuss some of the ways in which C&J manage to make it seem plausible.

The claim of premise (2) is that there must be an a priori conditional of the form, $(P \& T \& I) \supset M$ whenever the phenomena described in $M$ are reductively explicable. Although I have doubts about this, too, I shall stifle them for present purposes. I propose to grant the truth of *all* of the premises, indeed. Yet there is a further suppressed assumption that has to be made before we can draw the conclusion that phenomenal consciousness isn't reductively explicable. This is an assumption about the terms in which the target of a reductive explanation must be described. And as we will see from reflection on the demands of reductive explanation generally, this assumption is false. So it will turn out that there is no principled explanatory gap after all, and all's right with the world.

The plan of what follows is this. In section 2 I discuss the sort of case that C&J are able to make in support of their first two premises, and relate their views to more traditional treatments of reductive explanation in the philosophy of science. In section 3 I elaborate on the way in which purely recognitional concepts of experience generate the supposed explanatory gap. In section 4 I argue that there is a suppressed—and eminently deniable—premise that needs to be added, before we draw the conclusion that there is *actually* an explanatory gap. And finally, in section 5 I illustrate how some recent reductive accounts of phenomenal consciousness seem to have just the right *form* to yield a complete and successful reductive explanation. (Whether any of those accounts *is* successful is of course another question.)

---

[2] See, e.g. Jackson, 1986; Block, 1995; Chalmers, 1996; Loar, 1997; Tye, 1999; Carruthers, 2000; Sturgeon, 2000.

## 2. REDUCTIVE EXPLANATION AND
## A PRIORI CONDITIONALS

Chalmers (1996) makes out a powerful case in support of premise (1). On reflection it seems that we can see, just by thinking about it, that once the position and movement of every single microscopic particle is fixed (once all the microscopic facts are as they are), then there is simply *no room* for variation in the properties dealt with by macroscopic physics, chemistry, biology, and so forth—unless, that is, some of these properties are genuinely emergent, like the once-supposed *sui generis* life-force *élan vital*. So if we include in our description the claim that there exists nothing *except* what is entailed by the microphysical facts, then we can see a priori that the microphysical facts determine all the physical facts. And once we further add information about where in the microphysically described world *I* am and when *now* is, it looks as if *all* the facts (or all the facts not implicating phenomenal consciousness, at any rate) are determined. That is to say, some conditional of the form *(P & T & I) ⊃ M* can in principle be known to be true a priori.

Let us grant that this is so. Still, it is a further claim (made in the second premise of the C&J argument), that this has anything to do with reductive explanation. We could agree that such a priori conditionals exist, but deny that they are a requirement of successful reductive explanation. And this objection might seem initially well-motivated. For is there any reason to think that reductive explanation always aims at a suitable set of a priori conditionals? Nothing in such a claim seems to resonate with standard accounts of reductive explanation, whether those accounts are *deductive–nomological, ontic,* or *pragmatic* in form. So intuitively, there seems little support for the view that a priori conditionals are required for successful reductive explanation. But actually, there is some warrant for C&J's view that the practice of reductive explanation carries a *commitment* to the existence of such a priori conditionals, at least, as will emerge when we consider existing accounts of reductive explanation.

### 2.1. *The deductive–nomological account of explanation*

The theory of explanation that comes closest to warranting C&J's picture is surely the classical 'deductive–nomological' model (Hempel, 1965). On this account, explanation of particular events is by subsumption under laws. An event *e* is explained once we have a statement of one or more laws of nature, *L*, together with a description of a set of initial conditions, *IC*, such that *L* and *IC* together logically entail *e*. In which case the conditional statement, '(L & IC) ⊃ e' will be an a priori truth. When this model is extended to accommodate reductive explanation of laws, or of the properties contained in them, however, it is normally thought to require the postulation of a set of 'bridge laws', *BL*, to effect the connection between the reducing laws *RL* and the target *T* (Nagel, 1961). The full conditional would then have the form, *(RL & IC & BL) ⊃ T*. And this, too, can be supposed to be a priori, by virtue of expressing a conceptual entailment from the antecedent to the consequent.

Notice, however, that the bridge laws will themselves contain the target terms. For example, if we are explaining the gas temperature–pressure laws by means of statistical mechanics, then one bridge principle might be, 'The mean momentum of the molecules in the gas is the temperature of the gas.' This itself contains the target concept *temperature*, whose corresponding property we are reductively explaining. There is therefore no direct support here to be had for the C&J view, that in reductive explanation there will always be an a priori conditional whose antecedent is expressed in the reducing vocabulary and whose consequent is the target being explained. For on the present model, the conditional without the bridge laws, *(RL & IC) ⊃ T*, is *not* an a priori one—there is no logical entailment from statistical mechanics to statements about temperature and pressure unless the bridge principles are included.[3]

Let me approach the same point somewhat differently. Suppose that we have achieved full understanding of what is going on at the microlevel when a gas is heated in a container of fixed volume. It should then be manifest to us that the increased momentum transmitted by the faster-moving particles to the surface of the container would have the same effect as an increase in pressure, described at the macrolevel. In fact, it should be plain to us that the roles described at the microlevel—increased mean molecular momentum leading to increased transfer of momentum per unit area in a fixed volume—are isomorphic with those described at the macrolevel—namely, increased temperature leading to increased pressure in a fixed volume of gas. But this isn't *yet* an explanation of the higher-level facts. Correspondence of role doesn't entail identity of role. It remains possible, in principle, that the macrolevel properties might be *sui generis* and irreducible, paralleling the microlevel properties in their behavior. It is only considerations of simplicity and explanatory scope that rule this out.

But now this is, in fact, the role of the *'That's all'* clause in C&J's scheme. The microfacts don't entail the macrofacts by themselves, C&J grant. But they will do so when conjoined with the claim that the microfacts together with facts composed, constituted, or otherwise implied by the microfacts are all the facts that

---

[3] Moreover, our reason for belief in the reducing bridge principles will be abductive, rather than a priori, of course—we come to believe that temperature (in a gas) is mean molecular momentum because assuming that it is so is simpler, and because it enables us to explain some of the processes in which temperature is known to figure.

there are.[4] What emerges, then, is that the role of the 'That's all' clause in C&J's account is to do the same work as the bridge-principles or property identities in the framework of a classical reductive explanation, but in such a way that the target terms no longer figure on the left-hand side of the reducing conditional.

The classical deductive–nomological account of reductive explanation of properties can easily be extended to account for reductive explanation of particular facts or events, in cases where considerations of multiple realizability rule out intertheoretic reduction or reduction of properties. In place of a set of reducing laws, initial conditions, and bridge laws, we can now have reducing laws, initial conditions, and a *constituting conditional*, which states that the target phenomenon is constituted by some set of events described at the microlevel. These will together entail the presence of the target event *e*. And here, as before, C&J can claim that the constituting conditional (which contains the target terms) can be replaced by a *'That's all'* clause, yielding an a priori conditional in which the target terms figure only on the right-hand side.

Before moving on, we should note that the classical account of intertheoretic reduction, as described above, soon came under pressure from those who pointed out that reduced theories often require *correction* before they can be derived from the reducing theory together with bridge principles (Sklar, 1967; Schaffner, 1976). Yet we can still regard the target properties as having been reductively explained, provided the new corrected theory is strongly analogous to the original target, and provided we can explain why the original theory works as well as it does in its domain of validity. This point will prove to be of some importance in sections 4 and 5, when we come to discuss the possibility of reductive explanations of phenomenal consciousness.

I conclude, then, that a priori conditionals aren't what are directly aimed at by those seeking reductive explanations within the framework of a deductive–nomological account of explanation. What is actually aimed at, are the set of reducing facts together with bridge laws, identities, or constituting conditionals that can entail the target phenomenon. But it looks as if it will always be possible to construct from this an a priori conditional with the reducing facts and a *'That's all'* clause on the left-hand side, and some sort of description of the

---

[4] Are the implications here *conceptual* or *metaphysical*? What C&J actually say is that the *'That's all'* clause states that the world contains only the microfacts and *what is a priori implied by* the microfacts (317). This characterization might seem question-begging if their goal is to show that the microfacts together with the *'That's all'* clause (and the indexicality clause) *entails* the macrofacts with a priori warrant. But it isn't. Their thought is this. We can see from the microfacts alone that any world where such facts obtain will be a world in which there is temperature-like and pressure-like phenomena—this much is entailed a priori by the description of those facts. The microfacts by themselves, however, don't yet rule out that in *this* world temperature and pressure are *sui generis* irreducible properties, paralleling the microfacts in their behavior. But when we add that in this world there exists nothing *except* what is entailed by the microfacts, then we get our required explanation—temperature and pressure are actually constituted by the microphenomena, because there exists nothing else to constitute them.

target phenomenon on the right. (This also means that the role of simplicity and other epistemic considerations has become absorbed into the left-hand side.) So C&J's claim that successful reductive explanation requires the existence of a priori conditionals would appear to be vindicated, at least within the framework of a deductive–nomological approach.

## 2.2. *Ontic models of explanation*

It is fair to say that a deductive–nomological approach to explanation is now a minority position. A large part of the credit for this goes to Salmon (1984, 1989), who is one of the main proponents of an opposed 'ontic' conception of explanation. On this view, to explain something isn't to offer a deductive argument for it, but rather to specify some significant part of the causal process that brought it about. And a reductive explanation of some property or process will be a description of the causal mechanism that generates that property/process.

Ontic accounts of explanation have been broadened by others to include *non-causal* relations of identity and constitution (Kim, 1974; Achinstein, 1983; Ruben, 1990). So one can explain why the pH value of some solution is changing by saying that the concentration of hydrogen ions contained in the solution is changing; and one can explain why a gas has a given temperature on the grounds that it has a given mean kinetic energy; and so forth. The relations appealed to here aren't causal ones. But the resulting account can still be described as 'ontic', since there is no attempt to construct deductive arguments in which the explanandum figures as the conclusion. Rather, explanations proceed by telling us about the causes or the constitution of their targets.

From the perspective of ontic models it might initially seem rather unlikely that a priori conditionals will be required for successful reductive explanation. For the goal of such explanation is rather to describe the processes and mechanisms that constitute the target phenomenon. Our aim is to say something true and substantive about the world, not to construct a conditional whose truth we can see a priori. But C&J have a reply, here. For it does matter quite a lot how the target phenomena are described. Ontic explanation can't just be about relations among the properties in question *however described*. For I don't explain the rise in pH value by saying that there was a rise in pH value. It isn't identities *per se* that explain, but rather identities with a certain descriptive character.

C&J can claim, with some plausibility, that we will only ever be satisfied with a proposed reduction when the microphenomena mesh in the right way with the concepts used to characterize the target, in such a way as to warrant an a priori conditional. It is only when we can *see* that changing concentrations of hydrogen ions will produce just the kinds of changes distinctive of a changing pH value, that we will accept that the latter is constituted by the former. And in those circumstances it looks like a description of the microphenomena, combined with a '*That's all*' clause into which simplicity and other epistemic considerations have been absorbed, will a priori entail the change in pH value. And this is just what C&J claim.

By way of reinforcing this point, let us now look at the argument that C&J offer against attempts to find room for reductive explanations of phenomenal consciousness by means of bare psychophysical identities.

## 2.3. *The reductive role of identities*

Block and Stalnaker (1999) argue that general considerations adduced in support of physicalism, together with correlational data discovered by neuropsychologists, might be sufficient to warrant an *identity* between neurological facts, on the one hand, and the facts of phenomenal consciousness, on the other. This would then be sufficient for phenomenal consciousness to count as reductively explained, although (a) there is no a priori conditional consisting of just microphenomena and a '*That's all*' clause on the left and the facts of phenomenal consciousness on the right; and (b) there is no answer to the question *why* the facts of phenomenal consciousness are constituted as they are. For as Block and Stalnaker point out, although identities are *used* in explanations, they don't, themselves, characteristically *admit of* explanation. One cannot ask, 'Why is water $H_2O$?', for example (note: this is not to be confused with the question, 'Why do we *believe* that water is $H_2O$?', which isn't problematic)—the only answer will be, 'Because that's what water *is*.'

While conceding this last point, C&J argue first, that not all identities are explanatory; and second, that they only *are* explanatory when there exists a suitable a priori conditional in which all occurrences of the target terms figure on the right-hand side. For otherwise the identity will be left as a *brute*, epistemically basic, postulate, and the higher-level property or phenomenon won't have been reductively *explained*. And they are surely right about this. Would we think that the nature of water had been explained, for example, if *all* we had to go on was the bare identity, 'Water is $H_2O$', and if we couldn't use the fact of water's identity with $H_2O$ to generate explanations of its liquidity, potability, boiling point, properties as a solvent, and so forth? And given that we *can* use the properties of $H_2O$ to generate such explanations, we can construct an a priori conditional with the behavior of $H_2O$ described in detail on the left (together with a '*That's all*' clause) and the claim that there exists water, on the right.

Similarly, then, in respect of Block and Stalnaker's sort of psychophysical identity: the most that identities warranted by correlational data could explain would be the *time-course* of our phenomenally conscious experiences. But this isn't what puzzles us. We want to know what it is about such experiences that makes them available to introspective recognition, why they seem to have a distinctively subjective aspect, why they seem to their possessors to be intrinsic, ineffable, and private; and so on.[5] Since none of this would be explained, we shouldn't count a psychophysical identity—even if true—as a reductive explanation of phenomenal consciousness. The real explanatory work would still remain to be done. And if a brute psychophysical identity were the best that we could hope for, then it would be reasonable to conclude that there is, indeed, an unbridgeable explanatory gap between physical facts and the facts of phenomenal consciousness.

## 2.4. *Pragmatic accounts of explanation*

A number of writers have claimed that explanation is a pragmatic matter, and that what makes an explanation successful is a function of the needs, knowledge, and expectations of those people to whom the explanation is offered (van Fraassen, 1980; Achinstein, 1983; Lewis, 1986). Such claims come in various different strengths, and writers differ in how they think the pragmatic character of explanation relates to the accounts of explanation offered by deductive–nomological and ontic theories, of the sort discussed above. It should be plain, however, that there is nothing here that must necessarily undermine C&J's claim that successful reductive explanation requires the existence of an a priori conditional linking the reducing facts to the target. What everyone sympathetic to pragmatic accounts would insist on, however, is that whether or not an a priori conditional provides a successful reductive explanation of a target will depend crucially on the questions that puzzle us, and on whether the proffered conditional addresses those questions. This consequence is now widely accepted. And it seems to be reinforced by our discussion of the role of identities in explanation in section 2.3 above.

## 3. RECOGNITIONAL CONCEPTS AND THE EXPLANATORY GAP

It may be that we are committed to the truth of an a priori conditional, then, of the form, *(P & T & I) ⊃ M*, whenever we claim that the phenomena described in *M* are reductively explicable, or when we claim that those phenomena have been reductively explained. And for present purposes I shall accept that this is so. There exists a plausible hypothesis—endorsed by C&J—concerning the nature

---

[5] See Ch. 6 for a more extended discussion of the various *desiderata* for a reductive theory of phenomenal consciousness.

of our concepts for macrophenomena which explains why such conditionals are always available (given that a reductive explanation is available). This is that such concepts are all of them broadly *functional* or *causal role* ones. We can then see that, if the microphenomena behave in a certain way, those roles will get filled; and we can therefore see a priori that if the microphenomena *are* that way, and there is nothing else, then the macroproperties must be present as well.

For example, connected with our concept of (high) temperature will be such facts as *causing pressure to rise, causing damage to skin, causing plants to wilt,* and so on. When we understand the microstory in terms of mean molecular momentum, we can see that when the mean momentum in a gas or liquid is high there will be an increase in pressure, there will be increased damage to fragile cell-walls brought into contact with the fluid, and there will be increased evaporation from plants, causing them to wilt. Given the details of the micro-account, we can see a priori that if there is high mean molecular momentum (and there is nothing else) then there is high temperature.

Note that to say that our concepts for macrophenomena are broadly functional ones is *not* necessarily to say that they must be definable or analyzable into functional terms. C&J are insistent that their account needn't commit them to the existence of analyses for terms like 'temperature' and 'living thing'. It may be that most such concepts don't admit of analysis at all. And yet when we deploy those concepts we can discern certain connections with other concepts a priori. C&J offer the concept *knowledge* as an example to make the point. After many decades of failed attempts to analyze the concept of knowledge, it might be reasonable to conclude that there is no such analysis to be had. But for all that, when first presented with a Gettier example, we can still see a priori that it is a case in which someone lacks knowledge. C&J's point is that our intuitions about the application-conditions of our concepts in particular cases are prior to, and more basic than, any purported general analysis (assuming that the latter is possible at all).

It is now easy to see why there can't be any a priori conditionals of the form *(P & T & I) ⊃ C* (at least supposing that the descriptions of phenomenal properties in C take a certain canonical form). For if some of the concepts in C are purely recognitional ones, then they will *not* be broadly functional ones. And there will then be nothing with which our micro-account can mesh conceptually to yield an a priori conditional. If our recognitional concepts for some of the qualities of our phenomenally conscious states are *purely* recognitional, then they won't carry any commitments about the circumstances in which those properties would or wouldn't be tokened, besides their phenomenal content. So when we entertain some supposed reductive story in terms of neurological events, causal roles, or intentional contents, there will be nothing to force us to conclude that in such circumstances phenomenal consciousness must be present too.

It shouldn't be claimed that *all* of our concepts for phenomenally conscious states are purely recognitional ones, of course. It may be that some of our concepts in this domain are broadly functional in character, and that some contain a combination of functional and recognitional elements (Chalmers, 1996). Consider the concept *pain*, for example. It may be that our ordinary idea of pain contains such notions as, *is caused by tissue damage* and *tends to cause grimacing and nursing of the injured body-part*, as well as including a capacity to recognize pains—straight off and without inference—as and when one has them. But it will always be possible to carve out the purely recognitional component from this concept to form a distinct concept (*'this feel'*), which will then lack any conceptual connections with role-concepts. Indeed, it may be that many of us already possess such purely recognitional concepts, alongside a set of theoretically embedded functional-role ones.

We have, then, a pair of claims and a diagnosis. The claims are these: (1) in the case of all macrophenomena M not implicating phenomenal consciousness, there is an a priori conditional of the form *(P & T & I) ⊃ M*, and this conditional is a requirement for there to be a successful reductive explanation of the phenomena in M. (2) In the case of all phenomenally conscious facts and properties C (described using purely recognitional concepts of experience) there isn't any a priori conditional of the form *(P & T & I) ⊃ C* to be had; and so phenomenal consciousness doesn't admit of reductive explanation. And the diagnosis is that this difference derives from a difference in the concepts that we employ in the two domains—broadly functional, in the case of macrophenomena, and purely recognitional in the case of phenomenal consciousness.

## 4. TRANSFORMED TARGETS AND THICKLY INDIVIDUATED PROPERTIES

The suppressed premise in the argument for an explanatory gap, however, is that successful reductive explanations must respect the terms in which explanatory problems are posed. Our explanatory problem is, 'How can a physical system possess *this* sort of state?', where the *'this'* deploys a recognitional concept of some aspect of phenomenal consciousness. And I grant that there can be no a priori reducing conditional that has the statement, 'The system possesses *this* sort of state' on its right-hand side. Hence the appearance of an 'explanatory gap'. But what isn't yet ruled out is that we might construct an a priori conditional that has descriptions of phenomenal consciousness of some *other* sort on its right-hand side. This idea will be explored in a general way in the present section, and then illustrated with reference to recent reductive accounts of phenomenal consciousness in section 5 following.

Notice that in science generally, the targets of explanation don't always remain intact through the process of inquiry. In some cases we explain by *explaining away*. In the beginning our targets may be expressed in one way. But we may come to realize that they contain a false presupposition, or that the concepts with which they are expressed are in some way confused or in need of reform. For example, in astronomy we began with the explanatory problem, 'Why do the stars and the sun move across the sky in the way that they do?' But the explanation we ended up with didn't answer this question as posed. So we don't now have an a priori conditional with such-and-such facts described on the left, and the statement, 'The stars and sun move across the sky in such-and-such a way' on the right. Rather what we have is an account of the rotation of the earth, and of the movements of the earth, sun, planets, and stars in relation to one another, in terms of which we can explain why the sun and stars *appear* to move across the sky in the way that they do.

For another example of the same general type, consider evolutionary biology. Here we began (pre-Darwin) with an explanatory question: why do species exist? But now (post-Darwin) we see that there are no such things as species in the original intended sense. Rather, there exist a great many populations of individual organisms spread out over space and time that resemble one another more or less closely, and that stand in various inheritance relations to one another. The idea of *species* as some sort of underlying unifying essence has now been dropped. And what gets explained instead are the ways in which similarity relations amongst individuals shift over time, given facts of inheritance and facts about survival and reproduction. So here, too, there is no a priori conditional available to us that has a body of explanatory theory on the left-hand side and the statement (as originally intended), 'There are different species of living thing' on the right.

What makes these examples work, is that in the course of inquiry, and in the course of adopting our explanatory theories, we have realized that our initial questions made false presuppositions. So we have shifted to a new set of questions to which we can now provide direct answers. And it might be objected against any attempt to model our failures to produce a reductive explanation of phenomenal consciousness on this, that in the above cases we *do* finish with a priori conditionals with everything that we *currently* believe to be true on the right-hand sides. In the case of phenomenal consciousness, in contrast, the proposal would presumably have to be that all of our beliefs involving purely recognitional concepts would need to be left outside the scope of the explanatory conditional.

This is a fair point, and a significant difference. But in reply we can claim that the moral of the examples is really this: explanations succeed when there is nothing left to explain. Explanations are complete when every question that we *want* answered has *been* answered. And reflection can make us see that there are some questions that we might initially have been inclined to ask, that no longer require answers. (The question, 'Why am I lucky?' might be an example falling into this category.) And this is what many proposed reductive explanations suggest in respect of phenomenal consciousness, as we shall see in the next section. They offer a reductive account from which we could construct an a priori conditional concerning many facts about phenomenal consciousness. And at the same time they offer a reductive account of why there *can't* be any such reducing conditionals with statements containing purely recognitional concepts on their right-hand sides. So we are supposed to see, in the end, that every question that requires an answer has received an answer.

C&J might reply that even if—pragmatically—explanation stops when all the questions that we want answered have been answered, it is a further constraint on the success of a reductive explanation that *every* fact at the target level *could* be reductively explained *in principle*. In which case, by conceding that there are facts of phenomenal consciousness expressed using recognitional concepts that can't be reductively explained, we have accepted that phenomenal consciousness itself can't be explained.

Instead of challenging the premise of this argument, let me just accept it, and go on to draw some distinctions. First, as we noted in section 2.2, whether or not an explanation is successful can turn crucially on the way that the target is described, even from the standpoint of an ontic account of explanation. Some of the descriptions that figure on the right-hand side need to be drawn from the same *level* as the target, at least—e.g. involving phenomena that in one way or another pertain to *temperature*, described as such. *Which* descriptions from a given level are the relevant ones, though? Surely not *all*. The requirement cannot be that a successful reductive explanation should be able to generate *all* descriptions of the target phenomenon; for there will be infinitely many (indeed, uncountably many) of these. So even idealizing for limitations on time, memory and so on (C&J, 334), reductive explanation would become impossible. The relevant descriptions are the ones that puzzle us, perhaps, or that seem central to the characterization of the phenomena in question.

Now let me introduce a distinction between facts that are *thickly* and *thinly* individuated. In the first—*thick*—sense of 'fact', one fact may be the subject of many distinct thoughts. Here facts might be thought of as ordered n-tuples of individuals, properties, and relations. But in the second—*thin*—sense, facts are partly individuated in terms of the thoughts used to express them. In which case, whenever we use distinct concepts in characterizing a fact, we have thereby described a *distinct fact*. So in the thick sense, the fact that I am holding up five fingers, and the fact that the number of fingers that I am holding up is the smallest prime number larger than three, are the *same* fact. But in the thin sense, these are two distinct facts. Notice that we can draw the thick–thin distinction, not just *across* levels (with one given underlying thickly individuated fact being picked out by two distinct descriptions at a higher level, or by descriptions at two different levels), but also within the *same* level. For example, it is one and the same thickly individuated fact that is picked out by, 'John is thinking about ex-President Nixon' and, 'John is thinking about the President who resigned over the Watergate affair.'

Given the distinction between thick and thin facts, we can claim this. While it is a constraint on reductive explanation that the target should be described at the appropriate 'level'; and while it is a constraint on complete success in explanation that every *thickly individuated* fact at the target level should receive an explanation; it cannot be a rational constraint on explanation that every *thinly individuated* fact should be explained. There are just too many of them (infinitely many), for one thing. The suppressed assumption in the C&J argument for an explanatory gap can now be expressed more precisely. It is the assumption that reductive explanations must require a priori conditionals *in which all the thinly individuated facts concerning the target phenomena figure on the right-hand side.*

What I claim, then, is that this suppressed premise is false. A reductive explanation of phenomenal consciousness could be successful by doing the following. It could explain all that *needs* explaining at the target level, leaving no significant question unanswered; and it could be extended (in principle) to explain every thickly individuated fact in the target domain, described at the target level. But there will remain some *thinly individuated* facts (viz. those expressed using purely recognitional concepts) that remain outside the scope of the resulting a priori conditional. Yet our reductive account can at the same time explain just *why* such statements must remain outside the scope of the conditional. This, I argue, would be complete success.

## 5. THE FORM OF REDUCTIVE EXPLANATIONS OF THE PHENOMENAL

Phenomenally conscious properties can be characterized purely recognitionally, from a first-person perspective; which makes it hard to see initially how any reductive story could connect appropriately with those properties. But it is important to realize that phenomenally conscious properties *also* admit of third-personal characterization.[6] Most obviously, we can say that these are properties that are available to introspective recognition. We can say, too, that these properties have a 'fineness of grain' that gives them a richness well beyond our powers of

---

[6] The idea I make use of here is a derivative of Dennett's (1991) notion of *hetero-phenomenology*.

description and categorization. And we can add that people are strongly inclined to think of phenomenally conscious states as possessing intrinsic—that is, non-relational and non-intentional—properties, that are available for introspective classification; that people are inclined to think of these properties as ineffable and private; and that we are inclined to think that we have incorrigible, or at least privileged, knowledge of them.

Bundling these third-person characterizations into a third-person concept of phenomenal consciousness, we can then pick out each thickly individuated fact designated through the application of a purely recognitional concept by saying, 'It is the phenomenally conscious state that he/she is introspectively recognizing right now.' The claim is that each such fact—together with the various puzzling properties that make up the third-person concept of phenomenal consciousness—can in principle receive a reductive explanation.

Such third-person characterizations seem tailor-made for explanation from the perspective of 'intentionalist' or 'representationalist' theories of phenomenal consciousness, indeed—whether of a first-order sort (Kirk, 1994; Dretske, 1995; Tye, 1995, 2000) or of a higher-order kind (Dennett, 1978a, 1991; Lycan, 1987, 1996; Rosenthal, 1997; Carruthers, 2000). This is not the place to develop this claim in any detail; and of course there are important differences between the different reductive accounts on offer here.[7] But notice, for example, that an appeal to the 'analog' or 'non-conceptual' intentional content of our perceptual states can explain the fineness of grain associated with phenomenal consciousness. And notice, too, that any property that is the object of a bare-recognitional concept will be apt to seem intrinsic to someone deploying that concept.

Intentionalist explanations aren't yet *micro*-explanations, of course. So it is presupposed, first, that the facts of intentional psychology will in turn admit of reductive explanation in physical terms; and second, that intentional psychology can be carved off from anything involving phenomenal consciousness. Both presuppositions are to some degree controversial. There is much debate about whether, and if so how, intentional content can be reductively explained (Millikan, 1984; Fodor, 1990; Searle, 1992, 1997). And some deny that intentional content can be understood and characterized apart from phenomenal consciousness (Searle, 1992, 1997). But I don't need to enter into disputes about the naturalization of intentional content here. For my goal is not to defend the view that phenomenal consciousness can actually be reductively explained by micro-physics, but just that it is reductively explicable *in principle*.

---

[7] One important dimension of difference concerns the question of how much of our characterization of phenomenal consciousness—e.g. its rich and fine-grained character, or its possession of intrinsic non-relational properties (qualia)—is *explained*, and how much is explained *away* as resulting from some sort of illusion. (Many have alleged that Dennett's 1991 should really have been entitled, *Consciousness Explained Away*, for example.)

However, I do need to claim that Searle is mistaken in thinking that intentional content itself presupposes phenomenal consciousness. For otherwise the suggestion that the puzzling features of phenomenal consciousness can (even in principle) be explained by appeal to intentional content will be spurious. I shan't argue for this here, however, since Searle's position is endorsed by hardly anyone else working in the field (appeals to non-conscious intentional states are now routine in both philosophy and cognitive science), and since it isn't endorsed by C&J in particular.

It may be objected that intentionalist explanations don't in any case touch the core, or the defining feature, of phenomenal consciousness. This is its 'what it is likeness' (Nagel, 1974) that can only be characterized using our first-person recognitional concepts themselves. Yet we can have good reason to think, surely, that the properties picked out by our first-person recognitional concepts are the very same properties as those that figure in the third-person characterizations sketched above. And then a reductive account of those properties will be what we seek, provided it can answer all the questions that puzzle us. A successful reductive explanation that focuses on the third-person characterizations can give us good reason to think that phenomenal consciousness *per se* has been reductively explained.

Most importantly, a representational approach can deliver a third-person account of our recognitional concepts for the target properties that explains why, to anyone employing those concepts, the explanatory gap will seem unbridgeable. (For detailed proposals of this sort see Tye, 1999, and Carruthers, 2000.) For example, if we possess *purely* recognitional concepts of the form, '*This* type of experience'—with no a priori links to functional-role concepts or intentional concepts, in particular—then no matter what reductive account we are offered in causal-role or intentional terms, we will still be able to think, 'All that might be true without *this* type of experience being present.' But the property picked out by 'This experience' might be, nevertheless, the very same as the one given in the causal/intentional theory. And the success of that theory in accounting for the various third-person characterizations of the puzzling features of phenomenal consciousness can give us good reason to believe that it is.

The form that these various reductive proposals take, then, is this. There is a microstory (in this case cast in causal/intentional terms) from which we can see a priori that in any world in which it is true, the various puzzling facts about phenomenal consciousness will be true, in so far as those facts can be described without using our purely recognitional concepts. That is, we can see a priori that in any such world, people will be able to know immediately of the presence of their experiential states through introspective recognition, and they will be inclined to think that their experiential states possess properties that are ineffable, intrinsic, and private. Moreover, we can see a priori that in such a world, people will possess concepts for their experiences that (by virtue of their purely recognitional character) will rule out any sort of a priori reducing conditional that has statements expressed using those concepts on the right-hand side.

Does it follow from the microstory that in our world phenomenal consciousness is constituted by the truth of that story? No, not yet—any more than it follows from the microstory alone that in our world temperature in a gas is constituted by mean molecular momentum. Here (as in the case of temperature) we need to add a 'That's all' clause, warranted in the same way by considerations of simplicity and explanatory power. And then we can construct an a priori conditional of the form $(P \& T \& I) \supset C$, where what figures in $C$ aren't statements employing our recognitional concepts of experience, but rather third-person descriptions of the various puzzling facts about phenomenal consciousness (including, note, the fact that I can still think the thought, 'All of $P \& T \& I$ might be true, while I nevertheless lacked this', where 'this' expresses a recognitional concept of experience). And a third-person description of every phenomenally conscious property that is the object of such introspective recognition can also figure in $C$.

Notice that proposed reductive explanations of this form will only work by reconfiguring the terms in which the target is expressed. Instead of asking, 'How can any physical system have this sort of experience?' (deploying a recognitional concept in the *explanandum*), we now ask, 'How can any physical system have states that seem ineffable and private, etc., and which persistently induce the feeling of an explanatory gap?' But it is not at all unusual for successful explanations to require that their targets be reconfigured in this sort way. In astronomy, as we saw earlier, we had to stop asking, 'Why do the sun and the stars move across the sky in the way that we do?' and ask instead, 'Why do the sun and stars *appear* to move as they do?' The temptation to *see* the sun as moving still persists. But we no longer take it seriously. For we know that a rotating earth, together with a visual system that takes the earth as its frame of reference in perceptions of motion, will produce just such an impression.

Reductive explanations are successful when (a) all of the questions that puzzle us are answered, either directly, or indirectly by showing why the facts should *seem* a certain puzzling way to us when they are not; and when (b) every thickly individuated fact described at the target level can be reductively explained. And this is just what is claimed by the various causal/intentional reductive theories of phenomenal consciousness on the market. Where the C&J argument goes wrong, is in its assumption that reductive explanations require a priori conditionals in which the target phenomena *as initially characterized* are described on the right-hand sides, and in which *all* the *thinly individuated* target facts figure on the right-hand sides.

## 6. CONCLUSION

For purposes of argument I have conceded to C&J that successful reductive explanations require a priori reducing conditionals containing references to the target properties on their right-hand sides. But I have insisted that reductive explanation can often require a reworking of the terms in which the target phenomena are conceptualized, or the terms in which our explanatory questions are posed. And I have insisted, too, that while all the target facts (thickly individuated, but described at the appropriate level) need to figure on the right-hand sides of such conditionals, it *isn't* true that all *descriptions* of such facts need to be capable of figuring there. When these points are brought into proper focus, it is plain that there is no obstacle of principle, here, to the provision of a reductive explanation of phenomenal consciousness. Whether such an explanation can in fact be provided is, of course, a topic for another occasion.[8]

[8] See Carruthers (2000) and Chs. 3 through 6 below for detailed discussion, and also for development and defense of a novel form of dispositionalist higher-order thought theory, comparing it with alternatives.

# CHAPTER 3

# Natural Theories of Consciousness

Many people have thought that consciousness—particularly phenomenal consciousness, or the sort of consciousness that is involved when one undergoes states with a distinctive subjective phenomenology, or 'feel'—is inherently, and perhaps irredeemably, mysterious (Nagel, 1974, 1986; McGinn, 1991). And many would at least agree with Chalmers (1996) in characterizing consciousness as the 'hard problem', which forms one of the few remaining 'final frontiers' for science to conquer. But equally, there have been a plethora of attempts by philosophers at explaining consciousness in natural terms (Armstrong, 1968, 1984; Carruthers, 1996, 2000; Dennett, 1978a, 1991; Dretske, 1995; Flanagan, 1992; Gennaro, 1996; Kirk, 1994; Lycan, 1987, 1996; Nelkin, 1996; Papineau, 2002; Rosenthal, 1986, 1997; Tye, 1995, 2000).[1] This chapter surveys the prospects for success of such attempts, focusing particularly on the books by Dretske (1995), Tye (1995), Gennaro (1996), and Lycan (1996).[2] But it is by no means impartial; and the reader should note that I have my own axe to grind in this exercise. My overt agenda is to convince you of the merits of *dispositional higher-order thought theories* in particular, of the sort defended in my 1996, chs. 5 to 7.[3]

## 1. SOME DISTINCTIONS, AND A ROAD-MAP

One of the real advances made in recent years has been in distinguishing between different questions concerning consciousness (see particularly: Dretske, 1993; Block, 1995; Lycan, 1996). Not everyone agrees on quite *which* distinctions need to be drawn, however; and I shall be arguing later that one

[1] I leave to one side in this exercise the many attempts by psychologists at providing an account of consciousness, for simplicity only—my view is actually that there is no sharp line to be drawn between philosophical theories and psychological ones, in this area; both sets of theories are largely intended to be substantive and explanatory, with few a priori elements.

[2] For comment on Dennett, see my 1996, ch. 6 and my 2000, chs. 10 and 11. For comment on Kirk, see my 1992a and 1996, ch. 5. For comment on Nelkin, see my 1997. For some comments on Papineau, see Ch. 5 of the present volume. For comment on Rosenthal, see my 1996, ch. 6 and my 2000, ch. 8.

[3] In fact my main focus in those chapters was on the structure of *human* consciousness, since I was proposing to argue (1996, ch. 8) that natural language is crucially involved in human conscious thinking (see also Chs. 7 and 8 of the present volume). In developing an account of consciousness *as such* I am now inclined to drop the requirement that the higher-order thoughts, in virtue of availability to which a given mental state is conscious, must themselves be conscious ones. For the most detailed treatment of my considered current view, see my 2000.

crucial distinction (between worldly subjectivity and mental-state subjectivity) has been overlooked. But all are agreed that we should distinguish *creature* consciousness from *mental-state* consciousness. It is one thing to say *of an individual person or organism* that it is conscious (either in general or of something in particular); and it is quite another thing to say *of one of the mental states* of a creature that it is conscious.

It is also agreed that within creature-consciousness itself we should distinguish between *intransitive* and *transitive* variants. To say of an organism that it is conscious *simpliciter* (intransitive) is to say just that it is awake, as opposed to asleep or comatose. There don't appear to be any deep philosophical difficulties lurking here (or at least, they aren't difficulties specific to the topic of consciousness, as opposed to mentality in general). But to say of an organism that it is conscious *of such-and-such* (transitive) is normally to say at least that it is *perceiving* such-and-such. So we say of the mouse that it is conscious of the cat outside its hole, in explaining why it doesn't come out; meaning that it *perceives* the cat's presence. To provide an account of transitive creature-consciousness would thus be to attempt a theory of perception. No doubt there *are* many problems here; but I shall proceed as if I had the solution to them.

There is a choice to be made concerning transitive creature-consciousness, failure to notice which may be a potential source of confusion. For we have to decide whether the perceptual state in virtue of which an organism may be said to be transitively conscious of something must itself be a conscious one (state-conscious—see below). If we say 'Yes' then we shall need to know more about the mouse than merely that it perceives the cat, if we are to be assured that it is conscious of the cat—we shall need to establish that its percept of the cat is itself conscious. If we say 'No', on the other hand, then the mouse's perception of the cat will be sufficient for the mouse to count as conscious of the cat; but we may have to say that although it is conscious of the cat, the mental state in virtue of which it is so conscious isn't itself a conscious one. (This sounds strange, but it isn't really, once the distinction between creature consciousness and state consciousness is seen clearly enough.) I think it best to bypass all danger of confusion here by avoiding the language of transitive creature-consciousness altogether. Nothing of importance would be lost to us by doing this. We can say simply that organism O *observes* or *perceives* X; and we can then assert explicitly, if we wish, that its percept is or isn't conscious.

Turning now to the notion of *mental-state consciousness*, the major distinction is between *phenomenal consciousness*, on the one hand—which is a property of states that it is *like something* to be in, which have a distinctive 'feel'—and various functionally definable notions, such as Block's (1995) *access consciousness*, on the other. Most theorists believe that there are mental states—such as occurrent thoughts or judgments—that are conscious (in whatever is the correct functionally definable sense), but that aren't phenomenally conscious.[4] But there is considerable dispute as to whether mental states can be phenomenally conscious without also being conscious in the functionally definable sense—and even more dispute about whether phenomenal consciousness can be *explained* in functional and/or representational terms.

It seems plain that there is nothing deeply problematic about functionally definable notions of mental-state consciousness, from a naturalistic perspective. For mental functions and mental representations are the staple fare of naturalistic accounts of the mind. But this leaves plenty of room for dispute about the form that the correct functional account should take. Some claim that for a state to be conscious in the relevant sense is for it to be poised to have an impact on the organism's decision-making processes (Kirk, 1994; Dretske, 1995; Tye, 1995), perhaps also with the additional requirement that those processes should be distinctively *rational* ones (Block, 1995). Others think that the relevant requirement is that the state should be suitably related to higher-order representations—beliefs and/or experiences—of that very state (Armstrong, 1984; Dennett, 1991; Rosenthal, 1993; Carruthers, 1996, 2000; Gennaro, 1996; Lycan, 1996).

What *is* often thought to be naturalistically problematic, in contrast, is phenomenal consciousness (Nagel, 1984; McGinn, 1991; Block, 1995; Chalmers, 1996). And what is really and deeply controversial is whether phenomenal consciousness can be *explained* in terms of some or other functionally definable property. *Cognitive* theories maintain that it can—the contrast here being with those who think that phenomenal consciousness should be explained in neurological terms, say in terms of oscillation-patterns amongst neural spiking-frequencies (e.g. Crick and Koch, 1990).

Naturalistic theories of phenomenal consciousness may then usefully be sorted along a series of choice-points, as represented in Figure 3.1. First, the theorist has to decide whether to try to account for consciousness in *physical* and/or *neurological*, or rather in *cognitive* (representational and/or functional) terms.[5] Here I shall just assume that the correct choice is the latter. (See Chapter 1 of this volume.) We begin our discussion at the second choice-point: between theories that account for phenomenal consciousness in terms purely of first-order representations (FORs) of the environment (or of the subject's own body); and theories that involve higher-order representations (HORs) of the subject's own mental states. I shall argue that we ought to go for the right-hand branch. Then

---

[4] In my 1996, ch. 8, I disagreed—arguing that occurrent propositional thoughts can only be conscious (in the human case at least) by being tokened in imaged natural language sentences, which will then possess phenomenal properties. See also Chs. 7 and 8 of the present volume.

[5] *Cognitive* here need not mean *conceptual*. Both first-order representation (FOR) theories (Dretske, 1995; Tye, 1995) and higher-order experience (HOE) theories (Lycan, 1996) maintain that the features of mental states that render them phenomenally conscious consist in a certain sort of *non*-conceptual content.

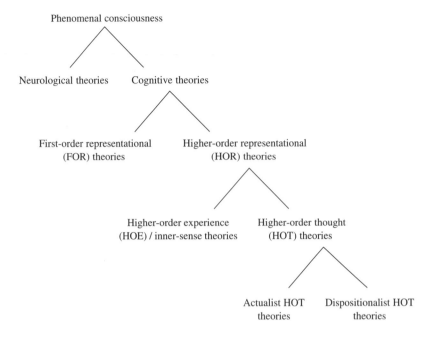

FIG 3.1 The tree of consciousness.

the third choice-point is between *inner-sense* models of consciousness, which conceive of the higher-order representations that render a given mental state conscious as being somewhat like *experience* (that is, higher-order experience, or HOE, models); and higher-order thought (HOT) theories, which explain consciousness in terms of thoughts or judgments about our mental states. Again I defend the right-hand branch. Then finally the choice is between accounts that require the *actual* presence of a HOT for a state to qualify as conscious; and accounts that characterize conscious states as those that are suitably *available* to HOTs. Once again I argue that the right-hand branch is to be preferred.[6]

## 2. FOR THEORIES

In two wonderfully written, lucid, and highly ambitious books, Dretske (1995) and Tye (1995) have independently developed very similar first-order

---

[6] It turns out, however, that dispositional HOT theory can *also* be considered to be a form of HOE theory, minus the commitment to any distinct organ of inner sense. For the theory claims that first-order perceptual states acquire, at the same time, higher-order analog contents, by virtue of their availability to a faculty of higher-order thought. See sections 5 and 8 below; and see Ch. 4 of the present volume.

representational (FOR) theories of phenomenal consciousness. In both cases the goal is to characterize all of the phenomenal—'felt'—properties of experience in terms of the representational *contents* of experience. So the difference between an experience of green and an experience of red will be explained as a difference in the properties represented—reflective properties of surfaces, say—in each case. And the difference between a pain and a tickle is similarly explained in representational terms—the difference is said to reside in the different properties (different kinds of disturbance) represented as located in particular regions of the subject's own body. In each case, a phenomenally conscious experience is said to be one that is *poised* to have an impact on the subject's beliefs and practical-reasoning processes in such a way as to guide behavior.

Perhaps the main consideration supporting such FOR theories is the so-called 'transparency' of consciousness, previously noted by a number of writers (e.g. Harman, 1990; McCulloch, 1988, 1993). Look at a green tree or a red tomato. Now try to concentrate as hard as you can, *not* on the colors of the *objects*, but on the quality of your *experience* of those colors. What happens? Can you do it? Plausibly, all that you find yourself doing is paying closer and closer attention to the colors in the outside world, after all. A perception of red is a state that represents a surface as having a certain distinctive quality—*redness*, of some or other particular shade—and paying close attention to your perceptual state comes down to paying close attention to the quality of the world *represented* (while being aware of it *as* represented—this will become important later). Of course, in cases of perceptual illusion or hallucination there may actually be no real quality of the world represented, but only a represent*ing*. But still, plausibly, there is nothing to your experience over and above the way it represents the world as being.

But what about bodily sensations, like itches, tickles, and pains? Are these, too, purely representational states? If so, *what* do they represent? It might seem that all there really is to a pain, is a particular sort of *non*-representational quality, which is experienced as unwelcome. But in fact, as Tye shows, the case for non-representational qualities (*qualia*) is no stronger in connection with pain than it is with color. In both cases our experience represents to us a particular perceptible property—in the one case, of an external surface, in the other case, of a region of our own body. In the case of color-perception, my perceptual state delivers the content, [*that* surface has *that* quality]. In the case of pain, my state grounds an exactly parallel sort of content, namely [*that* region of my body has *that* quality]. In each case the *that quality* expresses a recognitional concept, where what is recognized isn't a quale, but rather a property that our perceptual state represents as being instantiated in the place in question.

Dretske and Tye differ from one another mainly in the accounts that they offer of the representation relation. For Dretske (1995), the content of a representational state is fixed teleologically in terms of the objects/properties that the state is *supposed* to represent, given the organism's evolutionary and learning histories. For Tye (1995), in contrast, the content of a state is defined in terms of causal co-variance in normal circumstances—where the notion of *normal* circumstances may or may not be defined teleologically, depending upon cases. But both are agreed that content is to be individuated *externally*, in a way that embraces objects and properties in the organism's environment. I begin my discussion by suggesting that they have missed a trick in going for an externalist notion of content, and that their position would be strengthened if they were to endorse a *narrow* content account instead.

Consider the now-famous example of *Swampman* (Davidson, 1987), who is accidentally created by a bolt of lightning striking a tree-stump in a swamp, in such a way as to be molecule-for-molecule identical to Davidson himself. Dretske is forced to deny that Swampman and Davidson are subject to the same color experiences (and indeed, he must deny that Swampman has any color experiences at all), since his states lack *functions*, either evolved or learned. As Dretske admits, this consequence is highly counter-intuitive; and it is one that he has to chew on pretty hard to force himself to swallow. Tye, on the other hand, believes that he is better off in relation to this example, since he says that Swampman's circumstances can count as 'normal' by default. But then there will be other cases where Tye will be forced to say that two individuals undergo the same experiences (because their states are such as to co-vary with the same properties in circumstances that are normal for them), where intuition would strongly suggest that their experiences are different.

Thus, imagine that the lightning-bolt happens to create Swampman with a pair of color-inverting spectacles permanently attached to his nose. Then Tye may have to say that when Swampman looks at green grass, he undergoes the same experiences as Davidson does (who views the grass *without* such glasses). For in the circumstances that are normal for Swampman, he is in a state that will co-vary with greenness. So he experiences *green*, just as Davidson does. This, too, is highly counter-intuitive. We would want to say, surely, that Swampman experiences *red*.

Tye (in correspondence) replies that by *normal* he just means *ceteris paribus*, and that if Swampman has color-inverting spectacles in front of his eyes, then *ceteris* isn't really *paribus*. But now it looks easy to develop the example in such a way as to re-instate the point. Suppose that the bolt of lightning creates color-inverting lenses as part of the very structure of the corneas within Swampman's eyes. Then other things are, surely, equal *for Swampman* when he looks at green grass, in which case Tye's sort of first-order representational (FOR) theory will have to say that Swampman has an experience *as of* green; but again, intuition strongly suggests that his experiences will be the inverse of Davidson's.

Some may see sufficient reason, here, to reject a first-order account of phenomenal consciousness straight off. I disagree. Rather, such examples just motivate the adoption of a narrow-content account of representation in general, where contents are individuated in abstraction from the particular objects and properties in the thinker's environment. We might say, for example, that the representational content of the experience is the same whenever it is such that it *would* engage the very same recognitional capacity (note that this need not imply that the content of the experience is itself conceptualized). But explaining and defending such an account, and showing how it is fully consistent with— indeed, required by—naturalism about the mental, would take me too far afield for present purposes.[7] In the present context I must ask readers just to bracket any worries that they may have about externalist theories of perceptual content, accepting on trust that one could embrace a FOR naturalization of phenomenal consciousness while rejecting externalism.

This is not to say, of course, that I think FOR approaches to consciousness are unproblematic. On the contrary: over the next two sections I shall develop objections that seem to me to count decisively in favor of some sort of higher-order representational (HOR) approach.

## 3. FIRST PROBLEM: PHENOMENAL WORLD *VERSUS* PHENOMENAL EXPERIENCE

One major difficulty with FOR accounts in general is that they cannot distinguish between what the *world* (or the state of the organism's own body) is like for an organism, and what the organism's *experience of the world* (or of its own body) is like for the organism. This distinction is very frequently overlooked in discussions of consciousness. And Tye, for example, will move (sometimes in the space of a single sentence) from saying that his account explains what *color* is like for an organism with color-vision, to saying that it explains what *experiences of color* are like for that organism. But the first is a property of the world (or of a world-perceiver pair, perhaps), whereas the latter is a property of the organism's experience of the world (or of an experience-experiencer pair). These are plainly distinct (at least conceptually).[8]

It is commonplace to note that each type of organism will occupy a distinctive point of view on the world, characterized by the kinds of perceptual information that are available to it, and by the kinds of perceptual discriminations that it is

---

[7] See Botterill and Carruthers, 1999, ch. 7; and see Carruthers, 2000, ch. 4.

[8] A FOR theorist might allow that there is a *conceptual* distinction to be drawn here, but deny that there is any distinction in reality corresponding to it, denying that the *properties* of worldly subjectivity and mental-state subjectivity are distinct. Whether such a reply can be adequate will depend partly on how a FOR theorist proposes to handle the conscious/non-conscious distinction (see section 4 below), and partly on the adequacy of their attempts to account for our recognitional concepts of experience (see Ch. 5 of the present volume).

capable of making (Nagel, 1974). This is part of what it means to say that bats (with echolocation) and cats (without color vision) occupy a different point of view on the world from ourselves. Put differently but equivalently: the world (including subjects' own bodies) is *subjectively presented* to different species of organism somewhat differently. And to try to characterize this is to try to understand what the world for such subjects *is like*. But it is one thing to say that *the world* takes on a subjective aspect by being presented to subjects with differing conceptual and discriminatory powers, and it is quite another thing to say that the subject's *experience of the world* also has such a subjective aspect, or that there is something that the *experience* is *like*. Indeed, by parity of reasoning, this would seem to require subjects to possess information about, and to make discriminations amongst, their own states of experience. And it is just this that provides the rationale for higher-order representational (HOR) accounts as against FOR accounts, in fact.

According to HOR theories, first-order perceptual states (if non-conscious—see section 4 below) may be adequately accounted for in FOR terms. The result will be an account of the point of view—the subjective perspective—that the organism takes towards its world (and the states of its own body), giving us an account of what the world, for that organism, *is like*. But the HOR theorist maintains that something else is required in accounting for what an *experience* is like for a subject, or in explaining what it is for an organism's *mental states* to take on a subjective aspect. For this, we maintain, higher-order representations—states that meta-represent the subject's own mental states—are required. And it is hard to see how it could be otherwise, given that there is a real distinction between what the world is like for an organism, and what the organism's experience of the world is like.

We therefore need to distinguish between two different sorts of subjectivity— between worldly subjectivity and mental-state subjectivity. In fact we need to distinguish between 'phenomenal' properties of the world (or of the organism's own body), on the one hand, and phenomenal properties of one's experience of the world (or of one's experience of one's body) on the other. First-order representational (FOR) theories may be adequate to account for the former; but not to explain the latter, where some sort of higher-order theory is surely needed. Which of these two deserves the title 'phenomenal consciousness'? There is nothing (or nothing much) in a name; and I am happy whichever reply is given. But it is the subjectivity of experience that seems to be especially problematic— if there is a 'hard problem' of consciousness (Chalmers, 1996), it surely lies here. At any rate, nothing can count as a complete theory of phenomenal consciousness that can't explain it—as FOR theory plainly cannot.

But how are HOR theories to handle the point that conscious experiences have the quality of *transparency*? As we noted earlier, if you try to focus your attention on your experience of a bright shade of color, say, what you find yourself doing is focusing harder and harder on the color itself—your focus seems to go right *through* the experience to its objects. This might seem to lend powerful support to first-order accounts of phenomenal consciousness. For how can any form of higher-order representation (HOR) theory be correct, given the transparency of experience, and given that all the *phenomena* in phenomenal consciousness seem to lie in *what is represented*, rather than in anything to do with the mode of representing it?

Now in one way this line of thought is correct—for in one sense there is nothing in the content of phenomenally conscious experience beyond what a FOR theorist would recognize. What gets added by the presence of a HOR system is a dimension of *seeming* or *appearance* of that very same first-order content. But in another sense this *is* a difference of content, since the content *seeming red* is distinct from the content *red*. So when I focus on my experience of a color I can, in a sense, do other than focus on the color itself—I can focus on the way that color *seems* to me, or on the way that it *appears*; and this is to focus on the subjectivity of my experiential state. It is then open to us to claim that it is the possibility of just such a manner of focusing that confers on our experiences the dimension of subjectivity, and so that renders them for the first time fully phenomenally conscious, as we shall see in sections 5 and 8.

## 4. SECOND PROBLEM: CONSCIOUS *VERSUS* NON-CONSCIOUS EXPERIENCE

Another—closely related—difficulty with first-order representational (FOR) approaches is to provide an account of the distinction between conscious and non-conscious experience. (As examples of the latter, consider absent-minded driving; sleepwalking; experience during mild epileptic seizure; and blindsight. See also the 'two visual systems' hypothesis of Milner and Goodale, 1995, and Jacob and Jeannerod, 2003, according to which the experiences that guide our detailed movements on-line are all of them routinely non-conscious ones, the outputs of the parietal 'how-to' visual faculty.) For in some of these cases, at least, we appear to have first-order representations of the environment that are not only poised for the guidance of behavior, but that are actually controlling it.[9] So how can FOR theorists explain why our perceptions, in such cases, aren't

---

[9] Tye (1995) claims that blindsight is different, since in this case there is no behavior without prompting. Even imagined cases of Super-blindsight (Block, 1995)—where subjects become self-cueing, and act spontaneously on information gleaned from their blind fields—are said not to fit the bill, since what controls action here are propositional—conceptual—*thoughts*, not the kinds of non-conceptual, analog, representations that are characteristic of perceptual experience. What Tye overlooks, however, is the way in which perceptual information in the blind field can be involved in detailed, fine-grained, control of movement, such as reaching out to grasp an object (Marcel, 1998—but note that these results had in fact been circulating informally for many years). This looks much more characteristic of genuine perception.

phenomenally conscious? There would seem to be just two ways for them to respond. Either they can accept that absent-minded driving experiences *aren't* phenomenally conscious, and characterize what additionally is required to render an experience phenomenally conscious in (first-order) functional terms; or they can insist that absent-minded driving experiences *are* phenomenally conscious, but in a way that makes them inaccessible to their subjects.

Kirk (1994) apparently exemplifies the first approach, claiming that for a perceptual state with a given content to be phenomenally conscious, and to acquire a 'feel', it must be present to the *right sorts* of decision-making processes— namely those that constitute the organism's highest-level executive. But this is extremely puzzling. It is utterly mysterious how an experience with one and the same content could be sometimes phenomenally conscious and sometimes not, depending just upon the overall role in the organism's cognition of the decision-making processes to which it is present.[10]

Tye (1995) takes the second approach. In cases such as that of absent-minded driving, he claims that there is experience, which is phenomenally conscious, but which is 'concealed from the subject'.[11] This then gives rise to the highly counter-intuitive claim that there are phenomenally conscious experiences to which the subject is blind—experiences that it is *like* something to have, but of which the subject is unaware. And in explaining the aware/unaware distinction, Tye then goes for an actualist form of higher-order thought (HOT) theory. He argues that we are *aware* of an experience and its phenomenal properties only when we are actually applying phenomenal concepts to it. The dilemma then facing him, is *either* that he can't account for the immense richness of experience of which we are (can be) aware; *or* that he has to postulate an immensely rich set of HOTs involving phenomenal concepts accompanying each set of experiences of which we are aware—the same dilemma faced by any actualist HOT theorist, in fact (see section 7 below).[12]

## 5. THE EXPLANATORY POWER OF HOR THEORIES

I now propose to argue that phenomenal consciousness will emerge, of metaphysical necessity, in any system where perceptual information is made

---

[10] This point is developed at length in my 1992a, and in a different way in my 2000.

[11] Another variant of this approach would be to claim that the experience is phenomenally conscious, but is instantly forgotten (Dennett, 1991). This variant faces problems of its own (see my 1996, ch. 5); and it certainly cannot account for all cases.

[12] In the original version of this essay I also argued, at this point, that Tye's position may be incoherent—arguing that it makes no sense to talk about *subjective* properties that are unavailable to a *subject*. But I now think that this was a mistake. *Subjective* properties, in the present context, are the properties that *explain* the felt properties of experience, when tokened in the right sort of way within a subject. And those very properties might sometimes be tokened in such a way that there isn't any subject to whom they are available. See the final section of Ch. 4 of the present volume for further discussion.

available to higher-order representations (HORs) in analog form, and where the system is capable of recognizing its own perceptual states, as well as the states of the world perceived. For by postulating that this is so, we can explain why phenomenal feelings should be so widely thought to possess the properties of *qualia*—that is, of being non-relationally defined, intrinsic, private, ineffable, and knowable with complete certainty by the subject.[13]

I claim, in fact, that any subjects who instantiate such a cognitive system (that is, who instantiate a HOR model of state-consciousness) will normally come to form just such beliefs about the characteristics of their perceptual states—and they will form such beliefs, not because they have been explicitly programmed to do so, but naturally, as a by-product of the way in which their cognition is structured. This then demonstrates, I believe, that a regular capacity for HORs about one's own mental states must be a sufficient condition for the enjoyment of experiences that possess a subjective, phenomenal, feel to them.[14]

Let us consider, in particular, the thesis of non-relational definition for terms referring to the subjective aspects of an experience. This is a thesis that many people find tempting, at least. When we reflect on what is essential for an experience to count as an experience *as of red*, for example, we are inclined to deny that it has anything directly to do with being caused by the presence of something red. We want to insist that it is conceptually possible that an experience of that very type should normally have been caused by the presence of something green, say. All that is truly essential to the occurrence of an experience *as of red*, on this view, is the way that such an experience feels to us when we have it—it is the distinctive feel of an experience that defines it, not its distinctive relational properties or causal role (see Kripke, 1972).

Now any system instantiating a HOR model of consciousness will have the capacity to distinguish or classify perceptual states according to their contents, not by inference (that is, by self-interpretation) or description, but immediately. The system will be capable of recognizing the fact that it has an experience *as of red*, say, in just the same direct, non-inferential, way that it can recognize red. (This is just what it means to say that perceptual states are available to HORs, in the intended sense.) The system will, therefore, readily have available to it purely recognitional concepts of experience. In which case, absent and inverted

---

[13] In fact I focus here entirely on the question of non-relational definition. I shall then say something about intrinsicness in section 8 below. For the remaining points, see Ch. 6 of the present volume. Note that the term '*qualia*' is sometimes used more neutrally than I do here, as just another way of referring to the *what-it-is-likeness* of experience.

[14] What *sort* of sufficient condition? Not conceptual, surely, since the conceivability of zombies suggests that it is conceptually possible for a creature to have all the right representations of its own experiential states while lacking phenomenal consciousness. But to demand a conceptual sufficiency-condition is to place the demands on a naturalistic theory of consciousness too high. We just need to be told what phenomenal consciousness *is*. And a condition that is metaphysically sufficient can, arguably, do that. See Ch. 2 of the present volume for further discussion.

subjective feelings will immediately be a conceptual possibility for someone applying these recognitional concepts. If I instantiate such a system, then I shall straight away be able to think, '*This* type of experience might have had some quite other cause', for example.

I have conceded that there may be concepts of experience that are purely recognitional, and so that are not definable in relational terms. Does this then count against the acceptability of the functionalist conceptual scheme that forms the background to cognitive accounts of consciousness? If it is conceptually possible that an experience *as of red* should regularly be caused by perception of green grass or blue sky, then does this mean that the crucial facts of consciousness must escape the functionalist net, as many have alleged? I think not. For higher-order representational (HOR) accounts aren't in the business of conceptual analysis, but of substantive theory development. So it is no objection to those accounts, that there are some concepts of the mental that cannot be analyzed (that is, defined) in terms of functional or representational role, but are purely recognitional—provided that the nature of those concepts, and the states that they recognize, can be adequately characterized within the theory.

According to HOR theory, the properties that are in fact picked out (note: not *as such*) by any purely recognitional concepts of experience are not, themselves, similarly simple and non-relational.[15] When I recognize in myself an experience *as of red*, what I recognize is, in fact, a perceptual state that represents worldly redness, and that underpins, in turn, my capacity to recognize, and to act differentially upon, red objects. And the purely recognitional concept, itself, is one that represents the presence of just such a perceptual state, and tokenings of that concept then cause further characteristic changes within my cognition. There is nothing, here, that need raise any sort of threat to a naturalistic theory of the mind.

With the distinction firmly drawn between our recognitional *concepts* of phenomenal feelings, on the one hand, and the *properties* that those concepts pick out, on the other, we can then claim that it is metaphysically necessary that the subjective aspect of an experience of red should be caused, normally, by perception of red.[16] For a HOR account tells us that the subjective aspect of an experience of red just *is* an analog representation of red, presented to a cognitive apparatus having the power to distinguish amongst states in terms of their differing representational contents, as well as to classify and distinguish between the items represented. In which case there can be no world (where the laws of

---

[15] This is what makes me—in one good sense—a *qualia-irrealist*, since I claim that there *are no* non-relational properties of experience *qua* experience.

[16] Strictly speaking, what I say in this paragraph and in the ones following needs to be modified to allow for the fact that the representational contents in question may be individuated *narrowly*, in abstraction from their normal worldly causes. See my 2000, ch. 4, for discussion.

nature remain as they are, at least) in which the one exists but not the other. For there will, in fact, be no 'one' and 'other' here, but only one state differently thought of—now recognitionally, now in terms of functional role.

But isn't it possible—metaphysically as well as conceptually—that there should be organisms possessing color vision, that are sensitive to the same range of wavelengths as ourselves, but which nevertheless have their phenomenal feelings inverted from ours? I claim not, in fact. For the property of being the subjective feel of an experience of red is a functional/representational one, identical with possession of a distinctive causal/representational role (the role namely, of being a state that represents worldly redness, and that is present to a faculty of higher-order representation with the power to recognize its own perceptual states as such). In which case feeling-inversion of the type imagined will be impossible.

Since any organism instantiating a HOR model of state-consciousness will naturally be inclined to make just those claims about its experiences that human 'qualia-freaks' make about theirs, we have good reason to think that HOR theory provides us with a *sufficient* condition of phenomenal consciousness. But is there any reason to think that it is also *necessary*—that is, for believing that HOR theory gives us the truth about what phenomenal consciousness *is*? One reason for doubt is that a first-order (FOR) theorist, too, can avail himself of the above explanation (as Tye, 1995, does). For FOR theorists needn't deny that we humans are in fact capable of HORs. They can then claim that FOR theory gives the truth about phenomenal consciousness, while appealing to HORs to explain, e.g. the conceptual possibility of inverted spectra. To put the point somewhat differently: it may be claimed that what *underpins* the possibility of inverted spectra (i.e. phenomenal consciousness itself) is there, latent, in FOR systems; but that only a creature with the requisite concepts (HORs) can actually *entertain* that possibility.

This suggestion can be seen to be false, however, in light of the FOR theorists' failure to distinguish between worldly subjectivity and mental-state subjectivity (discussed in section 3 above) and in light of the FOR theorists' difficulties in explaining how we can have purely recognitional concepts of experience (see Chapter 5 of the present volume). In fact a system that is only capable of FORs will only have the raw materials to underpin a much more limited kind of possibility. Such a system may contain, let us say, FORs of *red*. Its states will then represent various surfaces as covered with a certain uniform property, for which it may possess a recognitional concept. This provides the raw materials for thoughts such as, '*That* property [*red*] may in fact be such-and-such a property [e.g. pertaining to reflective powers]'. But there is nothing here that might make it possible to entertain thoughts about spectra inversion. Lacking any way of distinguishing between *red* and *the experience of red*, the system lacks the raw materials necessary to underpin such thoughts as, 'Others may experience *red* as I experience *green*'—by which I mean not just that a FOR system will lack the concepts necessary to frame such a thought (this is obvious), but that there will be nothing *in the contents of the system's experiences and other mental states* that might warrant it.


## 6. CONSCIOUS STATES FOR ANIMALS (AND YOUNG CHILDREN)?

Having argued for the superiority of HOR theory over FOR theory, I turn now to the question of how widely distributed conscious mental states will be, on a higher-order representational account. For both Dretske (1995) and Tye (1995) claim—without any real argument—that this provides a decisive consideration in favor of their more modest FOR approach. I shall argue that they are right to claim that HOR theories must deny phenomenal consciousness to the mental states of animals (and very young children), but wrong that this provides any reason for accepting a FOR account.[17]

Gennaro (1996) defends a form of higher-order thought (HOT) theory. And he acknowledges that if possession of a conscious mental state M requires a creature to conceptualize (and entertain a HOT about) M *as M*, then probably very few creatures besides human beings will count as having conscious states. Let us focus on the case where M is a percept of green, in particular. If a conscious perception of a surface as green required a creature to entertain a HOT with the content *that I am perceiving a green surface*, then probably few other creatures, if any, would qualify as subjects of such a state. There is intense debate about whether even chimpanzees have a conception of perceptual states as such (see, e.g. Povinelli, 1996, 2000); in which case it seems very unlikely that any non-apes will have one. So the upshot might be that phenomenal consciousness is restricted to apes, if not exclusively to human beings.

This is a consequence that Gennaro (1996) is keen to resist. He tries to argue that much less conceptual sophistication than the above is required. In order for M to count as conscious one doesn't have to be capable of entertaining a thought about M *qua M*. It might be enough, he thinks, if one were capable of thinking of M as *distinct from* some other state N. Perhaps the content of the relevant HOT takes the form, *this is distinct from that*. This certainly appears to be a good deal

---

[17] I should stress that the argumentative structure of my position is definitely not this: first, form the opinion that non-human animals lack phenomenal consciousness; second, ask what it is that humans possess that animals lack; so third, endorse a HOR theory. On the contrary, I have no pre-theoretical axe to grind against animal consciousness. Rather, the argument goes like this: first, advance dispositional HOT theory as explaining what needs to be explained about phenomenal consciousness (see section 5 above, and sections 7 and 8 below); second, ask whether there is evidence of such thoughts in non-human animals; third, conclude that since such evidence is lacking, most animals are probably not phenomenally conscious.

less sophisticated. But appearances can be deceptive—and in this case I believe that they are.

What would be required in order for a creature to think, of an experience of green, that it is distinct from a concurrent experience of red? More than is required for the creature to think *of green* that it is distinct from *red*, plainly. For this wouldn't be a HOT at all, but rather a first-order thought about the distinctness of two perceptually presented colors. So if the subject thinks, *this is distinct from that*, and thinks something higher-order thereby, then something must make it the case that the relevant *this* and *that* are color experiences as opposed to just colors. What could this be?

There would seem to be just two possibilities. Either, on the one hand, the *this* and *that* are picked out as experiences by virtue of the subject deploying—at least covertly—a concept of *experience*, or some near equivalent (such as a concept of *seeming*, or *sensation*, or some narrower versions thereof, such as *seeming color* or *seeming red*). This would be like the first-order case where I entertain the thought, *that is dangerous*, in fact thinking about a particular perceptually presented cat, by virtue of a covert employment of the concept *cat*, or *animal*, or *living thing*. But this first option just returns us to the view that HOTs (and so phenomenal consciousness) require possession of concepts that it would be implausible to ascribe to most species of animal.

On the other hand, the subject's indexical thought about their experience might be grounded in a non-conceptual *discrimination of* that experience as such. We might model this on the sort of first-order case where someone—perhaps a young child—thinks, *that is interesting*, of what is in fact a colored marble (but without possessing the concepts *marble*, *sphere*, or even *physical object*), by virtue of their experience presenting them with a non-conceptual array of surfaces and shapes in space, in which the marble is picked out as one region-of-filled-space amongst others. Taking this second option would move us, in effect, to a *higher-order experience* (HOE) or 'inner sense' account of consciousness. Just such a view has been defended recently by Lycan (1996), following Armstrong (1968, 1984).[18]

How plausible is it that animals might be capable of HOEs? Lycan (1996) faces this question, arguing that HOEs might be widespread in the animal kingdom, perhaps serving to integrate the animal's first-order experiences for purposes of more efficient behavior-control. But a number of things go wrong here. One is that Lycan seriously underestimates the computational complexity required of the internal monitors necessary to generate the requisite HOEs. In order to perceive an experience, the organism would need to have the mechanisms to

---

[18] Gennaro (1996) alleges—surely wrongly—that there is no real distinction between HOE and HOT accounts. In fact the difference supervenes on the distinction between non-conceptual/analog content, on the one hand, and conceptual content, on the other. See Ch. 4 of the present volume.

generate a set of internal representations with a content (albeit non-conceptual) representing the content of that experience. For remember that both HOT and HOE accounts are in the business of explaining how it is that one aspect of someone's experiences (e.g. of movement) can be conscious while another aspect (e.g. of color) can be non-conscious. So in each case a HOE would have to be constructed that represents just those aspects, in all of their richness and detail. But when one reflects on the immense computational resources that are devoted to perceptual processing in most organisms, it becomes very implausible that such complexity should be replicated, to any significant degree, in generating HOEs.

Lycan also goes wrong, surely, in his characterization of what HOEs are *for* (and so, implicitly, in his account of what would have led them to evolve). For there is no reason to think that *perceptual integration*—that is, first-order integration of different representations of one's environment or body—either requires, or could be effected by, second-order processing. So far as I am aware, no cognitive scientist working on the so-called 'binding problem' (the problem of explaining how representations of objects and representations of color, say, get bound together into a representation of an object-possessing-a-color) believes that second-order processing plays any part in the process.

Notice, too, that it is certainly not enough, for a representation to count as a higher-order experience (HOE), that it should occur down-stream of, and be differentially caused by, a first-order experience. So the mere existence of different stages and levels of perceptual processing isn't enough to establish the presence of HOEs. Rather, those later representations would need to have an appropriate cognitive role—figuring in inferences or grounding judgments in a manner distinctive of second-order representations. What could this cognitive role possibly be? It is very hard to see any other alternative than that the representations in question would need to be able to ground judgments of *appearance*, or of *seeming*, helping the organism to negotiate the distinction between appearance and reality (see my 1996, ch. 5). But that then returns us to the idea that any organism capable of mental-state consciousness would need to possess *concepts* of experience, and so be capable of HOTs.

I conclude that higher-order representation theories will entail (when supplemented by plausible empirical claims about the representational powers of non-human animals) that very few animals besides ourselves are subject to phenomenally conscious mental states.[19] Is this a decisive—or indeed

---

[19] Does this have implications for our moral treatment of animals? I once used to think so—see my 1992b, ch. 8. But I now no longer do—see Chs. 9 and 10 of the present volume. My current view is that it is *first-order* (non-phenomenal) disappointments and frustrations of desire that are the most basic objects of sympathy and (possible) moral concern. (I still think that it is a distinctively moral question— to be addressed by moral theory—whether we are *required* to extend moral concern to animals; and on this my views haven't changed. See my 1992b, chs. 3–7.)

any—consideration in favor of FOR accounts? My view is that it isn't, since we lack any grounds for believing that animals have phenomenally conscious states. Of course, most of us do have a powerful intuitive belief that there is something which it is *like* for a cat or a rat to experience the smell of cheese. But this intuition is easily explained. For when we ascribe an experience to the cat we quite naturally (almost habitually) try to form a first-person representation of its content, trying to imagine what it might be like 'from the inside'.[20] But when we do this what we do, of course, is imagine a *conscious* experience—what we do, in effect, is represent one of our *own* experiences, which will bring its distinctive phenomenology with it. All we really have reason to suppose, in fact, is that the cat *perceives* the smell of the cheese. We have no independent grounds for thinking that its percepts will be phenomenally conscious ones. (Certainly such grounds aren't provided by the need to explain the cat's behavior. For this purpose the concept of perception, *simpliciter*, will do perfectly well. See Chapter 11 of the present volume.)

Notice that it isn't only animals, but also young children, who will lack phenomenal consciousness according to higher-order thought (HOT) accounts. For the evidence is that children under, say, the age of three[21] lack the concepts of *appearance* or *seeming*—or equivalently, they lack the idea of perception as involving *subjective* states of the perceiver—that are necessary for the child to entertain HOTs about its experiences. Dretske (1995) uses this point to raise an objection against HOT theories, which is distinct from the argument from animals discussed above. He asks whether it isn't very implausible that children older than three and children younger than three should undergo different *kinds* of experiences—namely, ones that are phenomenally conscious and ones that aren't. Granted, the one set of children may be capable of more sophisticated (and higher-order) thoughts than the other; but surely their experiences are likely to be fundamentally the same?

In reply, we may allow that the first-order contents of the two sets of experiences are very likely identical; the difference being that the experiences of the younger children will lack the dimension of *subjectivity*. Put differently: *the world* as experienced by the two sets of children will be the same, but the younger children will be blind to the existence and nature of their own experiences. This looks like a pretty fundamental difference in the mode in which their experiences figure in cognition!—fundamental enough to justify claiming that

[20] There is at least this much truth in so-called 'simulationist' accounts of mental-state attribution. See many of the papers in Carruthers and Smith, 1996.

[21] Many developmental psychologists would say that under the age of *four* most children lack a concept of false belief, and the related concepts of *seeming*, of *subjectivity*, and of *appearances*. I make the claim more cautiously, because increasingly sophisticated experimental techniques continue to push the age of 'theory-of-mind' acquisition lower; and because there is evidence that many younger children at least have an *implicit* conception of false belief. See Clements and Perner, 1994.

the experiences of the one set of children are phenomenally conscious while those of the other are not, indeed.

## 7. HOE *VERSUS* HOT, AND ACTUALIST *VERSUS* DISPOSITIONALIST

With the superiority of higher-order representational (HOR) over first-order representational (FOR) accounts of phenomenal consciousness now established, the dispute amongst the different forms of HOR theory is apt to seem like a local family squabble. Accordingly, this section will be brisk.[22]

The main problem for (inner-sense versions of) higher-order experience (HOE) theories, as opposed to higher-order thought (HOT) theories, is the problem of *function*. One wonders what all this re-representing is *for*, and how it could have evolved, unless the creature were already capable of entertaining HOTs. In fact this point has already emerged in our discussion of Lycan above—a capacity for higher-order discriminations amongst one's own experiences could not have evolved to aid first-order perceptual integration and discrimination, for example.[23] It is hard to see what function HOEs could serve, in fact, but that of underpinning, and helping the organism to negotiate, the distinction between *appearance* and *reality*. But this is already to presuppose that the creature is capable of HOTs, entertaining thoughts about its own experiences (i.e. about the way things *seem*). And then a creature capable of HOTs wouldn't *need* HOEs—it could just apply its mentalistic concepts directly to, and in the presence of, its first-order experiences (see below).

In contrast, there is no problem whatever in explaining (at least in outline) how a capacity for higher-order thoughts (HOTs) might have evolved. Here we can just plug-in the standard story from the primatology and 'theory-of-mind' literatures (see, e.g. Humphrey, 1986; Byrne and Whiten, 1988; Baron-Cohen, 1995). Humans might have evolved a capacity for HOTs because of the role that such thoughts play in predicting and explaining, and hence in manipulating and directing, the behaviors of others. And once the capacity to think and reason about the beliefs, desires, intentions, and experiences of others was in place, it would have been but a small step to turn that capacity upon oneself, developing recognitional concepts for at least some of the items in question. This would have brought yet further benefits, not only by enabling us to negotiate the appearance–reality

---

[22] For more detailed development of some of the points made here, see my 1996, chs. 5 and 6, and my 2000, chs. 8 and 9.

[23] Yet as a complex system it would surely have had to evolve, rather than appearing by accident or as an epiphenomenon of some other selected-for function. The idea that we might possess a faculty of 'inner sense' which wasn't selected for in evolution is almost as absurd as the suggestion that *vision* wasn't selected for—and that is an hypothesis that no one could now seriously maintain.

distinction, but also by enabling us to gain a measure of control over our own mental lives—once we had the power to recognize and reflect on our own patterns of thinking, we also had the power (at least to a limited degree) to change and improve on those patterns; so consciousness breeds cognitive flexibility and improvement. (See Chapter 8 of the present volume for further discussion.)

The main problem for *actualist* as opposed to *dispositionalist* HOT theories (and note that this is a problem infecting inner-sense theory, too, which is also actualist), is that of *cognitive overload*. There would appear to be an immense amount that we can experience consciously at any one time—think of listening intently to a performance of Beethoven's seventh symphony whilst watching the orchestra, for example. But there may be an equally large amount that we can experience *non*-consciously; and the boundaries between the two sets of experiences seem unlikely to be fixed. As I walk down the street, for example, different aspects of my perceptions may be, now conscious, now non-conscious, depending upon my interests, current thoughts, and saliencies in the environment. Actualist HOR theories purport to explain this distinction in terms of the presence, or absence, of a HOR targeted on the percept in question. But then it looks as if our HORs must be just as rich and complex as our conscious perceptions, since it is to be the presence of a HOR that explains, of each aspect of those perceptions, its conscious status. And when one reflects on the amount of cognitive space and effort devoted to first-order perception, it becomes hard to believe that a significant proportion of that cognitive load should be replicated again in the form of HORs to underpin consciousness.

The only remotely acceptable response for an actualist HOR theorist would be to join Dennett (1991) in denying the richness and complexity of conscious experience.[24] But this is not really very plausible. It may be true that we can only (consciously) *think* one thing at a time (give or take a bit). But there surely isn't the same kind of limit on the amount we can consciously *experience* at a time. Even if we allow that a variety of kinds of evidence demonstrates that the periphery of the visual field lacks the sort of determinacy we intuitively believe it to have, for example, there remains the complexity of focal vision, which far outstrips any powers of description we might possess.

---

[24] Dennett (1991) adopted, at the same time, a form of dispositional HOR theory, maintaining that it is a content's *availability* to higher-order thought and description which constitutes it as conscious— and it is because the counter-factuals embedded in the notion of *availability* are thought to lack determinate truth-values that we get the thesis of the radical *indeterminacy* of consciousness. There is an irony here if, as I suppose, the richness of conscious experience provides the main motive for preferring a dispositional HOT theory to its actualist counterpart. It is perhaps no accident, then, that Dennett has now shifted to a form of actualism, saying that consciousness is like *fame* (1995)—constituted by the (actual) effects of a content on surrounding systems, including linguistic description and long-term memory. (And by the way, the indeterminacy of fame is just the indeterminacy of vagueness—there is nothing very radical here any longer.)

Dispositional forms of HOT theory can neatly avoid the cognitive overload problem. They merely have to postulate a special-purpose short-term memory store whose function is, *inter alia*, to make its contents available to HOT. The entire contents of the store—which can, in principle, be as rich and complex as you please—can then be conscious in the absence even of a single HOT, provided that the subject remains *capable* of entertaining HOTs about any aspect of its contents. And note that the contents of the store are just first-order percepts, which can then be the objects of HOT (and hence also acquire a second-order content; see section 8 below)—no re-representation involving a faculty of 'inner sense' is needed.

It is easy to see how a system with the required structure might have evolved. Start with a system capable of first-order perception, ideally with a short-term integrated perceptual memory-store whose function is to present its contents, *poised*, available for use by various theoretical and practical reasoning systems. Then add to the system a 'theory-of-mind' or 'mind-reading' faculty with a capacity for HOTs, which can take inputs from the perceptual memory store, and allow it to acquire recognitional concepts to be applied to the perceptual states and contents of that store. And then you have it! Each of these stages looks as if it could be independently explained and motivated in evolutionary terms. And there is minimal metarepresentational complexity involved.[25]

## 8. DISPOSITIONAL HOT AND THE SUBJECTIVITY OF EXPERIENCE[26]

Isn't dispositionalism the wrong *form* for a theory of phenomenal consciousness to take, however? Surely the phenomenally conscious status of any given percept is an *actual*—and in some sense *categorical*—property of it, not to be analyzed by saying that the percept in question *would* give rise to a targeting higher-order thought (HOT) in suitable circumstances. In fact there is no real difficulty here. For presumably the percept is *really*—actually—contained in the short-term memory store in question. So the percept is categorically conscious even in the absence of a targeting HOT, by virtue of its presence in the store. It is merely that what constitutes the store as one whose contents are conscious lies in its availability-relation to HOTs.

---

[25] Ironically, Dretske (1995) himself provides us with just the materials needed, in the chapter (ch. 2) devoted to introspection. For 'introspection' just read 'potential introspection' throughout, and then you more-or-less have the correct account of phenomenal consciousness!

[26] This section has been added to the chapter for inclusion in the present volume, drawing on material used in the replies to the commentaries on the original article, which appeared in *Psyche*, 1999 & 2000.

But how do dispositions explain feel? How can the mere fact that perceptual contents are *available* to HOT transform them from states lacking phenomenal consciousness into states possessing the distinctive subjective properties of 'feel' and 'what-it-is-likeness'? For these latter properties certainly seem like categorical ones. Indeed, worse still, when I *do* make a higher-order judgment about the subjective properties of some experience, it is surely *because* that experience *already* has those properties that the judgment gets made. How, then, can a disposition to make higher-order judgments be constitutive of subjectivity?

The answer to the main question here—how a relation of mere availability can constitute subjectivity—is given by appeal to some or other version of consumer semantics. According to all forms of consumer semantics (including teleosemantics and various forms of functional and inferential role semantics) the intentional content of a state depends, at least in part, on what the down-stream consumer systems that can make use of that state are disposed to do with it. There are powerful reasons for preferring some form of consumer semantics to any kind of pure causal co-variance semantics (Botterill and Carruthers, 1999, ch. 7). And there are independent reasons to think that changes in consumer-systems can transform perceptual contents (and with it phenomenal consciousness), as in the classic experiments involving spatially-inverting lenses (Welch, 1978; Hurley, 1998).

Let me develop the point in connection with a different sort of example, however: prosthetic vision (Bach-y-Rita, 1995; Bach-y-Rita and Kercel, 2003). Blind subjects can be fitted with a device that transforms the output from a hand-held or head-mounted video-camera into a pattern of electrically induced tactile stimulation—in the original experiments, via a pad extending across the subject's back; in more recent experiments (and because of its greater sensitivity), via an attachment to the subject's tongue. Initially, of course, the subjects just feel patterns of gentle tickling sensations spreading over the area in question, while the camera scans what is in front of them. But provided that they are allowed to control the movements of the camera themselves, their experiences after a time acquire three-dimensional distal intentional contents, representing the positions and movements of objects in space.

Note that it isn't just that subjects learn to draw spatial *inferences* from the patterns of tactile stimulation; it is that those patterns themselves become imbued with spatial content. The subjects in question say that it has come to *seem* to them that there is a spherical object moving towards them, for example. And if a large object is moved suddenly towards the subject's face, he will 'instinctively' and immediately lurch away from it (even though the relevant patterns are occurring on his back). Moreover, the experiences in question can also guide actions, such as hitting a ball rolling towards the subject across a desk. Here everything on the input side remains the same as it was when they first began to wear the device; but the planning and action-controlling systems have learned to interpret those states differently. And as a result, the subjects' first-order intentional perceptual contents have become quite different.[27]

If consumer semantics is assumed, then it is easy to see how mere dispositions can transform contents in the way that dispositional HOT theory supposes. For notice that the consumer system for a given state doesn't actually have to be making use of that state in order for the latter to carry the appropriate content—it just has to be *disposed* to make use of it should circumstances (and what is going on elsewhere in the cognitive system) demand. So someone normalized to inverting spectacles doesn't actually have to be acting on the environment in order to see things right-side-up. He can be sitting quietly and thinking about something else entirely. But still the spatial content of his perceptual states is fixed, in part, by his dispositions to think and move in relation to the spatial environment.

According to dispositional HOT theory, then, the availability of a sub-set of our perceptual states (those in the 'consciousness-box', or 'C-box') to a 'theory of mind' or 'mind-reading' faculty is sufficient to transform the intentional contents of those states. Where before, in the absence of such a faculty, the states had merely first-order contents—containing analog representations of worldly color, texture, shape, and so on—now all of those states have, at the same time, higher-order, experience-representing, contents. Each state that is an analog representation of *red* is at the same time an analog representation of *seeming red* or *experience of red*, in virtue of the fact that the mind-reading system contains recognitional concepts of experience which can be applied to those very contents. So each of the perceptual states in the relevant sub-set acquires a dimension of *seeming* or *subjectivity*, by virtue of its availability to a (sufficiently sophisticated) mind-reading faculty.

Consider, here, the implications of some form of inferential role semantics in connection with a propositional example, for the sake of concreteness. What is it that confers the content $P \supset Q$ on some complex belief-state of the form '$P * Q$'? (The sign '$*$' here is meant as a dummy connective, not yet interpreted.) In part,

---

[27] One reason why I prefer this example to that of spatially inverting lenses, in order to make the consumer-semantic point, is that it is much more obvious in this case that the relevant changes occur down-stream of the perceptual system, in the way that the outputs of that system are consumed elsewhere. In the case of the visual system, it is already structured to generate 3-D representations of objects in space. So it would be possible for someone to claim that the effects of the inverting lenses occur on the input-side, using motor feedback to change the processing that takes place internal to the visual system, prior to the generation of a perceptual experience. But there is nothing on the input side of the tactile system that has prepared it to construct 3-D representations of objects in distal space. So it is highly likely that the relevant changes take place in the consumer systems for the tactile percepts, building links between the somasensory areas of the brain and the areas in visual cortex normally concerned with spatial representations, hence resulting in the changed intentional contents of those perceptions. And indeed, there exists brain-imaging data that suggests just this (Bach-y-Rita and Kercel, 2003).

plainly, it is that one is disposed to infer 'Q' from the premises 'P * Q' and 'P' (Peacocke, 1992). It is constitutive of a state with a conditional content that one should be disposed to deduce the consequent from it if one believes in the truth of the antecedent. But of course this disposition can remain un-activated on some occasions on which a conditional thought is entertained, if only because the antecedent isn't yet believed. For example, suppose that I hear the weather forecaster say, 'It will snow if it gets colder this afternoon', and that I believe her. Then I have a belief with a conditional content even if I do nothing else with it. Whether I ever form the belief that it will snow, will depend on my interests and background concerns, and on whether I subsequently form the belief that it will get colder in the afternoon. But my belief still actually has a conditional content—it has it categorically—in virtue of my inferential dispositions.

So a dose of consumer semantics is just what dispositional HOT theory needs to solve the categoricity problem. Indeed, to see the answer to the more particular challenge raised concerning the causation of judgments about phenomenally conscious states, notice from the example above that in any particular instance where I *do* exercise my inferential dispositions, and arrive at a belief in the consequent, we can cite my prior conditional belief as its partial cause. So it is *because* I *already* believed that it will snow if it gets colder (and believed that it will get colder) that I came to believe that it will snow. But for all that, my preparedness to engage in just such an inference is partly constitutive of the conditional content of my prior belief. So, too, then, in the case of phenomenal experience: if I think, 'What an interesting experience' of some perceptual state of mine, it can be *because* that state is *already* phenomenally conscious (i.e. has a higher-order analog content of *seeming experience*) that I come to entertain that higher-order thought; but it can also be by virtue of my disposition to entertain HOTs of just that sort that my perceptual state has the kind of content that is constitutive of phenomenal consciousness in the first place.[28]

But does this account really explain how the phenomenally conscious properties of my experiences can be *categorical*, in the strong sense of being intrinsic, non-relational, and non-dispositional? No, it does not. The sense of 'categoricity' that gets explained is just that there is a state actually occurring (an event in the 'C-box') that actually has the property (a higher-order analog intentional

---

[28] Notice, too, that this account of the subjectivity of phenomenally conscious experience makes essential appeal to analog higher-order representations. So in one sense it is quite right to accuse me of being a closet higher-order experience theorist. Like such theorists (e.g. Lycan, 1996) I believe that phenomenal consciousness constitutively involves higher-order analog (non-conceptual or only partly conceptual) contents. But I get these for free from dispositional HOT theory by appeal to some or other form of consumer semantics, as outlined above. No 'inner scanners', nor any special faculty of 'inner sense', needs to be postulated; nor are the states that realize the higher-order analog contents distinct from those that realize the corresponding first-order contents, in the way that higher-order experience theorists normally suppose.

content) that constitutes the state as a phenomenally conscious one (conferring on that state a subjective dimension). But in common with all other representational accounts, I claim that the property in question isn't intrinsic. Since the account explains phenomenal consciousness in terms of the occurrence of a certain sort of intentional content, it is committed to denying that the *feel* of experience is an intrinsic property of it.[29]

This would only be a problem if there were some way of demonstrating that the *feel* of experience *is* intrinsic. But there isn't. Granted, we have a strong temptation to say such a thing. But this temptation is easily explained. Part of the explanation may be that we have purely recognitional concepts for our phenomenally conscious states, as we saw in section 5 above. (So our concepts of such states treat them as though they were intrinsic.) And in part it may be that the relational character of the property in question isn't overtly represented within the content of the relevant intentional states. For it is easy to mistake a *lack* of representation of the relational character of a given property as a *representation* of its *intrinsic* character.

Consider color perception, for example. The first-order content of my experience of a red surface is that there is a certain uniform analog property distributed across the surface in question. The experience doesn't *represent* that property as being a relational, dispositional one. Yet that is just what it is (on many views of color, at least—see below). For the property is really a certain sort of disposition to reflect a given set of wavelengths of light, or to have a certain sort of effect on a normal perceiver. In consequence, before we start to think scientifically about perception it is easy for us to believe that colors are intrinsic, non-dispositional, genuinely categorical properties of objects. But this is an illusion.

Likewise in the case of the *feel* of my experience of color, then. According to dispositional HOT theory, this consists in the analog intentional content *experience of color*. My higher-order experience represents a certain property as occurring—*analog experience of red*, as it might be—without representing its relational, dispositional, character. And so it is entirely natural that we should pre-theoretically think that the property in question is an intrinsic and non-dispositional one. But again, this an illusion.

Of course there are some views of dispositional properties according to which they are to be identified with the categorical bases of the dispositions in question (Mumford, 1998). So colors would be identified with the categorical microproperties of a surface in virtue of which it reflects some wavelengths of light but not others. So on these views, there is nothing illusory about our perception of the

---

[29] Recall that I am a *qualia irrealist* (in the strong sense of 'qualia'). I deny that there are any intrinsic, non-relational, non-dispositional properties of experience *qua* experience. But I can nevertheless explain how we come to be under the illusion that there are. See Ch. 6 of the present volume for further discussion.

surface as having an intrinsic property. But then exactly the same move is available in connection with phenomenal consciousness, too. One could similarly identify the *feel* of experience with the categorical basis of the disposition to give rise to higher-order thoughts. This will be the categorical event of a computational or neural sort that takes place within some functionally defined system, and which *realizes* the phenomenally conscious experience.

## 9. CONCLUSION

What are the prospects for a naturalistic theory of phenomenal consciousness, then? Pretty good, I say. Even first-order (FOR) theories have the resources to reply to many of those who think that consciousness is essentially problematic, as Dretske (1995) and Tye (1995) have shown. And higher-order (HOR) theories—particularly some form of dispositional higher-order thought theory—can do even better on a number of fronts. It turns out that the 'hard problem' isn't really so *very* hard after all!

# CHAPTER 4

# HOP over FOR, HOT Theory

Following a short introduction, this chapter begins by contrasting two different forms of higher-order experience (HOE) or higher-order perception (HOP) theory of phenomenal consciousness.[1] These are inner-sense theory, on the one hand, and a dispositional kind of higher-order thought (HOT) theory, on the other. And I then give a brief statement of the superiority of the latter. Thereafter the chapter considers arguments in support of HOP theories in general. It develops two parallel objections against both first-order representational (FOR) theories and actualist forms of HOT theory. First, neither can give an adequate account of the distinctive features of our recognitional concepts of experience. And second, neither can explain why there are some states of the relevant kinds that are phenomenal and some that aren't. The chapter shows briefly how HOP theories succeed with the former task. (See Chapter 5 of the present volume for further elaboration.) And it then responds (successfully) to the challenge that HOP theories face the latter charge too. In the end, then, the dispositional HOT version of HOP theory emerges as the overall winner: only it can provide us with a reductive explanation of phenomenal consciousness which is both successful in itself and plausible on other grounds.

## 1. INTRODUCTION

I should begin by explaining the bad joke that forms my title. (It is bad because it does need some explanation, unfortunately.) On the one hand, I shall be arguing in this chapter for the superiority of higher-order perception (HOP) theories over both first-order representational (FOR) and actualist higher-order thought

---

[1] For these purposes, I regard the difference between higher-order *experience* (HOE) and higher-order *perception* (HOP) as merely terminological. Admittedly, to some people's ears the very idea of *experience* implicates phenomenal consciousness, so that the notion of a *non*-conscious experience is in some sense incoherent. (Note that for a higher-order experience theorist, the higher-order analog states that render our first-order perceptual states phenomenally conscious *aren't* themselves characteristically conscious.) My ears aren't like this. But in the present chapter I defer to those whose ears are more sensitive. It should be noted, however, that talk of higher-order *perception* has unfortunate connotations of its own, since it suggests the existence of *organs* of such perception. But in the version of HOE / HOP theory that I defend (and in contrast with 'inner sense' theory), there are no such organs. See the discussion that follows in this chapter.

(HOT) theories. (That is, I shall be arguing that *HOP* theories win out *over* both *FOR* theory and actualist *HOT theory*.) But on the other hand, I shall be arguing that the theory on which we should all converge (the theory that we should all *hop over for*) is actually a dispositional form of *HOT theory* (a form of HOT theory that, when combined with consumer semantics, can also count as a kind of HOP theory, as we shall see).

The topic of this chapter is phenomenal consciousness: the sort of conscious state that it is *like something* to have, or that has *feel*, or *subjective phenomenology*. More specifically, this chapter is about whether (and how) phenomenal consciousness can be reductively explained, hence integrating it with our understanding of the rest of the natural world. I shan't here pause to distinguish phenomenal consciousness from other forms of state-consciousness (specifically, from various forms of *access*-consciousness), nor from a variety of kinds of *creature*-consciousness; for these distinctions have been adequately drawn elsewhere, and should by now be familiar (Rosenthal, 1986; Block, 1995; Lycan, 1996; Carruthers, 2000, ch. 1). Nor shall I pause to consider 'mysterian' arguments that phenomenal consciousness lies beyond the scope of reductive explanation (McGinn, 1991; Chalmers, 1996; Levine, 2000). And accounts that attempt to explain phenomenal consciousness directly in terms of neurology or brain-function (e.g. Crick and Koch, 1990) are similarly excluded from discussion.[2] Somewhat more narrowly, then, this chapter is concerned with attempts to provide a reductive explanation of phenomenal consciousness in terms of some combination of *intentional* (or representational) *content* and *causal* (or functional) *role*.

Representational theories of phenomenal consciousness can be divided into two broad categories, each of which then admits of several further sub-divisions. On the one hand there are first-order theories of the sort defended, in different ways, by Kirk (1994), Dretske (1995), and Tye (1995, 2000). (For discussion of a number of other variants on this first-order theme, see Carruthers, 2000, ch. 5.) Such theories reduce phenomenal consciousness to a certain sort of intentional content (*analog* or *fine-grained*, perhaps; or maybe *non-conceptual*—these differences won't concern us here) figuring in a distinctive place in the causal architecture of cognition (perhaps as the output of our perceptual faculties, *poised* to have an impact on conceptual thought and behavior control). And then on the other hand there are a variety of higher-order theories that reduce phenomenal consciousness to some sort of higher-order awareness of such first-order analog/non-conceptual intentional states.

Here is one way of carving up the different forms of higher-order representational accounts of phenomenal consciousness. The basic contrast is between

---

[2] For direct critiques of both mysterian and neurological approaches to consciousness, see Carruthers, 2000, chs. 2–4.

theories that claim that the higher-order states in question are themselves perceptual or quasi-perceptual, on the one hand, and those that claim that they are conceptualized thoughts, on the other. Higher-order perception/theories propose a reduction of phenomenal consciousness to analog/non-conceptual intentional content which is itself the target of (higher-order) analog/non-conceptual intentional contents (Armstrong, 1968; Lycan, 1996; Carruthers, 2000). Actualist higher-order thought theory, on the other hand, reduces phenomenal consciousness to analog/non-conceptual contents that are the actual target, at the time, of a higher-order belief or thought. Or otherwise put, actualist HOT theory reduces phenomenal consciousness to analog/non-conceptual contents of which the subject is conceptually aware (Rosenthal, 1986, 1993, 1997).

One somewhat surprising thesis to be advanced in the present chapter is that both first-order representational (FOR) theories and actualist HOT theories (which superficially look very different from one another) turn out to be subject to quite similar kinds of difficulty. In point of fact, essentially the same arguments that can be used to defeat the one can also be used to defeat the other. This then leaves HOP theory as the only representational account left standing. But HOP theory, too, admits of a pair of sub-varieties, one of which turns out to be, at the same time, a (dispositional) form of HOT theory. This is where we begin, in section 2. But the range of different representational alternatives can be seen laid out in Figure 4.1.

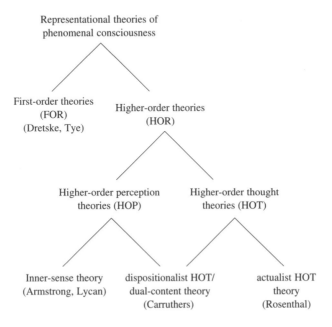

FIG 4.1 Representational theories of consciousness.

## 2. TWO KINDS OF HOP THEORY

The form of higher-order perception (HOP) theory that will be familiar to most people is so-called 'inner sense' theory, generally credited to John Locke (1690). It was reintroduced in our era by Armstrong (1968), and has been defended more recently by Lycan (1987, 1996). On this account, we not only have a set of first-order senses charged with generating analog/non-conceptual representations of our environment and the states of our own bodies, but we also have a faculty of *inner* sense, which scans the outputs of those first-order senses and generates higher-order analog/non-conceptual representations of (some of) them in turn. And while terminology differs, it would seem that it is these higher-order representations that are responsible for the *feel* of our phenomenally conscious states.[3] That is to say, our first-order perceptual states get to be phenomenally conscious by virtue of being targeted by higher-order perceptions, produced by the operations of our faculty of inner sense.

The contrasting, less familiar, form of HOP theory is a dispositional version of higher-order thought (HOT) theory (Carruthers, 2000), although it might equally be called a 'dual-content theory'. On this account, some of our first-order perceptual states acquire, at the same time, a higher-order analog/non-conceptual content by virtue of their availability to a HOT faculty, combined with the truth of some or other version of consumer semantics—either teleosemantics, or functional/conceptual role semantics.[4] (It is because it proposes a set of higher-order analog—or 'experiential'—states, which represent the existence and content of our first-order perceptual states, that the theory deserves the title of 'higher-order *perception*' theory, despite the absence of any postulated *organs* of higher-order perception.)

There is no faculty of 'inner sense' on this account; and it is one and the same set of states that have *both* first-order *and* higher-order analog/non-conceptual contents. Rather, a set of first-order perceptual states is made available to a variety of down-stream 'consumer systems' (Millikan, 1984), some concerned with first-order conceptualization and planning in relation to the perceived environment, but another of which is concerned to generate higher-order thoughts, including thoughts about those first-order perceptual states themselves. And it is by virtue of their availability to the latter consumer system that the perceptual

---

[3] Lycan (1996) describes first-order perceptual states as possessing *qualia*, irrespective of their targeting by higher-order perception; and the terminology of 'qualia' is normally reserved for states that are phenomenally conscious. But I think that what he has in mind is just that first-order perceptual states represent fine-grained colors, textures and so forth; and that those states only acquire a dimension of subjective *feel* (hence becoming phenomenally conscious) when they are higher-order perceived. At any rate this is what I shall assume in what follows. (Inner-sense theory seems to me devoid of interest otherwise.)

[4] For teleosemantics, see Millikan, 1984, 1989; Papineau, 1987, 1993. For functional or inferential role semantics, see Loar, 1981; Block, 1986; McGinn, 1989; Peacocke, 1992.

states in question acquire a dual content. Besides being first-order analog/non-conceptual representations of redness, smoothness, and so on, they are now also second-order analog/non-conceptual representations of seeming-redness, experienced-smoothness, and so forth; hence acquiring a dimension of *subjectivity*. And it is this dimension that constitutes those states as phenomenally conscious, on this account.

How can we adjudicate between these two very different versions of HOP theory? There are a pair of significant problems with inner-sense theory. One is that it is very hard to see any evolutionary reason for the development of an organ of inner sense. Yet such a faculty would be by no means computationally trivial. Since it would be costly to build and maintain, we need a good story about the adaptive benefits that it would confer on us in return. But in fact there are no such stories on offer. All of the various proposed functions of inner sense turn out, either not to require inner sense at all, or to presuppose a faculty for higher-order thought (HOT), or both (Carruthers, 2000, ch. 8). In contrast, it isn't difficult for dispositional HOT theory to explain why a HOT faculty should have evolved, nor why it should have access to perceptual contents. Here the standard stories about the adaptive benefits of sophisticated social—and perhaps 'Machiavellian'—thinking will surely suffice (Byrne and Whiten, 1988, 1998; Carruthers, 2000).

The other main problem with inner-sense theory is that it ought to be possible for such a sense organ to malfunction, just as our other senses sometimes do (Sturgeon, 2000). I can be confronted with a surface that is actually red, but which (due to unusual lighting conditions, or whatever) I perceive as orange. So, too, then, it ought to be possible for me to be undergoing an experience with the first-order analog/non-conceptual content *red* while my inner-sense faculty is producing the higher-order analog/non-conceptual content *seems orange* or *experienced orange*. In such circumstances I would be disposed to make the first-order recognitional judgment, 'It is red' (spontaneously, without inferring that the surface is red from background knowledge or beliefs about my circumstances), while at the same time being inclined to say that my experience of the object *seems orange to me*. Yet nothing like this ever seems to occur.[5]

In contrast once again, no parallel difficulty arises for dispositional HOT theory. For it is one and the same state that has both first-order and higher-order

[5] Another variant on this theme is that according to inner-sense theory it ought to be possible for me to undergo a higher-order perception with the analog/non-conceptual content *seems orange* while I am undergoing no relevant first-order perceptual state at all. (Just as, in the case of hallucination, my first-order senses can sometimes produce a state with the analog/non-conceptual content *red*, while there is nothing colored in my environment at all.) In such circumstances I would be inclined to make the first-order judgment that I see *nothing* colored (spontaneously, without inferring the absence of color from my knowledge of my circumstances and so on), while at the same time saying that I have an experience that seems orange to me. This combination of judgments seems barely coherent. Note, too, that similar problems can arise for actualist HOT theory; see Levine, 2000.

analog/non-conceptual content, on this account. (So there can be no question of the higher-order content existing in the absence of the first-order one.) And the higher-order content is entirely parasitic upon the first-order one, being produced from it by virtue of the latter's availability to a faculty of higher-order thought. There therefore seems to be no possibility that these contents could ever 'get out of line' with one another. On the contrary, the higher-order analog/non-conceptual state will always be a *seeming* of whatever first-order analog/non-conceptual content is in question.

There are difficulties for inner-sense theory that don't arise for dispositional HOT theory, then. Are there any comparable costs that attend the dispositional HOT version of HOP theory? Two are sometimes alleged, but neither seems to me very real or significant. It is sometimes said in support of inner-sense theory that this approach makes it more likely that phenomenal consciousness will be widespread in the animal kingdom (Lycan, 1996). Whereas it is rightly said that dispositional HOT theory will restrict such consciousness to creatures capable of higher-order thought (humans, and perhaps also the other great apes). But this alleged advantage is spurious in the absence of some account of the evolutionary function of inner sense, which might then warrant its widespread distribution. And our temptation to ascribe phenomenal consciousness quite widely amongst non-human animals is easily explained as a mere by-product of our imaginative abilities (see Chapter 9 of the present volume), and/or by our failure to be sufficiently clear about what really carries the explanatory burden when we explain other people's behavior by attributing phenomenally conscious states to them (see Chapter 11).

The other 'cost' of preferring dispositional HOT theory to inner-sense theory is that we are then required to embrace some form of consumer semantics, and must give up on any pure causal-covariance, or informational, mere input-side semantics. But this strikes me as no cost at all, since I maintain that all right-thinking persons should embrace consumer semantics as at least one determinant of intentional content, quite apart from any considerations to do with phenomenal consciousness (Botterill and Carruthers, 1999).

I conclude, then, that once the contrast is clearly seen between inner-sense theory, on the one hand, and dispositional HOT/dual-content versions of higher-order perception (HOP) accounts of phenomenal consciousness, on the other, then the latter should emerge as the winner overall. For there are powerful arguments against inner-sense theory, while there exist no significant arguments against dispositional HOT theory (which aren't just arguments against the higher-order character of the account, which both approaches share, of course).

This result is important, since many people are inclined to reject HOP accounts of phenomenal consciousness too easily. In fact, they see the weaknesses in inner-sense theory without realizing that there is an alternative form of HOP theory (dispositional HOT theory plus consumer semantics) which isn't really subject to those problems. The remainder of this chapter will now argue in support of HOP approaches in general, as against both first-order representational (FOR) and actualist HOT accounts. Combining those arguments with the points made briefly in the present section will then amount to an overall argument in support of a dispositional HOT form of HOP theory.

## 3. EXPLAINING HIGHER-ORDER RECOGNITIONAL JUDGMENTS

There is something of a consensus building amongst philosophers opposed to 'mysterian' approaches to phenomenal consciousness. It is that the right way to undermine the various thought experiments (zombies, inverted experiences, and suchlike) that are supposed to show that phenomenal properties don't supervene logically on physical, functional, or intentional facts, is to appeal to our possession of a set of *purely recognitional concepts* of experience (Loar, 1990, 1997; Papineau, 1993, 2002; Sturgeon, 1994, 2000; Tye, 1995, 2000; Carruthers, 2000).

The idea is that we either have, or can form, recognitional concepts for our phenomenally conscious experiences that lack any conceptual connections with other concepts of ours, whether physical, functional, or intentional. I can, as it were, just recognize a given type of experience as *this* each time it occurs, where my concept *this* lacks any conceptual connections with any other concepts of mine—even the concept *experience*. My possession of the concept *this* can consist in nothing more nor less than a capacity to recognize a given type of phenomenal state as and when it occurs.[6]

Given that I possess such purely recognitional concepts of experience, then it is easy to explain how the philosophical thought experiments become possible. I can think, without conceptual incoherence or contradiction, '*This* type of state [an experience *as of* red] might have occurred in me, or might normally occur in others, in the absence of any of its actual causes and effects; so on any view of intentional content that sees content as tied to normal causes (i.e. to information carried) and/or to normal effects (i.e. to teleological or inferential role), *this* type of state might occur without representing redness.' Equally, I can think, '*This* type of state [an experience] might not have been, or might not be in others, an *experience* at all. Rather it might have been/might be in others a state of some

---

[6] Proponents of the existence of such concepts are then committed, of course, to rejecting the (quite different) arguments put forward by Wittgenstein (1953) and Fodor (1998) against the very possibility of purely recognitional concepts. Fortunately, neither set of arguments is at all compelling, though I shan't attempt to demonstrate this here.

quite different sort, occupying a different position within the causal architecture of cognition.' Even more radically, I can think, 'There might have been a being (a zombie) who had all of my physical, functional, and intentional properties, but who lacked *this* and *this* and *that*—indeed, who lacked any of *these* states.'

Now, from the fact that we have *concepts* of phenomenally conscious states that lack any conceptual connections with physical, functional, or intentional concepts, it of course doesn't follow that the *properties* that our purely recognitional concepts pick out aren't physical, functional, or intentional ones. So we can explain the philosophical thought experiments while claiming that phenomenal consciousness is reductively explicable in physical, functional, or intentional terms. Indeed, it increasingly looks to me, and to others, that any would-be naturalizer of phenomenal consciousness needs to buy into the existence of purely recognitional concepts of experience.

Higher-order perception (HOP) theorists of phenomenal consciousness are well placed to explain the existence of purely recognitional concepts of experience. We can say the following. Just as our first-order analog perceptual contents can ground purely recognitional concepts for secondary qualities in our environments (and bodies), so our higher-order analog perceptual contents can ground purely recognitional concepts for our first-order experiences themselves. The first-order perceptual contents *analog-green, analog-smooth*, and so on can serve to ground the recognitional concepts, *green, smooth*, and so forth. Similarly, then, the higher-order perceptual contents *analog-experienced-green* and *analog-experienced-smooth* can serve to ground the purely recognitional concepts of experience, *this state* and *that state*. And such concepts are grounded in (higher-order) awareness of their objects, just as our recognitional concepts *green* and *smooth* are grounded in (first-order) awareness of the relevant secondary properties.

Neither first-order (FOR) theories of the sort defended by Dretske (1995) and Tye (1995, 2000), nor actualist higher-order thought (HOT) theories of the kind proposed by Rosenthal (1993, 1997) can give an adequate account of our possession of purely recognitional concepts of experience, however. Or so I shall briefly argue.[7]

According to FOR theories, phenomenal consciousness consists in a distinctive kind of content (analog or non-conceptual) figuring in a distinctive position in cognition (poised to have an impact upon thought and decision-making, say). Such contents are appropriate to ground first-order recognitional applications of concepts of secondary qualities, such as *green, smooth*, and so on. But what basis can they provide for higher-order recognition of those first-order experiences themselves? The perceptual content *analog-green* can ground a recognitional application of the concept *green*. But how could such a content ground a recognitional application of

---

[7] For further elaboration of some of these arguments, especially in relation to FOR theories, see Ch. 5 of the present volume.

the concept *this* [experience of green]? It isn't the right *kind* of content to ground an application of a higher-order recognitional concept. For if such concepts are to be applied recognitionally, then that means that they must be associated with some analog or non-conceptual presentation of the properties to which they apply. And that means, surely, a higher-order analog content or HOP.

One option for a FOR theorist here would be to say, as does Dretske (1995), that the higher-order concept applies to experience indirectly, via recognition of the property that the experience is an experience *of*. On such an account the putative recognitional concept *this* [experience *as of* green] is really a concept of the form, *my experience of this* [green]. But this then means that the concept is not, after all, a purely recognitional one. On the contrary, it is definitionally tied to the concept *experience*, and also to the presence of greenness. And then we can no longer explain the seeming coherence of the thoughts, 'This [experience *as of* green] might not have been an experience, and might not have been *of this* [green].'

Another option for a FOR theorist would be to defend a form of *brute-causal* account, as Loar (1990) seems tempted to do.[8] On this view the higher-order recognitional concept *this* [experience *as of* green] wouldn't have the quasi-descriptive content assumed by Dretske. Rather, applications of it would be caused by the presence of the appropriate kind of experience [*as of* green] without the mediation of any mental state, and more specifically, without the mediation of any higher-order perceptual state. But this view gets the phenomenology of higher-order recognitional judgment quite wrong. When I judge recognitionally, 'Here is *this* type of experience again', I do so on the basis of *awareness of* that which my judgment concerns—a given type of experience. I do not, as it were, judge *blindly*, as the brute-causal account would have it.

Finally, a FOR theorist might allow that we do have higher-order perceptions (HOPs) to ground our recognitional concepts of experience, while denying that this is what constitutes those experiences as phenomenally conscious ones. (Tye, 1995, sometimes seems tempted to adopt a position of this sort.) On the contrary, it might be said, all first-order analog perceptual contents are phenomenally conscious, but only some of these are targeted by higher-order perceptual contents in such a way as to ground purely recognitional concepts of experience.

One problem with this proposal, however, is that it requires us to accept the existence of phenomenally conscious states that are inaccessible to their subjects. That is, it requires us to believe that there can be phenomenally conscious states of which subjects cannot be aware. For as I shall note briefly in section 4 below, there is now robust evidence for the existence of perceptual systems whose outputs are inaccessible to consciousness, in the sense of being unavailable to higher-order awareness or verbal report. And it is one thing to claim that there

---

[8] For some alternative readings of Loar's position, see Ch. 5 of the present volume.

can be phenomenally conscious states that we happen not to be aware of through other demands on our attention (some have wanted to describe the 'absent minded driver' type of example in these terms), but it is quite another thing to claim that there are phenomenally conscious states in us that we *cannot* be aware of, or that we are *blind* to. This would be very hard to accept.

Another difficulty with the proposal is that it appears to confuse together two distinct forms of subjectivity. Any first-order perceptual state will be, in a sense, subjective. That is, it will present a subjective take on the organism's environment, presenting that environment in one way rather than another, depending on the organism's perspective and its discriminatory abilities. Thus any form of perception will involve a kind of subjectivity in the way that the world is presented to the organism. But phenomenal consciousness surely involves a much richer form of subjectivity than this. It involves, not just a distinctive way in which the world is presented to us in perception, but also a distinctive way that our perceptual states themselves are presented to us. It isn't just the world that seems a certain way to us, but our experiences of the world, too, appear to us in a certain way, and have a distinctive *feel* or phenomenology. And this requires the presence of some form of higher-order awareness, which would be lacking in the first-order representational (FOR) proposal made above.

FOR theories face severe difficulties in accounting for our possession of purely recognitional concepts of experience, then. Similar difficulties arise for actualist higher-order thought (HOT) theory, of the sort defended by Rosenthal (1993, 1997). On this account, an experience gets to be phenomenally conscious by virtue of the subject's conceptual awareness of the occurrence of that experience—that is to say, provided that the experience causes (and causes immediately, without self-interpretation) a higher-order thought to the effect that such an experience is taking place. But in the absence of any higher-order perceptual contents to ground such higher-order thoughts, this approach provides just another version of the 'brute-causal' account discussed above, and suffers from the same difficulties.[9]

Specifically, actualist HOT theory can't account for the way in which our higher-order thoughts about our experiences appear to be grounded in some sort of non-conceptual awareness of those experiences. Nor, in consequence, can it

---

[9] Does it make any difference, here, if instead of identifying a phenomenally conscious experience with an experience that is targeted by a higher-order thought, the higher-order theorist identifies the phenomenally conscious experience with a *complex* state consisting both of the first-order experience and the higher-order thought, perhaps with the contents of the two component states being suitably integrated with one another (Kriegel, 2003)? It makes no difference. The higher-order-thought component of the state is still *blind* in relation to the experience that it targets (see the discussion in the main text following this note). And there is still no explanation of why a first-order experience that gets 'bound' into a complex state containing a higher-order thought about itself should acquire the properties of subjectivity and *feel* distinctive of phenomenal consciousness (see the discussion in section 4 of this chapter). Moreover, there still remains the problem that parallels one of the main objections to inner-sense theory, namely that it ought to be possible to find cases where the contents of the two component states are out of line with one another, or cases where the higher-order component occurs in the absence of the first-order one.

explain how purely recognitional (higher-order) concepts of experience are possible which preserves their similarity to (first-order) recognitional concepts of color. Just as my judgments of 'green' are grounded in perceptual awareness of greenness (guided in their application by the content *analog-green*), so too my judgments of 'this state' are grounded in awareness of the state in question, which requires that they should be guided by a higher-order perceptual content such as *analog-experienced-green*.

According to actualist HOT theory, there is a sense in which my recognitional judgments of experience are made *blindly*.[10] I find myself making higher-order judgments about the occurrence of experience, but without those judgments being grounded in any other awareness of those experiences themselves. It is rather as if I found myself making judgments of color (e.g. 'Red here again') in the absence of any perceptual awareness of color. But higher-order judgment doesn't appear to be like that at all. When I think, 'Here is *that* experience again', I think as I do because I am aware of the experience in question. I can reflect on the appropriateness of my judgment, given the properties of the experience, for example. This requires the presence of higher-order perceptions (HOPs) of that experience.

## 4. WHY SOME STATES ARE PHENOMENAL AND SOME AREN'T

One difficulty for both first-order (FOR) theories and actualist higher-order thought (HOT) theories of phenomenal consciousness, then, is that neither can account adequately for the existence of purely recognitional judgments of experience. Another, equally powerful, objection is that neither can explain why some perceptual states are phenomenal and some aren't. That is to say, neither can give an adequate account of that in virtue of which some analog/non-conceptual states have the properties distinctive of phenomenal consciousness and some don't. But in order to make this point, I first need to say just a little about the conscious–non-conscious distinction as it applies to perceptual states.

The evidence for non-conscious perceptual states in all sensory modalities is now quite robust (Baars, 1997; Weiskrantz, 1997). Here let me concentrate on the case of vision. Armstrong (1968) uses the example of absent-minded driving to make the point. Most of us at some time have had the rather unnerving experience of 'coming to' after having been driving on 'automatic pilot' while our attention was directed elsewhere—perhaps day-dreaming or engaged in intense

---

[10] By this I *don't* mean that my higher-order judgments are *non-conscious*. For this isn't problematic. It is granted on all hands that the higher-order representations that render our first-order percepts conscious aren't themselves conscious ones, in general. Rather, I mean that for actualist HOT theory, higher-order judgments of experience aren't grounded in awareness of their objects; which debars them from counting as genuinely *recognitional*.

conversation with a passenger. We were apparently not consciously aware of any of the route we have recently taken, nor of any of the obstacles we avoided on the way. Yet we must surely have been *seeing*, or we would have crashed the car. Others have used the example of blindsight (Weiskrantz, 1986; Carruthers, 1996). This is a condition in which subjects have had a portion of their primary visual cortex destroyed, and apparently become blind in a region of their visual field as a result. But it has now been known for some time that if subjects are asked to *guess* at the properties of their 'blind' field (e.g. at whether it contains a horizontal or vertical grating, or whether it contains an 'X' or an 'O'), they prove remarkably accurate. Subjects can also reach out and grasp objects in their 'blind' field with something like 80 per cent or more of normal accuracy, and can catch a ball thrown from their 'blind' side, all without conscious awareness. (See Weiskrantz, 1997, for details and discussion.)

More recently, an even more powerful case for the existence of non-conscious visual experience has been generated by the *two visual systems theory* proposed and defended by Milner and Goodale (1995). (See Figure 4.2.) They review a wide variety of kinds of neurological and neuropsychological evidence for the substantial independence of two distinct visual systems, instantiated in the temporal and parietal lobes respectively. They conclude that the parietal lobes provide a set of specialized semi-independent modules for the on-line visual control of action; whereas the temporal lobes are primarily concerned with more off-line functions such as visual learning, object recognition, and action-planning in relation to the perceived environment. And only the experiences generated by the temporal-lobe system are phenomenally conscious, on their account.[11]

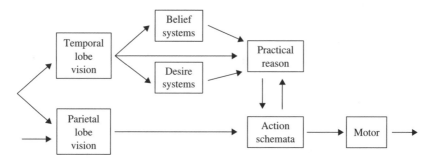

FIG 4.2 The dual-visual systems hypothesis.

[11] Note that this isn't the old and familiar distinction between *what* and *where* visual systems, but is rather a successor to it. For the temporal-lobe system is supposed to have access both to property information and to spatial information. Instead, it is a distinction between a combined *what-where* system located in the temporal lobes and a *how-to* or action-guiding system located in the parietal lobes. And note, too, that the two-visual-systems hypothesis has the resources to explain the blindsight data, by virtue of the inputs that are available to the parietal system independently of primary visual cortex (area V1).

To get the flavor of Milner and Goodale's hypothesis, consider just one strand from the wealth of evidence they provide. (For more extensive philosophical discussion, see Carruthers, 2000; Clark, 2002; Jacob and Jeannerod, 2003.) This is a neurological syndrome called *visual form agnosia*, which results from damage localized to both temporal lobes, leaving primary visual cortex and the parietal lobes intact. (Visual form agnosia is normally caused by carbon monoxide poisoning, for reasons that are little understood.) Such patients cannot recognize objects or shapes, and may be capable of little conscious visual experience, but their sensorimotor abilities remain largely intact.

One particular patient (D.F.) has now been examined in considerable detail. While D.F. is severely agnosic, she is not completely lacking in conscious visual experience. Her capacities to perceive colors and textures are almost completely preserved. (Why just these sub-modules in her temporal cortex should have been spared isn't known.) As a result, she can sometimes guess the identity of a presented object—recognizing a banana, say, from its yellow color and the distinctive texture of its surface. But she is unable to perceive the shape of the banana (whether straight or curved); nor its orientation (upright or horizontal, pointing towards her or across). Yet many of her sensorimotor abilities are close to normal—she would be able to reach out and grasp the banana, orienting her hand and wrist appropriately for its position and orientation, and using a normal and appropriate finger grip.

Under experimental conditions it turns out that although D.F. is at chance in identifying the orientation of a broad line or letter-box, she is almost normal when posting a letter through a similarly shaped slot oriented at random angles. In the same way, although she is at chance when trying to discriminate between rectangular blocks of very different sizes, her reaching and grasping behaviors when asked to pick up such a block are virtually indistinguishable from those of normal controls. It is very hard to make sense of this data without supposing that the sensorimotor perceptual system is functionally and anatomically distinct from the object-recognition/conscious system.[12]

There is a powerful case, then, for thinking that there are non-conscious as well as conscious visual percepts. While the perceptions that ground your thoughts when you plan in relation to the perceived environment ('I'll pick up *that* one') may be conscious, and while you will continue to enjoy conscious perceptions of what you are doing while you act, the perceptual states that actually guide the details of your movements when you reach out and grab the object will *not* be conscious ones if Milner and Goodale are correct.

---

[12] There are also syndromes in which the temporal-lobe object-recognition system is left intact, but in which the parietal-lobe how-to system is damaged. So what we have here is a *double*-dissociation. There is also experimental evidence from normal subjects showing that the two systems can be doubly dissociated. See Milner and Goodale, 1995.

But what implications does this have for *phenomenal* consciousness, as opposed to *access* consciousness (Block, 1995)? Must these non-conscious percepts also be lacking in *phenomenal* properties? Most people think so. While it may be possible to get oneself to believe that the perceptions of the absent-minded car driver can remain phenomenally conscious (perhaps lying outside of the focus of attention, or being instantly forgotten), it is very hard to believe that either blindsight percepts or D.F.'s sensorimotor perceptual states might be phenomenally conscious ones. For these perceptions are ones to which the subjects of those states are *blind*, and of which they *cannot* be aware. And the question, then, is: what makes the relevant difference? What is it about an access-conscious perception that renders it *phenomenal* that a blindsight perceptual state would correspondingly lack? Higher-order perception (HOP) theorists are united in thinking that the relevant difference consists in the presence of a higher-order perceptual content in the first case that is absent in the second, in virtue of the presence of which the state is one *of which the subject is perceptually aware.*

First-order (FOR) theories, by contrast, face considerable difficulties on this point. Unless the proponents of such theories choose to respond by denying the data, or by insisting that even blindsight and sensorimotor percepts are actually phenomenally conscious ones, then there is really only one viable option remaining. This is to appeal to the functional differences between percepts of the different kinds in explaining why one set is phenomenally conscious while the others aren't. For notice that the percepts constructed by the temporal-lobe system are available to conceptual thought and planning, but not to guide detailed movement on-line; whereas the reverse is true of the percepts produced by the parietal system. It is therefore open to a FOR theorist to say that it is *availability to conceptual thought* that constitutes an otherwise non-conscious perceptual state as phenomenally conscious (Kirk, 1994; Tye, 1995).

If what were being proposed were a brute identity claim, then such a position might be acceptable (or as acceptable as such claims ever are, if what we really seek is an *explanation*).[13] But proponents of FOR theories are supposed to be in the business of reductively *explaining* phenomenal consciousness. And it is left

---

[13] Block and Stalnaker (1999) argue that identities aren't the kinds of facts that *admit* of further explanation. Consider the identity of water and $H_2O$, for example. If someone asks, 'Why is water $H_2O$?', it looks as if we can only reply (vacuously), 'Because it is'. You can't *explain* the identity of water and $H_2O$. Rather, identity facts are *brute* ones (not further explicable). Now, it is true that identities can't be explained as such. But it is also true that, if the identity is to count as a successful reduction of the higher-level property involved, then it must be possible to deploy features of the property that figures on the reducing-side of the identity-claim in such a way as to explain the features distinctive of the property on the other side (the reduced property). Consider the identity of water and $H_2O$ again. Don't we think that it must be possible to deploy facts about $H_2O$, as such, in order to explain the distinctive properties of water—why it is colorless and odorless; why it is liquid at room temperatures; why it boils at 100 °C; and so forth? Likewise, then, with phenomenal consciousness. A postulated identity, here, can only be acceptable if we can deploy the properties involved in such a way as to explain some of the distinctive features of phenomenality.

entirely obscure why the presence of conceptual thought and/or planning should make such a difference. Why should a perceptual state with the content *analog-green*, for example, remain unconscious if it is available just to guide movement, but become phenomenally conscious if used to inform conceptualized thoughts (such as, 'That one is green' or 'I will pick up the green one')? Granted, there is a big difference between thinking and acting. But what reason is there for believing that this difference can explain the difference between phenomenality and its lack?

Actualist higher-order thought (HOT) theory faces essentially the same difficulty. In explaining why sensorimotor percepts aren't phenomenally conscious, a HOT theorist can point out that while such percepts guide movement, they don't give rise to higher-order thoughts and judgments. In contrast, the percepts produced by the temporal-lobe visual system are available to conceptual thought and reasoning in general, and to higher-order thought in particular. And the claim can then be made that those perceptual states produced by the temporal-lobe system are phenomenally conscious that are actually the target of a higher-order thought about themselves.

But why should the presence of a higher-order belief about the existence of a first-order perceptual state render that state phenomenally conscious? Why should higher-order *access* consciousness generate *phenomenal* consciousness? The first-order state remains the same, just as it was in the absence of the higher-order thought. (Or if it changes, this will be merely via a shifting of perceptual similarity-spaces, of the sort that is often caused by concept-application—as when I can make the aspect of a duck/rabbit figure alter by applying different concepts to it—not a change from the absence of subjective *feel* to its presence.) And the higher-order thought in question will characteristically not be a conscious one. It seems like actualist HOT theorists have no option but to advance a brute identity claim, saying that to be a phenomenally conscious state just *is* to be a perceptual state targeted by a HOT. But this is to give up on attempting a reductive *explanation* of the phenomena.[14]

## 5. DOES HOP THEORY FACE THE SAME OBJECTION?

I have argued then (in section 3) that both first-order (FOR) theories and actualist HOT theories face essentially the same problem in explaining how we can have purely recognitional concepts of experience; whereas higher-order perception

---

[14] For discussion of the demands placed on successful reductive explanation in general, and as applied to reductive explanations of phenomenal consciousness in particular, see Chs. 2 and 6 of the present volume.

(HOP) theories are well placed to provide such an explanation. And I have now argued (in section 4) that neither FOR theories nor actualist HOT theory can give an adequate account of the conscious–non-conscious distinction, explaining why some perceptual states are phenomenally conscious while some aren't. But how well do HOP theories perform in this latter respect? For ease of presentation, I shall now switch to framing the discussion in terms of the form of HOP theory that I actually endorse, namely dispositional HOT theory. On this account, phenomenal consciousness consists in the dual perceptual content (both first-order and higher-order) possessed by those perceptual states that are made available to HOT (given the truth of some or other form of consumer semantics).

Initially, the explanation of the difference between the states produced by the parietal and temporal-lobe visual systems is straightforward. The outputs of the sensorimotor system are first-order analog contents that are used merely to guide movement; and as such they aren't phenomenally conscious. The outputs of the temporal-lobe system, in contrast, are available to a variety of downstream consumer systems (such as action-planning), included in which is a faculty for higher-order thought (HOT). And it is by virtue of their availability to this HOT faculty that the first-order analog states that are produced by the temporal-lobe system come to acquire, at the same time, higher-order analog contents (given the truth of consumer semantics). And it is by virtue of having such dual content that the perceptual states in question are phenomenally conscious.[15]

Here is how an objection might go, however (Byrne, 2001). Even if we don't have any real examples, it surely *could* happen that dual-content perceptual states might occur without being accessible to their subjects (e.g. without being available to conscious thought and/or without being reportable in speech). For example, perhaps there could be a separate HOT faculty that monitors the outputs of the sensorimotor visual system for some reason, rendering those states, too, as dual-content ones. Then if I want to say that such states wouldn't really be phenomenally conscious ones, don't I have to appeal to functional-role considerations, just as FOR theory did above? Don't I have to say that phenomenally conscious states are dual-content perceptual states *that are reportable in speech*, or something of the sort? And then can't I, too, be charged with postulating a brute identity here, and giving up on reductive explanation?

An initial reply is that it is extremely unlikely that there should *actually* be such dual contents that aren't available to us. This is because higher-order thought doesn't come cheap. So far as we know, a capacity for it has evolved just

---

[15] Am I here holding dispositional HOT theory to a standard less demanding than that just imposed upon actualist HOT and FOR theories? No, because the dual-content idea *can* reductively explain the various features of phenomenal consciousness, particularly the latter's *subjective aspect* and the way in which it can ground purely recognitional concepts of experience. See Ch. 6 of the present volume.

once in the history of life on earth, somewhere in the great ape/hominid lineage (perhaps only with the appearance of *Homo*—see Povinelli, 2000, for a skeptical look at the mentalizing abilities of chimps). The idea that there might be a capacity for HOT attached to the outputs of the sensorimotor system, or embedded someplace within our color-discrimination module or whatever, is unlikely in the extreme. So I don't think that there are any *real* examples of non-access-conscious dual-content analog states (in the way that there *are* lots of real examples of non-access-conscious first-order perceptual states).

I concede, however, that it is logically possible that there could be dual-content events that aren't (in a sense) conscious. But here it really is important to emphasize the distinction between *phenomenal* consciousness and various forms of *access* consciousness. I bite the bullet, and commit myself to the view that it is logically possible for there to be phenomenally conscious events (analog perceptual states with dual content, hence perceptual states with a subjective dimension) that aren't access-conscious (that aren't available for reporting in speech or to figure in decision-making). And I think that intuitions to the contrary are easily explained away. I certainly don't see why one should *define* phenomenal consciousness in such a way as to entail (all forms of) access consciousness.[16]

This is where the fact that there are no real examples of dual-content perceptual states that aren't also widely access-conscious becomes important. For within our experience and to the best of our belief these two properties are always co-instantiated. It might be natural for us to assume, then, that the two are somehow essentially connected with one another—especially since imagination, when conscious and reflectively guided, always deploys states that are access-conscious. It is hard for us to imagine a phenomenally conscious state that isn't access-conscious. But that may just be because any image that we reflectively form is *de facto* access-conscious, given the way in which our cognitive system is actually structured.

What matters isn't what we can or can't imagine, but what we can or can't explain. And my contention is that dispositional HOT theory can reductively explain the distinctive features of phenomenal consciousness. In particular, by virtue of their dual analog content, perceptual states that are available to HOT will take on a subjective dimension. They will be both world-representing (or body-representing, in the case of pain and touch) and experience-representing at the same time. In such cases it isn't just the world that is presented to us in a certain way, but our own experience of that world will also be presented in a certain way to us. And by virtue of such higher-order presentings, we can form purely recognitional concepts targeted on those very experiential states.

---

[16] Of course, dual-content theory does entail *a* variety of access consciousness, where the *access* in question is to a faculty of higher-order thought.

This isn't the place to set out and explain in detail the way in which dispositional HOT theory/dual-content theory can provide a successful reductive explanation of the various distinctive features of phenomenal consciousness. (See Chapter 6 of the present volume.) But in addition to explaining how phenomenally conscious states possess a subjective dimension, this approach can also of course explain how such states possess properties that are available to introspective recognition, and how they can ground purely recognitional concepts, as we saw in section 3 above. We can therefore explain why, to anyone employing such concepts, the so-called 'explanatory gap' will seem to be unbridgeable. For such a person will always be able to combine, without incoherence, any proposed theory (including dual-content theory itself) with the thought, 'But someone might satisfy the conditions of the theory without possessing *this* kind of state' (thereby deploying their purely recognitional concept *this*).

Our account can also explain, too, how phenomenally conscious properties have a 'fineness of grain' that gives them a richness well beyond our powers of description and categorization. And it can be shown how people will then be strongly inclined to think of phenomenally conscious states as possessing intrinsic—that is, non-relational and non-intentional—properties; that people will be inclined to think of these properties as ineffable and private; and that we will be inclined to think that we have incorrigible, or at least privileged, knowledge of them.

Although there hasn't here been the space to develop these points in any detail, it should nevertheless be plain that it is the dual-content aspect of the theory rather than wider features of functional role (availability to planning and to speech, for example) that does the work in these explanations. This seems to me adequate motivation for the claim that phenomenal consciousness is constituted by dual-content perceptual states, wherever they might occur. To the best of our knowledge such states are also always actually accessible to the reasoning processes and reporting systems of their subjects. But there is nothing in my account of phenomenal consciousness as such that logically requires it.

## 6. CONCLUSION

I have argued that amongst higher-order perception (HOP) theories of phenomenal consciousness, dispositional higher-order thought (HOT) theory/dual-content theory is preferable to inner-sense theory. I have also argued that HOP theories are preferable to both first-order (FOR) theories and to actualist HOT theory. Neither of the latter can give an adequate account of purely recognitional concepts of experience, nor of the distinction between conscious and non-conscious perceptual states; whereas HOP theories are well placed in both of these respects. In the end, then, a dual-content theorist is what everyone ought to be.

# CHAPTER 5

# Phenomenal Concepts and Higher-Order Experiences

Relying on a range of now-familiar thought-experiments, it has seemed to many philosophers that phenomenal consciousness is beyond the scope of reductive explanation.[1] Others have thought that we can undermine the credibility of those thought-experiments by claiming that we possess purely recognitional concepts for the properties of our conscious mental states. This chapter is concerned to explain, and then to meet, the challenge of showing how purely recognitional concepts are possible if there are no such things as *qualia*—in the strong sense of intrinsic (non-relational, non-intentional) properties of experience.[2] It argues that an appeal to higher-order experiences is necessary to meet this challenge, and then deploys a novel form of higher-order thought theory to explain how such experiences are generated.

## 1. INTRODUCTION: THOUGHT-EXPERIMENTS AND QUALIA

There is now an array of familiar philosophical thought-experiments that are supposed to establish, not just that there are qualia that can vary independently of functional and intentional properties, but that qualia are non-physical in nature (Kripke, 1972; Jackson, 1982, 1986; Chalmers, 1996, 1999; Siewert, 1998). For example, I can think, '*This* type of experience [pain] might have occurred in me, or might occur in others, in the absence of any of the usual causes and effects

---

[1] Phenomenal consciousness is a form of state consciousness, which contrasts with *creature* consciousness, or *perceptual* consciousness. The different forms of state consciousness include various kinds of *access* consciousness, both first-order and higher-order—see Rosenthal, 1986; Block, 1995; Lycan, 1996; Carruthers, 2000. Phenomenal consciousness is the property that mental states have when it is *like something* to possess them, or when they have subjectively accessible *feels*; or as some would say, when they have *qualia* (see fn. 2 below).

[2] Some philosophers use the term 'qualia' in a weaker, theoretically neutral, sense than I do here, to mean whatever it is that renders a mental state phenomenally conscious (e.g. Sturgeon, 2000). Taken in this sense, to deny the existence of qualia would be to deny the very existence of phenomenal consciousness. But in the strong sense that I propose to adopt throughout this chapter, one can be a qualia irrealist—denying that experiences possess any mental properties that are intrinsic and non-intentional—while continuing to insist that some of our experiences possess subjectively accessible *feels*.

of pains. There could be someone in whom *these* experiences occur but who isn't bothered by them, and where those experiences are never caused by tissue damage or other forms of bodily insult. And conversely, there could be someone who behaves and acts just as I do when in pain, and in response to the same physical causes, but who is never subject to *this* type of experience.'

Equally, I can think, '*This* type of experience [as of red] might have occurred in me, or might normally occur in others, in the absence of any of its actual causes and effects. So on any view of intentional content that sees content as tied to normal causes (i.e. to information carried) and/or to normal effects (i.e. to teleological or inferential role), *this* type of experience might occur without representing *red*.'

Even more radically, indeed, it seems that I can think, '*This* type of state [an experience] might not have been, or might not be in others, an *experience* at all. Rather it might have been/might be in others a state of some quite different sort, occupying a different position within the causal architecture of cognition.' Or I can think, 'There might have been a complete physical/causal/intentional duplicate of me who failed to undergo *this* experience, or indeed any experience at all.'

What do these thought-experiments really establish? One popular response has been to claim that they show only that there is something distinctive about the way in which we conceptualize our experiences, not anything about the nature of those experiences themselves (Loar, 1990, 1997; Papineau, 1993, 2002; Sturgeon, 1994, 2000; Tye, 1995, 2000; Carruthers, 2000). Such thought-experiments only show, it is said, that we have some concepts of experience that are purely recognitional, in the sense of having no conceptual ties with physical concepts, or with concepts of causal role and/or concepts of intentional content. (Some use the term 'phenomenal concepts' in this regard.) The consensus amongst the authors listed above is that metaphysical claims about the nature of phenomenal properties can't be established by means of thought-experiments that turn crucially on the existence of purely recognitional concepts of experience. For we might well possess concepts of this type even if phenomenal properties are actually physical properties, or causal-role properties, or intentional properties of one sort or another.

It is true that not *every* philosopher who takes a physicalist/reductive attitude towards phenomenal consciousness is prepared to allow the existence of purely recognitional concepts of experience. Thus Dretske (1995), for example, thinks that we can only really refer to our own experiences indirectly, via the properties (*redness, roundness*, or whatever) that those experiences are experiences of. So when I think, '*This* type of experience [as of red] might have been F', I am really thinking, 'My experience *of this* [red] might have been F.' Dretske's difficulty, however, is then to provide a satisfactory explanation of how it is that I seem to be capable of thinking, '*This* type of experience [as of red] might not have been an experience *of this* [red].'

I shall not pursue the point here. I propose simply to assume, for the moment, that there are purely recognitional concepts of experience (returning to the issue briefly in section 4). I shall assume, that is, that it is possible to form a concept of a type of experience that consists in nothing more and nothing less than the capacity to recognize that type of experience when it occurs in one's own mental life. Such concepts will have no conceptual connections with any of our physical, causal-role, or intentional-content concepts—not even with the concept *experience*, if this is functionally specified by the characteristic place of experiences in the causal architecture of cognition. Our task will be to see how the existence and features of such purely recognitional concepts are best explained if there are no qualia.[3]

This chapter will be concerned to confront an important challenge. This is to explain how purely recognitional concepts are even so much as *possible* if qualia (in the strong sense) *don't* exist. For as we shall see, it can be difficult to under-stand how purely recognitional concepts of experience—of the sort that we mani-festly seem capable of possessing—are possible unless qualia are the properties being recognized. This challenge will form the topic of the remainder of the chapter. Sections 2 and 4 will outline and develop it, while sections 3 and 5 will show how the challenge can best be met. I shall be arguing, first, that purely recognitional concepts of experience need to be grounded in higher-order experiences of our (first-order) perceptual states; and second, that the most plausible version of higher-order experience theory is not the 'inner sense' theory of Armstrong (1968, 1984) and Lycan (1996), but rather one that can be derived from disposi-tional higher-order thought theory, of the sort defended by Carruthers (2000).

I should emphasize at the outset, however, that although the higher-order theories in question (whether of 'inner sense' or of higher-order thought) are normally intended and presented as reductive explanations of phenomenal consciousness, this is not their role in the present context. Our task is to explain how purely recognitional concepts of experience are possible without invoking qualia (thus blocking some of the main arguments *against* the reductive explic-ability of consciousness), not to propose any particular reductive explanation. Someone who rejects higher-order thought theory as a reductive account of phenomenal consciousness, as such, might still be able to accept the present

---

[3] I shall therefore set to one side the various direct attacks on purely recognitional concepts of experience that have been offered by such disparate authors as Wittgenstein (1953) and Fodor (1998). My view is that no version of Wittgenstein's famous argument against private concepts can succeed without drawing on anti-realist assumptions about the nature of the mind, or the nature of concepts, or both. And my view is that Fodor's argument—that recognitional concepts cannot be actual because such concepts *don't compose*—makes a false assumption. This is, that if recognitional concepts are possible at all, then it is possible for concepts composed out of recognitional concepts to be recognitional also. But I shall not attempt to substantiate these points here. My interest is in the *conditional* question: supposing that there can be purely recognitional concepts of experience, what then follows?

proposals for explaining the existence of purely recognitional concepts of experience.[4]

I should also emphasize that the dispute between qualia theorists and their opponents cuts across the debate between non-physicalists and physicalists about phenomenal consciousness. For there are those who believe in intrinsic qualia who are nevertheless physicalists about such properties (McGinn, 1991; Block, 1995). I shall have nothing to say to such people here. While I believe it would be a bad thing for aspiring physicalists if they were required to believe in qualia, I shall not attempt to substantiate this claim in the present context. My focus is on those who either reject or don't want to be committed to qualia in the strong sense, but who nevertheless wish to make appeal to purely recognitional concepts in blocking the arguments against physicalism. My targets therefore include Sturgeon (2000), Tye (2000) and Papineau (2002); indeed, they include any physicalist who thinks that we can hope for more than bare identities between phenomenally conscious states and physical states, and who wishes to propose a reductive story in terms of some combination of causal roles and/or intentional contents.

In fact the main goal of the present chapter is to argue for the following conditional claim:

> If there are purely recognitional concepts of experience (with the properties that we believe such concepts to have), and there are no intrinsic qualia, then there are higher-order experiences that serve to ground the application of those concepts.

A subsidiary goal is to contrast two accounts of higher-order experience. One is inner-sense theory, which is briefly criticized in section 3. And the other is that provided by dispositional higher-order thought theory, sketched in section 5. Many questions about the latter account remain, of course; and no attempt is made here at a full defense. My goal is to say just enough to indicate how higher-order experiences may be possible without inner sense (see Carruthers, 2000, for further development and discussion).

## 2. HOW ARE PURELY RECOGNITIONAL CONCEPTS OF EXPERIENCE POSSIBLE?

A concept is recognitional when it can be applied on the basis of perceptual or quasi-perceptual acquaintance with its instances. And a concept is *purely*

---

[4] I shall return to this point once again briefly at the end of the chapter. Note, however, that one way in which the issue of reductive explanation impacts upon our present topic is this. It seems unlikely that anyone would want to endorse inner-sense theory who *didn't* think that it provided a successful reductive explanation of phenomenal consciousness. For there would seem to be no *other* motives for believing in an organ of inner sense. In contrast, since dispositional higher-order thought theory doesn't need to appeal to anything that most people don't believe in anyway, many will be able to accept the present account of purely recognitional concepts who don't accept higher-order thought theories as reductive accounts of phenomenal consciousness as such.

recognitional when its possession-conditions (in the sense of Peacocke, 1992) make no appeal to anything other than such acquaintance. A concept is purely recognitional when nothing in the grasp of that concept, as such, requires its user to apply or appeal to any other concept or belief. A purely recognitional concept *of experience* is then a higher-order recognitional concept, which applies to another mental state (viz. an experience), and whose possession-conditions don't presuppose any other mental-state concepts (not even the concept *experience*).

Now, in one sense it is relatively easy to understand how we might possess purely recognitional concepts of experience, even in the absence of any qualia. Suppose that experiences are events that fall into a variety of distinct kinds, whether physical, functional, or intentional. Then it is easy enough to imagine that there could be a causal mechanism that would generate, from the presence of one of these states of kind $K$, the judgment that one is in K.[5] Since the mechanism is a causal one, it might qualify as a kind of quasi-perceptual acquaintance. But since it is also *brute*-causal—in the sense that its operation is independent of any of the subject's other mental states—it can also count as purely recognitional.[6] So where's the problem? Why should the existence of purely recognitional concepts of experience put any pressure on us to allow the existence of intrinsic qualia?

One source of difficulty with the above proposal is this. Although there may be no conceptual connection between recognitional concepts of types of experience and related functional or intentionally characterized concepts, it seems that there *are* such connections with other purely recognitional concepts. For example, subjects can know a priori that the state that they recognize when deploying a particular recognitional concept *is* an experiential state, provided that the latter, too, is picked out by a recognitional concept (albeit a more abstract one). Possessing a generalized recognitional concept of *experience*, and possessing the purely recognitional concept *this type of state* [a particular kind of experience], subjects can know, as soon as they reflect, that the items picked out by *this* are actually experiences. But of course, the mere fact that one concept tracks instances of kind $K$ (or has as its function to track instances of that kind, or whatever), while another tracks instances of kind $E$ (where the extension of $K$ is included in $E$) wouldn't enable a thinker to know a priori that all Ks are Es.

Qualia theorists, in contrast, can easily explain these a priori connections amongst our recognitional concepts of experience. They can claim that we have

---

[5] See Papineau (1993) where a model of our capacity to recognize our own experiences of just this kind is presented and defended. I shall return to consider alternative possible models, including Papineau's most recent views, in section 4 below.

[6] I should stress that by a 'brute-causal' account of purely recognitional concepts, I don't mean a causal/informational account of the *content* of those concepts, as opposed to a teleosemantical or inferential-role one. I just mean an account of the application-conditions of those concepts that doesn't make appeal to any other mental states besides the one the concept is applied to.

available a generalized concept of *experience* that is the concept of a state that just *feels* a distinctive way to the subject, being available for immediate introspective recognition. For a qualia theorist, the concept of experience is primarily that of a state possessing certain kinds of introspectible properties. On this account 'experience' stands to '*this state*' [a quale] just as 'color' stands to 'red'— perhaps it is by first possessing the capacity to recognize qualia of various kinds, and abstracting, that one gets the generalized concept of experience. So, possessing this sort of concept of experience, and also being capable of recognizing *this state* [quale], subjects can of course tell that what they have just recognized is an experience (viz. a state possessing one of a range of distinctive inner feels).[7]

In contrast, if we deny the existence of qualia, then the story is much less easy to tell. One option would be to claim that the generalized concept of experience is functional/intentional. But although one's functionalist concept of experience may include the fact that experiences are apt to issue in, or to be available to, purely recognitional judgments, in any particular case where one makes such a judgment one will only be able to tell that it is an *experience* that one has recognized as a result of a metaconceptual inference. That is, only if one knows *that* the concept that one has just employed is a purely recognitional one, will one be able to know that the item recognized is an experience. This looks highly counterintuitive.

So, one who denies the existence of qualia must somehow claim that the concepts *this* [type of experience] and *that* [experience in general] are both purely recognitional, while at the same time allowing for the idea that the subject can discern the relationship between their instances a priori in something like the way that one can discern the relationship between instances of *red* and of *color*. Qualia theorists can claim that qualia are directly *present to* the concept-wielding mind, being available to purely recognitional classification while also being objects of immediate awareness. If qualia are rejected, in contrast, then some account has to be given of the acquaintance relation that underpins purely recognitional applications of experience concepts. And the only candidate on the table at the moment, is a brute-causal account (others will be considered in section 4). But this doesn't have the resources to explain the character of our awareness that the grounds for applying the recognitional concept *this* [type of experience] are included amongst the grounds for applying the recognitional concept *that* [experience in general].

---

[7] I should emphasize that the appeal to a process of *abstraction*, here, is for purposes of illustration only. The real point concerns, not the genesis of our concepts, but rather our awareness of that which grounds their application. Possessing a recognitional concept of *this* [type of experience], and possessing a recognitional concept of *that* [type of state, namely experience in general], I can see by mere reflection that anything of *this* type is of *that* type, in something like the way that someone possessing a recognitional concept of *red* and a recognitional concept of *color* can see by reflection that anything red is colored.

Another problem for the brute-causal account being mooted here, is that there seems to be a particularly intimate connection between the content of the recognitional judgment, '*This* [experience] is a K' and the specific nature and/or content of the state that grounds that judgment. What I recognize when I deploy a recognitional concept of experience is in some sense presented to me (albeit non-conceptually) *as* an experience. I don't merely find myself judging '*This* is a K', as it were blindly, or for no reason. Rather, I think that I am aware of, and can inspect and reflect on the nature of, the event that evokes that recognitional judgment.[8]

How is this possible? Again, qualia theorists can provide an answer—it is because the property that my recognitional concept picks out is both intrinsic and directly present to the concept-wielding mind. Qualia are supposed to be properties that we are aware of, and that we can come to have immediate recognitional capacities for by virtue of that awareness. In contrast, it is much less obvious what a defender of the brute-causal account can say here. For if the property whose instantiation causes an application of the recognitional concept K is a physical, or functional, or intentional one, then it is far from clear how such properties could figure in the right way in the content of awareness. Indeed, given that the connection between the concept and its instances is supposed to be *brute*-causal, it seems plain that the account does *not* have the resources to capture the relevant mode of presentation of those instances.

So what is it that I am recognizing when I apply a recognitional concept of experience, if not a quale? How can what I am recognizing be presented to me *as* an experience, given that it doesn't have to involve any conceptualization of it as such, unless what I recognize possesses the distinctive and (on this view) defining properties of phenomenally conscious experience (i.e. qualia)?

## 3. HOES TO THE RESCUE?

Inner-sense theorists, who believe that we are subject to higher-order experiences (HOEs), have answers to these problems (Armstrong, 1968, 1984; Lycan, 1996). On this view, humans not only have first-order non-conceptual and/or analog perceptions of states of their environments and bodies, they also have second-order non-conceptual and/or analog perceptions of their first-order states of perception. Humans (and perhaps other animals) not only have sense organs

---

[8] Another way of putting this point is that the brute-causal account cannot adequately capture the distinction between the *sense* of a recognitional concept (or its *mode of presentation* of its instances), and its referent. When I apply a recognitional concept to my experience, that experience seems to be presented to me in a distinctive way, and it is this mode of presentation that grounds my application of the relevant concept.

that scan the environment/body to produce fine-grained representations which can then serve to ground thoughts and actions, but they also have *inner* senses, charged with scanning the outputs of the first-order senses (i.e. experiences) to produce equally fine-grained, but higher-order, representations of those outputs (i.e. to produce higher-order experiences).[9]

Now, there are important issues here concerning the proper characterization of the contents of perception. In particular, should we say that those contents are *non-conceptual* (as Tye, 1995, argues), or should we merely say that they are *analog* (that is, being more fine-grained than any concepts we possess; which is the view defended in Carruthers, 2000)? The former entails the latter, but the latter need not entail the former. For there remains the possibility that perceptual contents might be *both* fine-grained *and* imbued with concepts. Important as these issues are, they need not detain us here. Since experiences are analog (or 'fine-grained') on either view, I propose to adopt this way of talking. And in what follows I shall adopt the convention of marking terms referring to perceptual contents with a sub-scripted '*a*' for analog.

An experience *as of* red, say, is a state with the first-order analog content $red_a$. A higher-order experience targeted on that very state, will be one with the second-order analog content *seems $red_a$* or *experience of $red_a$*. Such a higher-order experience can then serve to ground a higher-order recognitional concept. This can either be a recognitional application of the theoretically embedded concept *experience of red*, or it can be a concept that is purely recognitional. A purely recognitional concept of experience that is deployed in the presence of, and guided in its application by, a second-order analog content will be a recognition *of* a state of *experience of $red_a$*, but without conceptualizing it *as* what it is—an experience of red.

A higher-order experience is just that—an experience whose non-conceptual/analog content represents the non-conceptual/analog content of a first-order experience. A higher-order experience of an experience of red will be a state with the analog content *experience of $red_a$*. An application of a higher-order recognitional concept that is driven by the content of this higher-order experience will therefore have at least a non-accidental connection with the experiential status of what is recognized, in the same sort of way that recognitional applications of the concept *red* that are driven by the content of a first-order state with the analog content $red_a$ have an intrinsic connection with the redness of what is recognized.

---

[9] Since some people hear the term 'experience' in a sense that entails phenomenal consciousness, I should emphasize that this is not the intention here. No higher-order experience theorist believes that higher-order experiences are themselves (normally) phenomenally conscious. Those who have trouble with this terminology should substitute 'higher-order perceptual state' throughout, replacing 'HOE' by 'HOP' wherever necessary.

Consider someone who has experiences with the analog content $red_a$, and who also possesses the recognitional concept *red*, where the latter is guided in its application by the former. Their application of the concept *red* will not be brute-causal or 'blind', but will rather be guided by their awareness of the redness recognized. And if they also have experiences with the contents $green_a$, $blue_a$, and so on, they may also possess a more generalized recognitional concept *color*. (And given that they *also* have experiences with the contents $smooth_a$, $loud_a$, $sour_a$, and so on, they may even have a generalized recognitional concept of *perceptible property*.)

So, too, then, for someone who has higher-order experiences with the analog content *experience of $red_a$*, and who also possesses a purely recognitional concept *this* [experience of red]—their application of the concept *this* will not be brute-causal, either, but will rather be guided by their higher-order perceptual awareness of the experience recognized. And given that they also have higher-order experiences with the contents *experience of $green_a$*, *experience of $smooth_a$*, *experience of $loudness_a$*, and so on, they may be capable of possessing a generalized recognitional concept *that* [state of experience in general]. In which case, anyone deploying the higher-order recognitional concept *this* will be able to discern, a priori, the connection with their higher-order recognitional concept *that*, in just the same way that someone deploying the recognitional concept *red* will be able to discern the conceptual connection with their generalized recognitional concept *color*.

It seems that higher-order experiences provide us with just what we need in order to answer the qualia theorist's challenge. They enable us to explain how we can possess purely recognitional concepts of experience whose application can be grounded in awareness of the properties recognized, and in such a way that there can be a priori connections discernible amongst such concepts themselves. And higher-order experiences, too, provide just the necessary modes of presentation that intuition seems to require for our recognitional concepts of experience. But these benefits are provided at a considerable cost. For there are powerful objections to theories of inner sense.

One objection is this. If there really were such an organ of inner sense, then it ought to be possible for it to malfunction, just as our first-order senses sometimes do (Sturgeon, 2000). And in that case, it ought to be possible for someone to have a first-order percept with the content $red_a$ causing a higher-order percept with the content *seems $orange_a$*. Someone in this situation would be disposed to judge, 'It is red', immediately and non-inferentially (i.e. not influenced by beliefs about the object's normal color or their own physical state), which would normally be sufficient grounds for us to say that the object seems red to them. But at the same time they would be disposed to judge, 'It *seems* orange.' Not only does this sort of thing never apparently occur, but the idea that it might do so conflicts with a powerful intuition. This is that our awareness of our own experiences is *immediate*, in such a way that to *believe* that you are undergoing an experience of a certain sort *is* to be undergoing an experience of that sort. But if inner-sense theory is correct, then it ought to be possible for someone to believe that they are in a state of *seeming-orange$_a$* when they are actually in a state of *seeming-red$_a$*.

Another objection to inner-sense theories is developed by Carruthers (2000). It is that, on the one hand, the computational demands placed on an organ of inner sense would surely be considerable (perceiving perceptions is going to be a task no easier than perceiving physical objects); and yet, on the other hand, there is no plausible story to be told about the powerful evolutionary pressures that would have been necessary to provide the incentive to build and maintain such an organ.

I shall not pursue these objections to inner-sense theory here. (See Chapter 4 of the present volume.) Rather, I shall show shortly (in section 5) that there may be a way of getting all of the benefits of this theory without any of the costs, by deploying a particular version of higher-order thought theory. First, however, I shall return to consider the alternatives in more detail. Are there any ways to explain our capacity for purely recognitional concepts of experience that *neither* appeal to intrinsic qualia *nor* to higher-order experiences (HOEs)?

## 4. CAN WE DO WITHOUT HOES?

Loar (1997) claims that phenomenal concepts (viz. purely recognitional concepts of experience) pick out the physical properties to which they refer *directly*, without the mediation of anything else. (Since Loar's account is designed to defend physicalism, the physical properties in question are those that are identical to, or that realize, the phenomenal properties of our experiences.) Put differently, he says that the physical properties of the brain that are also phenomenal properties *provide their own modes of presentation*—when identifying such a property recognitionally, there is no distinction between the property recognized and its mode of presentation to the subject.

It would seem, on the face of it, that this is just another version of the brute-causal account discussed earlier. Our recognitional judgments of experience are directly caused by (the physical states that are) our experiences, without the mediation of any further mental state. And it is apparent, too, that the account is subject to just the same difficulties as before. In particular, it cannot accommodate the powerful intuition that we are *aware of*, and can introspect and contemplate, that which grounds our applications of our purely recognitional concepts. For on Loar's account, *nothing* grounds their application except the physical state-types that cause them. Nor can the account explain the a priori connections between recognitional concepts of particular experience-types and a recognitional concept of experience in general.

There are two alternative readings of Loar's (1997) position, however. One is that he intends to allow his anti-physicalist opponents the existence of qualia, in the strong sense adopted in this chapter. Loar himself does not use this language; but he does stress that he can grant his opponents all of their initial intuitions and still block their argument to an anti-physicalist conclusion. Loar may simply be concerned to defend the view that qualia are (strictly indentical with) physical states of the brain. And if this *is* his position, then he doesn't fall within the scope of my arguments here. As I emphasized in section 1 above, my goal is to establish that purely recognitional concepts of experience *without qualia* require higher-order experiences.

The second possible alternative reading of Loar is that he is assuming some sort of representationalist or intentionalist reduction of phenomenal properties. For at the outset of his paper he allows that the phenomenally conscious properties of visual experience might coincide with 'internally determined intentional structure, so that it is an introspectable and non-relational feature of a visual experience that it represents things visually as being thus and so' (Loar, 1997, 597). This looks, on the face of it, like an identification of phenomenal properties with narrowly individuated intentional content. If so, then the position is no longer consistent with the existence of qualia, and is vulnerable to the arguments I shall present against Sturgeon immediately below.

Sturgeon (2000) develops an account of the relation between phenomenal consciousness and our recognitional concepts that is neutral as to the nature of the former, and yet that purports to explain the so-called 'explanatory gap' between them. But he also wants to claim that the explanatory gap isn't in itself metaphysically troubling—once we understand the nature of the gap and how it arises, we should see that people committed to physicalism and/or naturalism needn't be concerned by it. If this is to be successful, however, then it is crucial that he should have an account of the relationship between phenomenal consciousness and our recognitional concepts, together with a view of the nature of the latter, that will work *whatever* the true nature of phenomenal consciousness should turn out to be.

Since Sturgeon (2000) is plainly sympathetic towards a form of intentionalist—or representational—approach to phenomenal consciousness, let me work through the commitments of his account under that assumption. So suppose that intentionalism is the truth about phenomenal consciousness; suppose that phenomenally conscious states are just states possessing a certain sort of (analog and/or non-conceptual) intentional content. Can his account be made to work, in that case, without introducing higher-order experiences?[10]

---

[10] Sturgeon wishes to remain neutral on *whether* intentionalism is true. But he also wants to claim that his account is *consistent with* intentionalism. What I shall argue is that such consistency requires higher-order experiences in order to succeed. He therefore can't avoid our question by pleading that he is neutral on the question of the *truth* of intentionalism.

Well, if there aren't any higher-order analog contents involved, then all that exists to ground a purely recognitional judgment of *this* [experience of red] is the analog intentional content $red_a$. This is a first-order intentional content, appropriate to ground a first-order judgment of *red*. How does it give rise to the higher-order judgment *this*? 'No problem', Sturgeon may say, 'it causes it.' But this would just be a return to a form of brute-causal account.

The point is that our judgments of *this* [experience of red] seem related to the experience (which is, on the intentionalist hypothesis under consideration, none other than the first-order analog content $red_a$), in just the sort of manner that judgments of *red* are related to redness. That is, they are recognitional judgments grounded in some sort of non-judgmental analog awareness of their objects. When I make judgments about my own experiences, they seem to be presented to me in something like the way that redness is presented to me when I make judgments of color—I am aware of a fineness of grain in what I recognize that slips through the mesh of my conceptual net, for example. But the first-order analog content $red_a$ isn't the right *sort* of content to ground an awareness of the experiential state itself. It can ground recognition of redness, but not experienced redness. What I am aware of, by virtue of being in a state with the analog content $red_a$, is redness, not experienced redness. And all the fineness of grain in its content has to do with redness, not with the experience itself.

It does then seem that Sturgeon can't transcend a brute-causal account if he tries to operate without appeal to either higher-order experiences or to qualia. In contrast, as soon as higher-order analog contents are admitted, the problems go away. A recognitional judgment of *red* is grounded in the analog content $red_a$, and a recognitional judgment of *this* [experience of red] is grounded in the analog content *experience of* $red_a$ or *seems* $red_a$, which takes the experience of red as its object in something like the way that $red_a$ takes redness as its object.

Papineau (2002) proposes a somewhat different theory. He now argues that purely recognitional concepts of experience can be formed on the back of our first-order recognitional concepts of colors, textures and so on, by prefacing such concepts with an operator of the form, 'The experience: . . . .' We can set such an account a dilemma, however, depending on how the content of the experience-operator is said to be fixed.

Suppose, on the one hand, that the embedding concept of experience is in broad terms theoretical. Suppose, that is, that experience is here characterized in terms of causal role, or intentional content, or both. But in that case the experience-operator can't do the necessary work of explaining the content of phenomenal concepts. This is because the latter concepts can be free of any a priori connections with any causal role or intentional-content concepts (hence the conceivability of zombies, etc.). As we noted at the outset of the paper, I can think, 'Items of *this* type [experiences of red] might normally have been caused by decisions to speak', and so on.

Then suppose, on the other hand, that the embedding concept of experience is itself purely recognitional in the sense that it refers directly to the property of being an experience, without theoretical mediation. (Papineau, 2002, speculates that its content might be fixed through some form of teleosemantics.) This enables us to meet one of our *desiderata*, at least—we can explain how it can be a priori for users of purely recognitional concepts of experience that what they are recognizing are experiences. This is because the concept 'experience' is actually a component in all such recognitional judgments.

The trouble, though, is that the account still can't accommodate our sense that we are directly *aware of* what grounds the application of a phenomenal concept, in a way that need involve no a priori connections with non-phenomenal concepts. For notice that on this account, when I recognize in myself a particular type of experience (as of red, say), what is actually going on is that I make a judgment of 'red' while prefacing it with an experience-operator. In which case it would surely have to be a priori that experiences of this type have something to do with redness. But in fact I can think, 'Experiences of *this* type might normally have been caused by greenness, or might even have occupied the causal role now occupied by pains.'

Tye (2000) inhabits a position that seems to vacillate between those of Sturgeon and Papineau. Tye is a first-order representationalist about phenomenal consciousness itself (see also his 1995). He maintains that phenomenally conscious states are those with a certain sort of intentional content (non-conceptual and abstract), provided that they are poised in the right sort of way to have an impact on conceptual thinking and belief-formation. And he sometimes appears to suggest that phenomenal concepts are purely recognitional concepts that can be applied in the face of just such intentional contents. For example, he writes, 'The phenomenal concepts I apply and the features to which I apply them are the same in both the perceptual and the introspective cases' (1995, 167). That is, whether I am judging *red* or *experience of red*, just the same concepts are involved. But this won't do. Recognitional judgments of color are one thing, recognitional judgments of experiences of color quite another. And the latter cannot be grounded in first-order contents representing colors alone, as we saw in our discussion of Sturgeon above.

In other passages, on the other hand, Tye appears to suggest that the concept *experience* will always be a component in any recognitional judgment of experience. For example, he writes, 'Introspective awareness of phenomenal character, I maintain, is awareness-*that*—awareness that *an* experience with a certain phenomenal character is present' (2000, 52).[11] But then this is really no different from the view of Dretske (1995), which we briefly mentioned and set aside in section 1 above—despite Tye's rhetoric concerning 'introspection' and 'recognitional concepts', the view is that we know of our experiences via awareness of the objects of our experience. Moreover, it runs up against the main difficulty we noted for Papineau: if phenomenal concepts like *this* [experience of red] are really concepts of the form, 'This experience *of this* [redness]', then there is the problem of explaining how I can nevertheless think, '*This* [experience of red] might not have been an experience *of this* [redness], and might not have been *an experience* at all, but rather a decision to speak.'

There are things Tye could say here, of course, perhaps drawing a distinction between *roles* and *role occupiers* (following Lewis, 1980). That is, he could explain the possibility represented when I think of circumstances in which *this* [type of experience] would exist but without any of its actual normal causes and effects, by saying that this is to think of the brain-state that actually occupies the causal role in question (experience of red, say) occurring, but in some other role ('mad experience of red'). And he could explain the possibility represented when I think of circumstances in which all the normal causes and effects of an experience of red are present, but without *this* [type of experience] occurring, by saying that this is to think of the causal role in question being occupied by a different type of physical state than in the actual circumstances ('Martian experience of red').

Such maneuvers cannot do justice to the original intuitions, however. For when we entertain thoughts of the form, '*This* type of experience could be/could have been F', we don't seem to be thinking thoughts of the form, 'The type of state that actually occupies such-and-such a causal role could be/could have been F.' Indeed, it seems possible to think, '*This* type of experience. . . .' without *any* specification of a causal role figuring in the content of the thought (not even one governed by an actually-operator). In fact the phenomenology of such cases isn't that I think *through* a causal role to the type of state (whatever it is—presumably a brain-state) that actually occupies that causal role. It is rather that I think of a type of state that doesn't need to be specified by partly indexical description, because I am directly aware of it. The referent of the phrase '*This* type of experience' seems to be present to consciousness, not 'hidden' beneath a causal role as the actual bearer of that role. And higher-order experience theory explains how this can happen.

In conclusion, it would appear that we have no real alternative if we wish to explain how purely recognitional concepts of experience are possible without appealing to qualia, but to frame our account in terms of higher-order experiences. I now propose to sketch how this can be done without having to appeal to an organ

---

[11] Note that for Tye the phenomenal characters of an experience are the characters *represented* in the content of that experience—redness, greenness, or whatever.

of 'inner sense', by deploying a form of dispositional higher-order thought theory—a task that will occupy us through the final section of the chapter.

## 5. HOW TO GET HOES FROM HOTS (FOR FREE)

There are a number of different higher-order thought (HOT) theories on the market. The account to be presented here unites elements of a number of them, and then combines that account with an appeal to some or other form of consumer semantics to explain how higher-order experiences (HOEs) will automatically be generated by the operations of a HOT faculty.

Rosenthal (1986, 1993) provides an account in terms of the *actual* occurrence of higher-order thoughts. For a state to be conscious is for it *actually* to be targeted by a higher-order thought at the time, where that thought is non-inferentially produced. Dennett (1978a, 1991) offers a *dispositional* account, claiming that conscious status resides in *availability* to higher-order thought; but he also distinctively claims that these thoughts are to be expressed in natural language (so consciousness is essentially language-involving). Carruthers (1996) agrees with Dennett in offering an account that is dispositional, while dropping the alleged connection with natural language. But Carruthers also claims that the higher-order thoughts in question must themselves be available to higher-order thought (hence explaining conscious experience in terms of availability to *conscious* thought—he calls this 'reflexive thinking theory'). The present account shares the dispositionalism of Dennett (1991) and Carruthers (1996). But it rejects the language-involvement of the former, while also rejecting the latter's claim that the higher-order thoughts involved should be conscious ones. So it agrees with Rosenthal in allowing that the higher-order thoughts in virtue of (availability to) which a state is conscious will characteristically be *non*-conscious.

According to dispositional higher-order thought theory (Carruthers, 2000), the conscious status of a mental state or event consists in its non-inferential availability to a 'theory of mind' or 'mind-reading' system capable of higher-order thought. And a conscious experience, in particular, will be an experience that is available to cause higher-order thoughts about the occurrence and content of that very experience. We can then utilize some or other form of consumer semantics (either teleosemantics, or some form of functional or inferential-role semantics) in order to explain how our experiences acquire higher-order analog contents by virtue of their availability to higher-order thought.[12]

---

[12] For exposition and defense of different forms of teleosemantics, see Millikan (1984, 1986, 1989) and Papineau (1987, 1993). For some varieties of inferential role semantics, see Loar (1987, 1982), McGinn (1982), Block (1986), and Peacocke (1986, 1992).

According to all forms of consumer semantics, the intentional content of a state depends, at least in part, on what the down-stream consumer systems that can make use of that state are disposed to do with it. And there is independent reason to think that changes in consumer systems can transform perceptual contents, and with it phenomenal consciousness. (See Hurley, 1998, for presentation and discussion of a wide range of examples that are interpretable in this light.)

Consider the effects of spatially inverting lenses, for example (Welch, 1978). Initially, subjects wearing such lenses see everything upside-down, and their attempts at action are halting and confused. But in time—provided that they are allowed to move around and act while wearing their spectacles—the visual field rights itself. Here everything on the input side may remain the same as it was when they first put on the spectacles; but the planning and action-controlling systems have learned to interpret those states inversely. And as a result, intentional perceptual contents become normalized.[13]

If consumer semantics is assumed, then it is easy to see how mere dispositions can transform contents in the way that dispositional higher-order thought theory supposes. For notice that the consumer system for a given state doesn't *actually* have to be making use of that state in order for the latter to carry the appropriate content—it just has to be *disposed* to make use of it should circumstances (and what is going on elsewhere in cognition) demand. So someone normalized to inverting spectacles doesn't actually have to be acting on the environment in order to see things right-side-up. He can be sitting quietly and thinking about something else entirely. But still the spatial content of his perceptual states is fixed, in part, by his dispositions to think and move in relation to the spatial environment.

Consider, here, the implications of some form of inferential role semantics, in connection with a different example. What is it that confers the content *P&Q* on some complex belief-state of the form 'P#Q'? (The sign '#' here is meant as a dummy connective, not yet interpreted.) In part, plainly, it is that one is disposed to infer 'P' from 'P#Q' and 'Q' from 'P#Q' (Peacocke, 1992). It is constitutive of a state with a conjunctive content that one should be disposed to deduce either one of the conjuncts from it. But of course this disposition can remain un-activated on some occasions on which a conjunctive thought is entertained. For example, suppose that I hear the weather forecaster say, 'It will be windy and it will be cold', and that I believe her. Then I have a belief with a conjunctive content even if I do nothing else with it. Whether I ever form the belief that it will be windy, in

---

[13] I should emphasize that while consumer semantics provides a possible and plausible explanation of the inverting-lenses phenomenon, this isn't actually forced on us. For there remains the possibility that the righting of visual experience may be caused by feedback from motor systems to the visual system, giving rise to alterations in the internal operations of the latter. This would then be an explanation in terms of changes on the input side of conscious experience, rather than an account in terms of changes on the output side using consumer semantics. See Ch. 3 of the present volume, however, for discussion of examples of prosthetic vision that don't suffer from this weakness.

particular, will depend on my interests and background concerns, and on the other demands made on my cognitive resources at the time. But my belief still actually has a conjunctive content in virtue of my inferential dispositions.

According to dispositional higher-order thought theory, then, the availability of our perceptual states to a 'theory of mind' or 'mind-reading' faculty is sufficient to transform the intentional contents of those states. Where before, in the absence of such a faculty, the states had merely first-order contents—containing analog representations of worldly color, texture, shape, and so on—now all of those states will have, at the same time, higher-order analog, experience-representing, contents. Each state that is an analog representation with the content $red_a$ is at the same time an analog representation with the content *experience of $red_a$*, in virtue of the fact that the mind-reading system contains concepts of experience that can be applied to those very states.

We are now in position to explain how purely recognitional concepts of experience are possible, obtaining all of the advantages of 'inner-sense' theory without any of the associated costs. Here is how the story should go. We begin—both in evolutionary terms and in normal child development—with a set of first-order analog contents available to a variety of down-stream consumer systems. These systems may include a number of dedicated belief-forming modules, as well as a practical reasoning faculty for figuring out what to do in the light of the perceived environment together with background beliefs and desires. One of these belief-forming systems will be a developing mind-reading system.

When our mind-reading faculty has reached the stage at which it confers on us an understanding of the subjective nature of experience, and/or a grasp of the it/seems distinction, then we will easily—indeed, trivially—become capable of second-order recognitional judgments of experience, with these judgments riding piggy-back on our first-order recognitional concepts (in something like the way that Papineau, 2002, outlines, as discussed in section 4 above). So if subjects had a recognitional concept *red*, they will now acquire the concept *seems red*, or *experience of red*, knowing (a) that whenever a judgment of 'red' is evoked by experience, a judgment of 'seems red' is also appropriate on the very same grounds; and (b) that a judgment of 'seems red' is still appropriate whenever a disposition to judge 'red' has been blocked by considerations to do with abnormal lighting or whatever. Note that at this stage the higher-order concept in question is still a theoretically embedded one, with conceptual connections to worldly redness (it is, after all, a seeming *of red*). What one recognizes the state *as* is a state whose normal cause is worldly redness, and so on.

This change in the down-stream mind-reading consumer system is sufficient to transform all of the contents of experience, rendering them at the same time as higher-order ones. So our perceptual states will not only have the first-order analog contents $red_a$, $green_a$, $loud_a$, $smooth_a$, and so on, but also and at the same time the higher-order analog contents *experience of red_a, experience of green_a, experience of loudness_a, experience of smoothness_a,* and so on. The subject will then be in a position to form recognitional concepts targeted via just these higher-order contents, free of any conceptual ties with worldly redness, greenness, loudness, and smoothness. And once possessed of such concepts, it is possible for the subject to wonder whether other people have experiences of *this* sort when they look at a ripe tomato, to conceive of worlds in which zombies perceive red without undergoing *this experience,* and so on.

Here we have an account of our purely recognitional concepts of experience that appeals to higher-order experiences, but without the need to postulate any sort of organ of inner sense. So (in contrast with inner-sense theory) there should be no problem in telling some sort of evolutionary story concerning the emergence of higher-order experience. This now reduces to the problem of explaining the emergence of our 'theory of mind' capacity, and some or other version of the 'Machiavellian intelligence' hypothesis might suffice here (Byrne and Whiten, 1988, 1998). Moreover, it should also be obvious why there can be no question of our higher-order analog contents getting out of line with their first-order counterparts, on this account—in such a way that one might be disposed to make recognitional judgments of *red* and *seems orange* at the same time, for example. This is because the content of the higher-order experience *seems red_a* is parasitic on the content of the first-order experience *red_a,* being formed from it by virtue of the latter's availability to a 'theory of mind' system.

Before closing I should stress once again that although the present account of how purely recognitional concepts of experience are possible is drawn from higher-order reductive theories of phenomenal consciousness, that is not how it is being used in the present context. First-order theorists of phenomenal consciousness like Dretske (1995) and Tye (1995) might agree with the present use of higher-order thought theory to explain the possibility of purely recognitional concepts of experience, while rejecting that theory as an account of phenomenal consciousness as such. They merely need to claim that phenomenal consciousness is already present in creatures that lack any capacity for higher-order thought, and also perhaps in perceptual states in us that are unavailable to such thought.[14]

In fact the present account should be acceptable to a wide range of different theorists, provided only that they are prepared to endorse some form of

---

[14] In fact, since Dretske (1995) endorses a form of teleosemantics, while Tye (1995) opts for a form of pure causal-covariance (or input-side) semantics, the present proposals could be acceptable to Dretske but not to Tye. I should stress, however, that the concessive tone taken here (accepting that first-order theorists might appeal to higher-order experiences in explaining how recognitional concepts of experience are possible) doesn't mean that first-order theories are ultimately defensible. For there are good reasons, in particular, to think that phenomenal consciousness is tied to the existence of the higher-order experiences themselves, without yet being present in the first-order experiences that they target. See Ch. 6 following. And see also the criticisms of first-order theories set out earlier in Chs. 3 and 4.

consumer semantics as one determinant, at least, of intentional content. For it should then be plain that higher-order experiences with higher-order analog contents can come to exist by virtue of the availability of first-order analog contents to a faculty of higher-order thought, without any need to postulate 'inner scanners' or any organ of inner sense. And it can be by virtue of the existence of such higher-order experiences we come to form purely recognitional concepts of experience, grounded in those higher-order analog contents. In any case, anyone of reductionist sympathies who does *not* endorse consumer semantics in general (or the particular use being made of it here), and who is reluctant to believe in the existence of an organ of inner sense, is still left with the challenge of explaining how purely recognitional concepts are possible without qualia.

# CHAPTER 6

# Dual-Content Theory: the Explanatory Advantages

Over the course of the last three chapters various different arguments have been sketched in support of my dual-content theory of phenomenal consciousness, as well as against a variety of opponents (first-order representational theories, inner-sense theories, and actualist higher-order thought theories, in particular). Likewise in Carruthers (2000) multiple lines of argument were presented, both in support of my own views, and against a number of different opponents. Even in the chapter of that book where the main argument against first-order theories was laid out (chapter 6), the lines of reasoning were complex, with different real or imaginary opponents being in my sights at various different points throughout it, and frequently requiring reference to the arguments of earlier and later chapters as well (especially chapters 4, 7, and 9). Within this welter of different arguments it isn't easy to keep one's eye on the ball. What I propose to do in the present chapter is to lay out the *main* line of reasoning supporting dual-content theory as against what I take to be the strongest, most plausible, form of first-order theory. I shall also take up the question that has now begun to be broached in Chapter 5 of the present volume, which is whether a first-order theorist can *also* accept the higher-order analog contents postulated by dual-content theory, and can thereby obtain all of the advantages of the latter while retaining their distinctively first-order account of phenomenal consciousness itself.

## 1. SOME BACKGROUND

One of my arguments against first-order theories of phenomenal consciousness (of the sort espoused by Dreske, 1995, and Tye, 1995, for example; see Chapters 2 and 3 for explanation and discussion) has been that such theories can't account adequately for the distinction between conscious and non-conscious perceptual states. (Such a distinction is warranted by the two-visual-systems hypothesis of Milner and Goodale, 1995; see also Jacob and Jeannerod, 2003; see Chapters 4 and 11 of the present volume for elaboration.) But there is a version of first-order theory that can easily *seem* invulnerable to that argument.[1] Let me explain.

I have in mind someone who accepts the dual-systems theory of vision, and who accepts that while the perceptual states produced by the ventral/temporal system are phenomenally conscious ones, the perceptual states produced by the dorsal/parietal 'how-to' system aren't. But it might be felt that this is just the result that someone who endorses a version of Tye's (1995) first-order theory of phenomenal consciousness might predict. For according to that account, phenomenally conscious experiences are those that are poised to have an impact on the belief-forming and conceptual-reasoning systems of the agent in question. And the outputs of the dorsal/parietal system *aren't* so poised (rather, they are made available for on-line fine-grained control of movement). Only the outputs of the ventral/temporal system are. So such a first-order theory will predict that the dorsal/parietal perceptual states won't be phenomenally conscious, whereas the ventral/temporal states will be phenomenally conscious—just as we seem to find to be the case.

All this is perfectly true; and it is a possible combination of views that I addressed at some length in Carruthers (2000). My objection is that it isn't *explanatory*. Each of the dorsal/parietal and ventral/temporal visual systems produces analog intentional contents, representing distal properties of the environment (motion, shape, color, and so forth). So it is mysterious why the availability of such contents to conceptual thought and reasoning should transform them into states with the distinctive properties of phenomenal consciousness, whereas the availability of such contents to guide movement shouldn't.

To this it can be remarked that consciousness is mysterious in any case; hence the mystery in question is only to be expected; hence there is no objection to a first-order theory here. But this would be to miss the *whole* point, which is that representational theories of phenomenal consciousness are in the business of proffering reductive explanations of their target. They are in the business of *explaining* the distinctive features of phenomenal consciousness, not just in finding natural properties that happen to be co-extensive with those features. Nor is it adequate for them merely to postulate a brute identity between phenomenal consciousness, on the one hand, and the properties that figure in the theory (availability to first-order conceptual thought, as it might be), on the other. For an identity, even if true, can only count as a successful reduction when we can use the properties proposed in order to explain the distinctive properties of the target—just as we can use the properties of $H_2O$ in explaining why water boils at $100°$ C, why it is such a good solvent, and so on (see Chapters 1 and 2).

---

[1] I am grateful to Shriver and Allen (2005) for impressing this upon me.

In fact my ultimate argument against first-order theories is that they are incapable of explaining the distinctive, puzzling, to-be-explained features of phenomenal consciousness; whereas dispositional higher-order thought theory *can* explain those features. (Seen from this perspective, the contrast between conscious and non-conscious experience isn't even strictly necessary to the argument; although it does help greatly to make the point more vivid.) I shall spend the remainder of this chapter elaborating this claim.

## 2. THE PHENOMENA TO BE EXPLAINED

What are the main *desiderata* for a successful reductive theory of phenomenal consciousness? I shall lay out six of them.[2]

First and foremost, a reductive account of phenomenal consciousness should explain why phenomenally conscious states have a *subjective aspect* to them, meaning that it is *like something* to undergo them, and that they should each have a distinctive subjective *feel*. This is more or less the defining feature of phenomenal consciousness, and any adequate explanation needs to be able to account for it.

Second, a successful theory should explain why there should seem to be such a pervasive *explanatory gap* between all physical, functional, and intentional facts, on the one hand, and the facts of phenomenal consciousness, on the other. (See Chapter 2.) At a minimum, it seems that one can take any proposed explanatory story—including one framed in terms of dispositional higher-order thought theory, it should be stressed—and think, 'All of that might be true, and still *this* [type of experience] might be different or absent.' So a successful explanation needs at the same time to explain *why* such thoughts will always remain thinkable.

---

[2] It might easily seem that a seventh should also be listed. This is that a successful theory should be able to explain the difference between conscious and non-conscious experiences. But in the context of the present debate this isn't really a distinct *desideratum*. For both sides (first-order representationalism, on the one hand, and my dual-content theory, on the other) are agreed in *predicting* that the difference between phenomenally conscious and non-phenomenally conscious experience should fall where it seems to, in the outputs of the ventral/temporal and dorsal/parietal visual systems respectively. What is at issue is whether those theories can successfully *explain* the distinctive properties of our phenomenally conscious states; and this is what my six *desiderata* are intended to capture. Moreover, once we widen the scope of the debate to include other versions of first-order theory, some of which claim that dorsal/parietal percepts *are* (or might be) phenomenally conscious despite not being *access*-conscious, then it is obvious that explaining why the conscious–non-conscious distinction should fall where it seems to is no longer an appropriate constraint on a theory of *phenomenal* consciousness. This is because such theorists will deny the reliability of our intuitive beliefs about which of our experiences fail to be phenomenally conscious. For they claim that these beliefs may merely reflect the inaccessibility of those states to conceptual thought and verbal report. (Against this alternative form of first-order theory my objection is essentially the same: it still can't satisfy the *desiderata* for a successful theory of phenomenal consciousness.)

Now in fact there is an emerging consensus amongst would-be naturalizers of consciousness that the key to explaining (and to defusing) the explanatory gap lies in the existence of purely recognitional concepts of experience—sometimes called 'phenomenal concepts'—which have no conceptual connections to physical, causal-role, or intentional-content concepts (Loar, 1997; Tye, 1999; Carruthers, 2000 and Chapter 5 of the present volume; Sturgeon, 2000; Papineau, 2002). In which case, this second *desideratum* amounts to saying that a successful theory needs, *inter alia*, to be capable of explaining the existence of purely recognitional concepts of experience.

Third, a successful theory ought to be able to explain why people should have such a persistent intuition that the properties of their phenomenally conscious states are *intrinsic* ones, being non-relationally individuated. When we reflect on the distinctive qualities of an experience of red, for example, it seems to us that those properties don't depend upon the existence of the worldly property *red*, nor upon the experience in question occupying any particular sort of functional role within our mental lives (Kripke, 1972). Rather, those properties seem to us to be intrinsic to the experience. This is the *qualia-intuition*, which all representational theories of consciousness (whether first-order or higher-order) are committed to denying, and to explaining *away*.[3]

Fourth, a successful theory of phenomenal consciousness ought to be capable of explaining why phenomenally conscious experiences should seem to their possessors to be peculiarly *ineffable* (indescribable and incommunicable). When I reflect on the distinctive qualities of any experience that I am currently undergoing—say a perception of a warm vibrant shade of red—I seem to be aware of qualities that slip through the net of any descriptive scheme that I attempt to impose on them. I can say, 'It is an experience of a warm vibrant red', of course, or, 'It is an experience of a bright scarlet.' But such descriptions feel wholly inadequate to the task of expressing what I am aware of. And I can *exhibit* the red object to another person, of course, saying, 'It is the experience of *this* color.' But then I am aware that I am *neither* describing *nor* exhibiting the experience itself, and am forced to rely upon the presumed similarities between our respective perceptual systems in order to communicate my meaning.

Fifth, and relatedly, a successful reductive theory ought to be able to explain why the properties of phenomenally conscious experiences should seem in some way *private* to their possessors. We are strongly tempted to say that only we ourselves can truly know what our own experiences are *like*, and that others can only approximate to that knowledge by means of a more or less shaky inference. (For a recent

---

[3] Some writers use the term 'qualia' in a weak sense, to refer just to whatever the properties are that render our experiences phenomenally conscious. See Sturgeon (2000), for example. Throughout this chapter I adopt the more standard philosophical usage, in which 'qualia' is used in a strong sense, to mean the alleged intrinsic, non-relational, properties of phenomenally conscious experience.

elaboration on this sort of view, see Block, 2002.) Yet if any representational theory of consciousness is correct, of course, then the relevant properties *aren't* private ones. On the contrary, they are in the public domain, knowable in principle by others as well as by oneself. So again there is a thesis here that needs to be denied, and a persistent tendency that needs to be explained away.

Finally, and again relatedly, a successful theory ought to be able to explain why it should seem to people that they have *infallible* (and not just *privileged*) knowledge of the properties of their phenomenally conscious experiences. There is a strong temptation to insist that we can be completely certain of the qualities of our own conscious states, in a way that we couldn't be certain of any physical, causal-role, or intentional-content property. This, too, is a thesis that will need to be resisted by any representational theory, and our sense of infallibility will have to be explained away.

## 3. HOW MUCH CAN A FIRST-ORDER THEORY EXPLAIN?

How much progress can a first-order theory of the sort espoused by Tye (1995, 2000) and others make with these six *desiderata*?

First, it is plain that the core property of possessing a *subjective aspect* can't get explained by anything distinctive about the *contents* of the first-order perceptual experiences in question. Granted, the percepts produced by the ventral/temporal system must involve a subjective *take* on some aspects of the environment and not others, determined by the properties of the subject's perceptual apparatus.[4] But the same is equally true of the percepts produced by the dorsal/parietal system. And granted, the percepts produced by the ventral/temporal system have a distinctive sort of analog and/or non-conceptual intentional content, different from the digital/conceptual contents of belief and judgment.[5] But the same is also true of the non-conscious percepts produced by the dorsal/parietal system. So there aren't the resources, here, with which to explain the distinctive subjectivity—the 'what-it-is-likeness'—of the former set of percepts.

[4] In Ch. 3 of the present volume I refer to this as the 'subjectivity of the world', contrasting it with the 'subjectivity of experience' that is truly distinctive of phenomenally conscious experience. All perceptual states have *worldly* subjectivity, in that they possess a distinctive representational profile, determined by the properties of the perceptual apparatus in question. (Only some wavelengths of light are detected by the visual system, for example, and some wavelengths are perceived as being more similar to, or as being the opposites of, others.) But only phenomenally conscious percepts have *experiential* subjectivity; only they possess, themselves, a subjective dimension or *feel*.

[5] Intentional contents are *analog* when they have a finer grain than any concepts that the subject can possess and recall. Intentional contents are *non-conceptual* when their existence is independent of any concepts that the subject possesses. The latter implies the former, but not vice versa. I therefore work with the weaker notion of analog content throughout this chapter.

The only option for a first-order theorist, then, is to attempt to explain the subjectivity of ventral/temporal percepts in terms of their distinctive functional role. In particular, it might be said that such percepts are, by virtue of their availability to conceptual thought and judgment, *available to the subject* in a way that the dorsal/parietal percepts aren't. Now, one might wonder with what right *the subject* should get identified with the concept-deploying sub-systems of the mind rather than with the sensorimotor ones. Why shouldn't percepts that are available to guide the actions of a subject count as 'available to the subject' just as much as are percepts that are available to inform belief and judgment? For each is in fact available to less than the whole person, but rather to sub-systems that nevertheless form essential parts of the whole person. Although this is a powerful criticism, it isn't really the main point, as I shall now try to explain.

From the perspective of a first-order theorist, the sense in which ventral/temporal percepts are available to the subject can't be that the subject is capable of introspecting and identifying those percepts as such. For this would then be a higher-order theory, not a first-order one. Rather, it is just that the percepts in question are apt to give rise to beliefs and judgments about the worldly (and bodily) items that those percepts concern. So my perception of a red tomato is apt to give rise to the belief that I am confronted by a red tomato; my perception of a moving light causes me to judge that something is in motion; and so on. And it just isn't clear why this sort of availability should give rise to the subjective *feel* that is distinctive of phenomenally conscious states. Why *should* the functional role of causing first-order judgments give rise to states that it is *like* something to undergo, when the functional role of guiding action doesn't? The connection is far from transparent, to say the least.

In fact at this point first-order theorists are reduced to postulating a brute *identity* between phenomenal consciousness, on the one hand, and percepts that are available to first-order thought, on the other. But this is to give up on the goal of seeking a reductive *explanation* of phenomenal consciousness. We want to know *why* it should be *like* something to undergo perceptual states that are available to first-order judgment and decision-making. Whereas the best that a first-order theorist can do, is to tell us that this is just what it *is* for a state to be phenomenally conscious. And that isn't good enough.[6]

What, then, of the second *desideratum*: that a good theory should be capable of explaining the existence of purely recognitional concepts of experience, necessary to explain (and explain away) the explanatory gap? It should be obvious, I think, that first-order theories lack the resources to explain the existence of such concepts. I have argued this at length elsewhere (see Chapters 4 and 5). But here

---

[6] See Chs. 1 and 2 of the present volume for arguments that identities need to be backed up by reductive explanations if they are to count as successful reductions.

let me point out, first, that a recognitional concept *of experience* is inevitably higher-order rather than first-order in character; and second, that there is nothing in the content of a first-order percept that could serve to ground the application of such a higher-order concept. A perceptual state with the first-order analog content *red* is of the right sort to ground a first-order recognitional judgment of *red*; but not of the kind required to ground a higher-order recognitional judgment of *this* (where the object of recognition is a state of seeming red, or an experience of red).[7]

Might a recognitional judgment of experience be grounded, not in the first-order *content* of the experience, but rather in the *occurrence* of that experience? A first-order theorist might try claiming that the higher-order purely recognitional judgment *this* [experience of red] is grounded, not in the analog content *red* (nor in any higher-order analog content, either, as dual-content theory claims—see below), but rather in the *state* of perceiving red. Such claims can't do justice to the distinctive character of our purely recognitional concepts of experience, however. In particular, they can't explain the manner in which we have awareness of that which grounds our judgments. For when making a judgment of *this* I am aware of a fineness of grain in the object of my judgment that seems to slip through the mesh of my conceptual net. Indeed, the proposal on offer would seem to be a species of 'brute causal' account, of the sort that is criticized extensively in Chapter 5.

First-order theories can seem a bit more successful with the third *desideratum*, which is to explain the *qualia-intuition*. But for the explanation to work, two distinct sources of confusion have to be postulated. Recall that the qualia-intuition is the belief that our phenomenally conscious perceptual states possess non-relational (non-intentional, non-functionally individuated) properties. A first-order theorist *might* be able to explain why we have the intuition that there are properties of the world (or of our own bodies) that are intrinsic ones—for example, the property of being red. For a percept of red doesn't *represent* the relational character of the property that it represents. (It certainly doesn't represent it *as* represented, for example.) Rather, it just represents the surface in question as covered with a distinctive recognizable property. So if (as seems plausible) we have a tendency to confuse an absence of representation with a representation of absence, we might come to believe that the property of being red isn't a relational one.

---

[7] Does the displaced-perception account of introspective awareness proposed by Dretske (1995) serve as a counter-example to this claim? On this view, when I make an introspective judgment of *this* [experience of red] what I am really doing is judging that I am experiencing *this* [redness]. In which case the experience of redness *is* of the right kind to ground an introspective judgment, contrary to what I claim. However, on this account the recognitional concept in question turns out not to be *purely* recognitional, after all. On the contrary, it has embedded within it a concept of experience. And this is then sufficient to preclude Dretske from explaining all of the intuitions that can seem to give rise to an explanatory gap. See Ch. 5 of this volume.

But even if this were convincing (and I will return in a moment to argue that it isn't), it doesn't yet explain the intuition that the experience of red itself (and not just the redness experienced) possesses non-relational properties. For that, we have to postulate a second source of confusion: between the properties presented in or represented by our experiences, and the properties *of* those experiences. So we have to suppose that people have a tendency to move from thinking that there is a fine-grained intrinsic property (*redness*) represented by an experience, to thinking that this is really a fine-grained intrinsic property of the experience itself.[8]

There may well be some such tendency. (Thus Dennett, 1991, for example, argues that we mistake the richness and unlimited detail of the world perceived for an equivalent richness in our own perceptions of the world.) But I believe that this explanation of the *qualia-intuition* fails at the first hurdle. For we don't actually possess the intuition that redness is an intrinsic property of external surfaces. The relational nature of color is a deeply ingrained part of common-sense belief. For we know that the colors that objects appear to have will vary with the lighting conditions, and with the state of the perceiver. So even if our perceptions of color don't represent the relational character of the colors represented, most of us nevertheless believe firmly in their relational nature.

As for the fourth *desideratum*, first-order theories can make *some* progress with the *ineffability intuition*. This is because of the fine-grained (analog or non-conceptual) character of the first-order perceptual contents in question. Our color-percepts represent subtle variations in shade that far outstrip our capacities for classification and description, for example. (Similar things are true of perceptible properties in each of the various sense modalities.) So when I am forced to think about or describe the color of the object that I am seeing in comparatively coarse-grained conceptual terms, it is well-nigh inevitable that I should feel that the property in question is indescribable (even though it *can* be *exhibited* to others).

But this is all about the ineffability *of* color, not about the ineffability of our experience of color. The latter is an intrinsically higher-order phenomenon. (To say that an experience of color is ineffable is to say that there is something about the experience that outruns our capacity for higher-order conceptual thought and/or our capacity for higher-order linguistic description.) And while the fine-ness of grain of our first-order percepts can explain why we can't give a satisfy-ing higher-order *description* of those experiences—I am forced to say, 'It is an experience *of red*', while being aware that there is much more detail than that present in the objects of my experience—it *can't* explain why we should feel that we can't even *exhibit* the relevant properties of those experiences to another

[8] This would be the inverse of the tendency famously postulated by Hume (that the mind has a tendency to 'spread itself onto' the world): it is a tendency of the world to spread itself onto the mind. In contrast with Hume's *projectivism*, then, this tendency might be labeled 'back-projectivism'.

person. (So it can't explain why the experience should seem fully *incommunicable* and not just *indescribable*.) For if all that were present were a first-order representation of a fine-grained property of a surface of the object, then I *should* be able to exhibit the experience to others just as I can exhibit the relevant property, by saying, 'It is the experience *of this*', while demonstrating the object that I am perceiving.[9]

For related reasons a first-order theory can't, as such, explain the intuition that our conscious experiences are *private*, and unknowable to others. For knowledge of experience is necessarily a higher-order phenomenon. If you are *aware of* your experience of red, or know *that* you are undergoing an experience of red, then you must be *representing* that experience; and this is, of course, a higher-order representation. Moreover, there is nothing about the content of a first-order experience that should suggest privacy. While I can indeed wonder whether other people are really tuned to the same external properties as myself when I perceive things (and hence while I can know that they can be subject to the very same doubts concerning myself), it ought to be equally obvious that this will be relatively easy for others to test. It is just a matter of determining whether or not our discrimination-profiles are sufficiently similar.

Likewise, then, with the intuition that we have *infallible* knowledge of our own phenomenally conscious experiences: since knowledge *of* experience is intrinsically higher-order, infallible knowledge would have to be so too. And there is nothing in the story that a first-order theorist tells us that can explain why we should be so tempted to believe that our higher-order knowledge of the character of our experiences should be infallible. Certainly there is nothing in the content of a first-order experience of red, say, that should suggest any sort of infallibility.

## 4. THE EXPLANATORY POWER OF DUAL-CONTENT THEORY

In contrast with first-order theories, dispositional higher-order thought theory *can* meet each of our six *desiderata* in a satisfying way. According to this account, the percepts produced by the ventral/temporal visual system acquire *dual* analog intentional contents, because they are available to higher-order thought,

---

[9] Admittedly, with a little bit of background theory it will be possible to wonder whether other people have sense organs that tune them to the very same external properties (e.g. the reflective properties of surfaces) as do mine. So in exhibiting a red surface to another person, I can doubt whether I have succeeded in exhibiting the *relevant* property (the property that forms the object of my own perception). But this should give me no reason to feel that the property in question *cannot* in principle be communicated to others. On the contrary, it will be fully *effable* to other people on condition that their perceptual systems are relevantly like my own.

and by virtue of the truth of some or other form of consumer semantics (either teleosemantics, or causal or inferential role semantics). Those experiences become both world-representing (e.g. with the analog content *red*) and experience-representing (e.g. with the analog content *seems red* or *experience of red*) at the same time. In contrast, the percepts produced by the dorsal/parietal system retain analog intentional contents that are merely first-order in character, representing properties of the world (e.g. red), but not properties of our experience of the world. For the latter percepts *aren't* available to higher-order thought.

This immediately gives us an account of the key subjectivity, or 'what-it-is-likeness', of phenomenally conscious experience. For by virtue of possessing a dual analog content, those experiences will acquire a subjective aspect. This is their higher-order analog content. Hence they come to present *themselves* to us, as well as presenting properties of the world (or of the body) represented.[10] Moreover, recall that by virtue of having the first-order analog content *red*, there is something that *the world* is *like* to one who has that experience. But now by virtue of having, in addition, the higher-order analog content *seems red*, there is something that the experience itself is *like* for the one who has it. So dual-content theory ascribes to our conscious experiences both *worldly* subjectivity and *experiential* subjectivity, with the contents of the latter being parasitic upon, and exactly mirroring, the contents of the former. And the 'what-it-is-likeness' of phenomenally conscious experiences is thereby explained.

In similar manner, dual-content theory gives us a satisfying explanation of the possibility of purely recognitional concepts of experience ('phenomenal concepts'). I have explained this at length elsewhere (see Chapter 5). But in brief, the idea is that the higher-order analog contents of experience enable us to develop purely recognitional concepts of experience, in just the same sort of way that the first-order contents of experience enable us to develop recognitional concepts of secondary qualities like redness and smoothness. The first-order analog content *red* (of some specific shade) serves to ground, and to guide the application of, a recognitional concept of red. Likewise, according to dual-content theory, the higher-order analog content *seems red* or *experience of red* (again, where the *seeming* is of some specific shade) can serve to ground, and to guide the application of, a purely recognitional concept *this* [experience of red].

---

[10] See Ch. 8 of the present volume for further discussion of this idea. Note that I ought really to say, strictly speaking, that it is by virtue of having higher-order analog contents that our experiences come to present themselves *to their consumer systems*, rather than to *us*, if I am to avoid the objection that I leveled earlier against first-order theories. (With what right, it might be objected, do I assume that by virtue of their availability to the sub-systems responsible for higher-order thought and for linguistic judgment, our dual-content experiences are thereby available *to the subject*?) This then leaves open as a (remote) conceptual possibility that there might be phenomenally conscious (= dual content) experiences that are *inaccessible* to the systems that govern practical reasoning and linguistic report, as I duly acknowledge in Ch. 4 of the present volume.

Such a recognitional concept need have no conceptual connections with any physical, functional-role, or intentional-content concepts. (This is what it means to say that it is *purely* recognitional.)[11] And hence it is possible for someone deploying such a concept to entertain thoughts like the following: 'It might be possible for someone to be undergoing a perceptual state with the dual analog contents *red* and *experience of red*, while nevertheless lacking *this* [experience of red].' But of course this needn't prevent us from accepting that the property picked out by the recognitional concept *this* just *is* a perceptual state with the analog content *red*, recognized via its higher-order analog content *seeming red* (supposing that we were convinced of the virtues of dual-content theory overall). So the so-called 'explanatory gap' between physical, functional-role, and intentional facts, on the one hand, and the facts of phenomenal consciousness, on the other, is both explained and explained away.

What, then, of the *qualia-intuition*? How does dual-content theory explain the persistent tendency for people to believe that phenomenally conscious experiences possess properties that are *intrinsic* and non-relational in character? The explanation comes in two parts. The first part is conceptual. Since the concept *this* [experience of red] need have no conceptual connections with functional-role and/or intentional-content concepts, the concept *this* doesn't represent the property that it picks out *as* a relational one. And then the second part of the explanation is perceptual. The dual analog content of my phenomenally conscious experience of red neither represents the first-order property in question (redness) by its relations with anything else, nor does it represent the second-order property (experienced redness) relationally, either. Rather, just as the first-order contents of the experience seem to present to us an intrinsic property of the surface of the object perceived, so the second-order content of the experience seems to present to us an intrinsic (but introspectible) property of the experience itself.

But in contrast with first-order perception, we have no common-sense theory of introspection that might lead us to believe that the properties introspected are really relational in character after all. Although the first-order content of an experience of red seems to present us with an intrinsic, non-relational, property of the surface perceived, we have enough theoretical knowledge of the nature of perception to believe that redness is, really, a relational property of objects. In contrast, there is nothing to stop us from taking the higher-order content of a phenomenally conscious experience of red at face value, hence coming to *believe*

[11] In contrast, the recognitional concept *red* isn't a *purely* recognitional one, since it is embedded in a proto-theory of vision; whereas the recognitional concept *this* [experience of red] can be independent of any sort of proto-theory of introspection. And recall from Ch. 5 that it is vital that we should be able to explain how we can have a concept here that is *purely* recognitional, or we shan't be able to explain the intelligibility of some of the philosophically problematic thoughts, such as, 'Someone might have *this* occupying some quite different role within their cognitive system' (e.g. without it even being an *experience*, considered as a state that is functionally individuated).

that the experience possesses an intrinsic property, just as its higher-order analog content seems to present it as having.

It is only natural, then, since our experiences seem to present us with intrinsic properties of our experiences themselves, and since we aren't required to conceptualize those properties as *non*-intrinsic, that we should come to believe that our phenomenally conscious experiences possess properties that are intrinsic and non-relationally individuated (*qualia*, in the strong sense). But for all that, of course it is possible for us to believe, with dual-content theory, that there *are no* intrinsic properties of experience qua experience, since all of the relevant properties are in fact representational ones.[12]

The *ineffability-intuition*, too, is neatly explained by dual-content theory. Recall that both the first-order and higher-order contents in question are analog, or fine-grained, in character. So not only will the distinctive properties of the objects perceived (e.g. a particular shade of redness) seem to slip through the mesh of any conceptual net that we use to describe them, but so too will the distinctive properties of the perceptions themselves (e.g. a *seeming* of a particular shade of redness), presented to us by their higher-order analog contents. So we will have the persistent sense that our phenomenally conscious experiences cannot be adequately described to others. But then nor, of course, can they be *exhibited*. While I can exhibit the object of my first-order experience (e.g. a red surface), I can't exhibit the object of my higher-order experience (e.g. an experience of redness). So by virtue of the kind of awareness that I have of my own experiences, I shall have the persistent feeling that they are wholly *incommunicable* to others—for I can neither describe, nor exhibit to others, the object of my awareness.

Although the ineffability-intuition is powerful, and is explained by dual-content theory, it is nevertheless misguided if the explaining theory is correct. For if my phenomenally conscious experience of a particular shade of red is nothing other than a dual-content perceptual state with the analog contents *red* and *experience of red*, then it will be possible, in principle, to describe that experience fully to another person. But actually providing such a description may have to wait on an adequate theory of intentional content. For only when that theory is in hand will we be able to specify fully the distinctive properties of the experience in question, in virtue of which it has the particular analog contents that it has (representing both a specific *shade* of red and a *seeming* of that very shade).

The *privacy-intuition* is likewise both explained and undermined by dual-content theory. For if the properties of our phenomenally conscious experiences are apt to seem ineffable, such that we can neither describe nor exhibit them to

---

[12] It is vital to this explanation, of course, that one should keep straight the distinction between *concepts* (mental representations), on the one hand, and *properties* (features of the world or the mind represented), on the other. And one should have a robust, 'thick', conception of the latter, allowing that one and the same property can be picked out by a number of distinct concepts. See Carruthers, 2000.

others, then it is quite natural to conclude that they cannot be known to other people, either. One will be apt to think something like the following: 'How can another person ever know that I have *this* [experience of a specific shade of red], given that I can't adequately describe it to them, and given that I can't exhibit it to them for their inspection, either?' But if the properties in question are dual-content ones, then plainly it should be possible, in principle, for others to know of them—provided that the intentional properties in question can be known to others, of course. (Here, too, detailed knowledge of the kind required may have to wait on a worked-out theory of intentional content.)

Finally, what of the *infallibility-intuition*? Can dual-content theory explain why people should be so tempted to believe that they have infallible knowledge of the properties of their own conscious experiences, when they have them? Indeed, it can. For notice that the higher-order analog contents postulated by the theory are entirely parasitic upon their first-order counterparts, only coming to exist by virtue of the availability of the first-order analog contents in question to a faculty of higher-order thought. So, in contrast with so-called 'inner sense' theories of higher-order perceptual content (Armstrong, 1968; Lycan, 1996),[13] there is no possibility of the higher-order contents getting out of line with the first-order ones. On the contrary, whenever a percept has the first-order analog content F, that state will also possess the higher-order analog content *seems F* or *experience of F*—at least, provided that the state in question is available to a higher-order thought faculty of the right sort, and given the truth of some or other kind of consumer semantics.

According to the dispositional higher-order thought version of dual-content theory, our higher-order experiences really do track our first-order ones in a way that is infallible. This is a consequence of the fact that the former are parasitic upon the latter. So whenever we have a higher-order analog experience with the content *seems F*, we must be undergoing a first-order experience with the content *F*. In which case there is barely any room for error when we make immediate recognitional judgments about our own phenomenally conscious experiences, while we are having them.[14] Since there is no scope for *misperceiving* our own experiences (in the way that we *can*, of course, misperceive properties of the world) the only remaining room for error lies in various forms of mental disorder, which might in one way or another interfere with our conceptual abilities.

---

[13] Such theories postulate that we have inner sense-organs, designed to deliver higher-order perceptions of (some of) our perceptual states, just as we have outer sense-organs designed to deliver perceptions of our environments and bodies. It will therefore be possible for such sense organs to malfunction, yielding higher-order *mis*-perceptions of our own first-order experiences. See Ch. 4 of the present volume.

[14] When it comes to *remembering* our phenomenally conscious experiences, of course, our judgments will be just as liable to failure as are any other judgments about the past. Equally, we can of course be mistaken about the *causes* of our experiences, and in judgments that require some sort of mental operation to be performed on the immediate contents of experience, such as counting the sides of a mentally imaged figure, or making comparative judgments between one experience and another.

## 5. WHAT CAN A FIRST-ORDER THEORIST GAIN BY EMBRACING DUAL CONTENT?

I have argued that dual-content theory does a fine job of meeting the various *desiderata* that we laid down in section 2 for a successful theory of phenomenal consciousness, whereas first-order theories don't. So far, then, dual-content theory is winning 'hands down'. But it might seem that there is a further option open to first-order theorists, at this point. For couldn't they *also* believe in the existence of dual-analog contents? And couldn't they thereby get all of the explanatory advantages of dual-content theory while remaining first-order theorists about phenomenal consciousness as such?[15] I shall elaborate on this idea first, before turning to evaluate it.

It is plain that first-order theorists can accept that some of our first-order perceptual states (specifically, in the case of vision, those produced by the ventral/temporal system) are made available to a faculty of higher-order thought, which is capable of forming partly recognitional concepts that apply to the first-order states in question.[16] And it is also plain that first-order theorists can accept some or other form of consumer semantics. In which case first-order theorists might believe that our phenomenally conscious experiences are *also* dual-content states, having both first-order and higher-order analog intentional contents. But they will insist that it isn't in virtue of possessing dual analog contents that the states in question are phenomenally conscious ones, and thus come to have *experiential* as well as *worldly* subjectivity. Rather, their phenomenally conscious status will derive from the fact that they have *first-order* analog contents available to conceptual thought and conceptual judgment.

Now, if first-order theorists can think that phenomenally conscious states are also dual-content ones, then they can surely endorse many of the explanations offered in section 4 above, hence fulfilling the relevant *desiderata* of a theory of consciousness. For example, they can explain the existence of purely recognitional concepts of experience as being grounded in the higher-order analog contents of our perceptual states, in something like the way that first-order recognitional concepts of color are grounded in the first-order analog contents of

---

[15] Tye (1995, 2000) sometimes seems to come close to endorsing this combination of views. I am grateful to Keith Frankish for pushing this idea on my attention.

[16] At this initial stage the concepts, although recognitional, will still be theoretically embedded. Subjects who understand what an experience is will know that, whenever they are inclined to make a judgment of 'red', they are also entitled to make a judgment of 'seems red' or 'experience of red'. The component concepts of *seeming* and *experience* here are theoretical ones. It is only when the perceptual states in question thereby acquire higher-order analog contents that the subject can acquire *purely* recognitional concepts of experience, making judgments of 'this again' grounded in the higher-order perceptual contents in question.

our experiences. But they can do this while continuing to claim that all and only those mental states that possess first-order analog intentional contents that are available to conceptual thought are phenomenally conscious ones.

One might be tempted to respond to this suggestion by saying that phenomenal consciousness is, surely, whatever it is that gives rise to the 'hard problem' of consciousness (Chalmers, 1996). And it is the various features laid out in our six *desiderata* that make the problem of explaining phenomenal consciousness seem particularly hard. (This is especially obvious in respect of the second feature, which is precisely that phenomenal consciousness seems to give rise to a persistent 'explanatory gap'.) But what has now emerged from the discussion in sections 3 and 4 above, is that it is the dual-analog content of our perceptual states, rather than their first-order analog contents, that gives rise to the appearance of a 'hard problem'. In which case phenomenal consciousness itself should be identified with states possessing a dual-analog content, rather than more generally with first-order analog states that are available to conceptual thought.

There is some danger that the disagreement between first-order theorists and higher-order theorists may become merely verbal at this point, however. Each would be agreeing that the various puzzling features of phenomenal consciousness are to be explained by appeal to dual-analog contents. But the first-order theorist would be insisting on identifying phenomenal consciousness itself with the *object* of those puzzles—with what we are thinking *about* when we worry about the intrinsic properties of our experience or the ineffability of a sensation of red, say. And a higher-order theorist, too, should agree that what we are thinking about in such cases is a first-order analog perceptual state (albeit one that is presented to us via a higher-order analog representation of itself). But the higher-order theorist would be insisting, on the contrary, that phenomenal consciousness itself should be identified with that which *gives rise to* the various puzzles. And this is the higher-order analog content of our conscious perceptual states, as we have seen.

It is unclear, at this point, whether there would be anything substantive remaining in this disagreement. For it is unclear whether anything of theoretical importance turns on the question whether phenomenal consciousness should be identified with what we are thinking *about* when we are puzzled by the 'hard problem', or rather whether it should be identified with that which *gives rise to* the puzzles that constitute the 'hard problem'.

I believe that the dispute is *not* merely verbal, however. Recall from section 2 that the distinctive subjectivity, or 'what-it-is-likeness', of our phenomenally conscious experiences was said to be the defining feature of them. A phenomenally conscious state just *is* a state possessing the relevant kind of subjectivity. But we also said that first-order theory as such lacks the resources to explain it; whereas dual-content theory provides the needed explanation. If these claims are correct, then first-order theory (even when combined with a belief in dual analog contents) isn't an acceptable theory of phenomenal consciousness. For it is the higher-order analog content, not the first-order content, that constitutes the defining feature of such consciousness (its subjective *feel* or 'what-it-is-likeness').

Does this reply commit me to any kind of objectionable *qualia*-realism? By insisting that the subjectivity of our phenomenally conscious states is a real (and defining) property of them, standing in need of explanation, have I let in *qualia* by the back door? Not at all. For there is, indeed, a real but naturalistically acceptable property here: it is the higher-order analog content possessed by the experiences in question. This gives those experiences a subjective dimension, making them available to their subjects in something like the way that first-order analog contents make available to us properties of our environments (and bodies).

Moreover, the higher-order analog content of the content-bearing states with which my sort of higher-order theorist identifies phenomenal consciousness serves to mark a real and substantial difference between the perceptual states produced by the ventral/temporal visual system (which possess such content) and those forming the output of the dorsal/parietal system (which don't). So we have identified a real difference between the states of the two kinds, which marks out the former as phenomenally conscious and the latter as not, in a way that is thoroughly relevant to their phenomenally conscious status. A first-order theorist, in contrast (even one who accepts that dual analog contents are differentially possessed by the ventral/temporal states) is committed to *denying* that it is the presence of the higher-order analog content that renders these states phenomenally conscious. On the contrary, it will have to be something about the wider functional role of those states (e.g. their availability to first-order thought and planning) that constitutes them as phenomenally conscious. And we have already seen the inadequacies of this approach (see section 3 above).

I conclude, then, that although first-order theorists can accept the existence of dual analog contents, and can hence reap the benefits of explaining many of the puzzling facts about phenomenal consciousness, they still can't provide an adequate account of what phenomenal consciousness itself *is*. For they can't explain the key subjectivity, or *what-it-is-likeness* of such consciousness. For this, they would have to accept that phenomenal consciousness should be *identified* with states possessing dual analog contents. But that, of course, would be a higher-order theory and not a first-order theory. Indeed, it is my own theory.

## 6. CONCLUSION

In summary, then, the case against first-order theories of phenomenal consciousness is that they are incapable of providing a reductive explanation of all of the various distinctive and problematic features of phenomenal consciousness.

In contrast, the kind of higher-order dual-content theory that arises from combining dispositional higher-order thought theory with some suitable form of consumer semantics *can* explain those features. This provides us with powerful reasons for rejecting first-order theories, and for embracing dual-content theory instead.[17, 18, 19]

[17] The case against other varieties of higher-order theory (specifically, inner-sense theory and actualist higher-order thought theory) needs to be made rather differently. It should be obvious that inner-sense theory can meet the first five of our six *desiderata*, since it, too, postulates the existence of higher-order analog contents targeted on (some of) our first-order experiences. But the theory predicts that our inner sense-organs should sometimes malfunction, just as our outer senses do. In which case there should be instances where people are inclined to judge, spontaneously and without theoretical influence, 'The surface is red' while at the same time judging, 'The surface *seems* orange.' This seems barely coherent. There are, moreover, no good evolutionary reasons why an organ of inner sense should have evolved. See Carruthers, 2000, and Ch. 4 of the present volume for further discussion. Actualist higher-order thought theory, in contrast, can't meet our *desiderata* as such, since it fails to postulate higher-order analog contents. It *can* make appeal to such contents by accepting some version of consumer semantics; but then the motivation for being actualist rather than dispositionalist will evaporate, since all kinds of consumer semantics are dispositionalist in form. In addition, actualist higher-order thought theory faces essentially the same evolution-based objections as does inner-sense theory, since it is mysterious why evolution should have ensured the generation of so many higher-order thoughts on a regular basis. See Carruthers, 2000, and Ch. 4 of the present volume for further discussion.

[18] Note that if it also follows (when dual-content theory is supplemented by suitable premises concerning the cognitive powers of non-human animals) that non-human animals aren't subject to phenomenally conscious mental states, then that is a conclusion with which we are somehow going to have to learn to live. This topic is taken up at length in Chs. 9, 10, and 11 of the present volume.

[19] I am grateful to Keith Frankish, Robert Lurz, Benedicte Veillet, and an anonymous referee for Oxford University Press for their thoughtful comments on a draft of the present chapter.

# CHAPTER 7

# Conscious Thinking: Language or Elimination?

Do we conduct our conscious propositional thinking in natural language? Or is such language only peripherally related to human conscious thought-processes? In this chapter I shall present a partial defense of the former view, by arguing that the only real alternative is *eliminativism* about conscious propositional thinking. Following some introductory remarks, I shall state the argument for this conclusion, and show how that conclusion can be true. Thereafter I shall defend each of the three main premises in turn.

## 1. INTRODUCTION

How are language and thought related to one another? While almost everyone allows that language-use, in any full-blooded sense, requires thought, there is considerable dispute about whether thought, in turn, requires or involves natural language. On the one hand there are those who espouse what can be called *the cognitive conception* of language, who maintain that language is crucially implicated in thought—as well as being used for purposes of communication, of course (Wittgenstein, 1921, 1953; Vygotsky, 1934; Whorf, 1956; Davidson, 1975, 1982; Dummett, 1981, 1991; Dennett, 1991; as can be seen, they are a varied bunch). And on the other hand there are defenders of what can be called *the communicative conception* of language, who maintain that language is *not* essentially implicated in thinking, but rather serves only to facilitate the communication of thought (Russell, 1921; Grice, 1957, 1969; Lewis, 1969; Fodor, 1978; Searle, 1983; Pinker, 1994; again a varied list, though perhaps not quite *so* varied).

While this chapter is concerned to defend a form of cognitive conception of language, it is important to see that the version in question is a relatively weak one, in at least two respects. *First*, the thesis that language is constitutively involved in human thought is here put forward as holding with, at most, *natural* necessity. It is certainly not claimed to be conceptually necessary. So there is a contrast in this respect with some of the main defenders of the cognitive conception (specifically, Davidson and Dummett), who have claimed that their thesis is an a priori conceptual one. For reasons that I don't intend to go into now, this strikes me as highly implausible (see my 1996, ch. 1, for some brief discussion). On the contrary, the case for the *conceptual* independence of thought from language is, I believe, a very powerful one. But that leaves open the possibility that there may still be some sort of naturally necessary involvement. *Second*, the thesis that language is involved in human thought is not here maintained universally, but is restricted to specific *kinds* of thought, particularly to *conscious propositional* thoughts. I shall make no attempt to show that *all* thought constitutively involves natural language. Indeed, my own belief is that it doesn't (see Chapter 12).

While the version of cognitive conception to be defended in this chapter is relatively weak, the question is still of considerable interest and importance. For what is at issue is the overall place of natural language in human cognition. According to the communicative conception, the sole function and purpose of natural language is to facilitate communication (either with other people, in the case of written or spoken language, or with oneself, by means of 'inner speech'— see below). Spoken language thus serves only as the medium, or conduit, through which thoughts may be transmitted from mind to mind, rather than being involved in the process of thinking itself. Something like this is now the standard model employed by most of those working in cognitive science, who view language as an isolatable, and largely isolated, *module* of the mind, which is both innately structured and specialized for the interpretation and construction of natural language sentences (Fodor, 1978, 1983, 1987; Chomsky, 1988; Levelt, 1989; Pinker, 1994). According to the (weak form of) cognitive conception of language, in contrast, natural language is constitutively involved in some of our conscious thought-processes, at least. So language is not (or *not just*—see my 1998) an isolated module of the mind, but is directly implicated in central cognitive processes of believing, desiring, and reasoning.

Now, many of us are inclined to report, on introspective grounds, that at least some of our conscious propositional thinking is conducted in imaged natural-language sentences—either spoken (in motor imagery) or heard (in the form of auditory imagery). And certainly, the systematic introspection-sampling studies conducted by Hurlburt (1990, 1993) found that, while proportions varied, *all* subjects reported at least some instances of 'inner speech'.[1] So the existence of inner speech, itself, isn't—or shouldn't be—in doubt. The question concerns its status, and its explanation. According to the weak form of cognitive conception to be defended here, inner speech is partly constitutive of thinking. According to

---

[1] In these studies subjects wore a modified paging-device, which issued a series of beeps through an ear-phone at irregular intervals during the course of the day. Subjects were instructed to 'freeze' their introspective consciousness at the precise moment of the beep, and immediately to jot down notes about those contents, to be elaborated in later interviews with the experimenters. Subjects reported finding, in varying proportions, visual imagery, inner speech, emotive feelings, and purely propositional— non-verbal—thoughts.

the communicative conception, in contrast, inner speech is merely *expressive* of thought, perhaps being the medium through which we gain access to our thoughts.

One final clarification (and qualification) is in order, before I present the argument for my conclusion. This is that I am perfectly happy to allow that *some* conscious thinking *doesn't* involve language, and nothing that I say here should be taken to deny this. Specifically, it seems plain that conscious manipulation of visual or other images can constitute a kind of thinking (recall what might run through your mind as you try to pack a number of awkwardly shaped boxes into the trunk of your car, for example), and a kind of thinking that seems clearly independent of language. However, since it also seems likely that such imagistic thoughts are not fully propositional, having contents that can only awkwardly and inaccurately be reported in the form of a that-clause, I can restrict my claim to conscious *propositional* thought. And the standard arguments that refute imagistic theories of meaning, or imagistic theories of thought, can be used to show that there is a space here to be occupied, since imagistic thinking cannot be extended to colonize the whole domain of conscious thought (unless, that is, the images in question are images *of natural language sentences*—see below).

## 2. THE ARGUMENT

The argument for the claim that conscious propositional thinking is conducted by means of natural language sentences is as follows.

1. Conscious thinking requires immediate, non-inferential, non-interpretative, access to our own occurrent thoughts, and that access is distinctively different from our access to the thoughts of other people.

2. Occurrent propositional thoughts either receive articulation in inner speech, or they don't; and if they do, then inner speech is either constitutive of the thought-tokens in question (the cognitive conception), or not (the communicative conception).

3. If the manipulation of natural language sentences in imagination (in 'inner speech') *isn't* constitutive of propositional thinking, then our access to those of our thoughts that receive expression in inner speech is interpretative, and similar to the sort of access that we have to the thoughts of other people, when they speak; and hence such thoughts of ours don't count as conscious (by 1).

4. The form of access that we have to those of our occurrent propositional thoughts that *don't* receive expression in inner speech also involves self-interpretation, and hence such thoughts, too, fail to count as conscious (by 1).

5. So if we engage in conscious propositional thinking at all, then natural language sentences must be constitutively involved in such thinking (from 1, 2, 3, and 4).
6. But we do sometimes engage in conscious propositional thinking.
7. So natural language is constitutively involved in conscious thought (from 5 and 6).

The argument itself is plainly valid. Premise 2 presents us with a three-branched disjunction. Two of these disjuncts are then closed off by premises 3 and 4 respectively (relying upon premise 1), leaving the third disjunct to be conditionalized in premise 5. Now, premise 2 is just a truism. So if premises 1, 3, and 4 are held firm (supposing that they can be adequately supported by further argument, as I shall try to show respectively in sections 4, 5, and 6 below), then our choices are: to give up premise 6, hence becoming eliminativists about conscious propositional thought; or to accept 7, thus endorsing a version of the cognitive conception of language.

For many people, I suspect, the correct response to such a dilemma will seem straightforward—if there is a conflict between the communicative conception of language, on the one hand, and the belief that we sometimes entertain conscious propositional thoughts, on the other, then, plainly, it is the former that should be given up. But this would be much too swift. For many of the arguments against eliminativism about the mental in general (Horgan and Woodward, 1985; Fodor, 1987) don't extend to eliminativism about conscious propositional thought in particular. Specifically, the arguments from the indispensability and success of common-sense psychology can cut little ice in this more restricted domain, since it is not at all clear whether, or why, we really *need* the assumption of *conscious* thought for purposes of intentional explanation and prediction. Nor can this sort of restricted eliminativism be immediately refuted by any kind of appeal to introspective phenomenology, since it is, in fact, quite easy to explain how we might come to be under the illusion that we engage in genuinely conscious thinking, as we shall see in sections 5 and 6 below.[2]

Despite what I have just said, it does seem to me somewhat more reasonable to accept premise 6 than it is to reject the cognitive conception of language (represented by the conclusion in 7). But this involves examining, and disarming, the various arguments that have been put up against the cognitive conception of language, and in favor of the communicative conception. I shall not attempt to

---

[2] This isn't to deny, of course, that the belief that we sometimes entertain conscious propositional thoughts might be very deeply embedded in our common-sense conception of ourselves. Thus Burge (1996) argues, for example, that the belief that we have non-inferential, non-interpretative, access to our own occurrent thoughts is crucial to our status as *critical reasoners*—and ultimately, perhaps, to our status as persons. But even if this is correct, it doesn't really provide us with any independent argument against eliminativism, unless we have some further ground for believing that we actually *are* critical reasoners, in Burge's restrictive sense, as opposed to being under the illusion that we are such reasoners.

do this here. (See my 1996, much of which is taken up with consideration and rebuttal of such arguments.) For present purposes I shall have to be content to leave it to my readers to decide which way they want to jump. (But note that even a disjunctive conclusion has considerable bite, since there are many people who think that they can combine a belief in premise 6 with the denial of 7.)

It *is* important to see, however, how the conclusion in 7 can possibly be true, consistent with the other premises; for it is natural to wonder how natural language *can* be constitutive of conscious thinking, if the latter requires non-inferential, non-interpretative, access, as claimed in premise 1. It is also important to recognize the strength of the empirical commitments that we would take on by accepting 7. So in the next section I shall try to show how the manipulation of natural-language sentences in imagination *can* be partly constitutive of propositional thinking; and if it is, how we would have the right sort of non-inferential access to some of our occurrent thoughts for them to count as conscious ones.

## 3. THE POSSIBLE TRUTH OF 7: ON THINKING LINGUISTICALLY

Suppose that imaged sentences have the causal roles distinctive of occurrent thoughts. That is, suppose that it is *because* I entertain, in judgmental mode, the sentence, 'The world is getting warmer, so I must use less fuel', that I thereafter form an intention to walk rather than to drive to work. If the imaged natural-language sentence is a crucial part of the process that causes the formation of an intention, and is thus, ultimately, part of what causes my later action, then this might seem sufficient for it to be constitutive of the occurrent thought.

This would, however, be too swift. For a defender of the communicative conception can allow that there are some chains of reasoning that cannot occur in the absence of an imaged natural-language sentence (Clark, 1998). If it is, for example, by virtue of our thoughts causing the production of imaged natural-language sentences that we gain access to their contents and occurrences, then any chain of reasoning that requires us to have such access will constitutively involve an imaged sentence. But, by hypothesis, the imaged sentence is not *itself* the thought, but is merely what gives us *access to* the thought. So rather more needs to be done to get at the intended idea behind (this version of) the cognitive conception of language.

The obvious thing to say, in fact, is that an imaged sentence will occupy the causal role of a thought if it has the distinctive causes and effects of that thought, but *without* these being mediated by events that themselves carry the same (or a sufficiently similar) content. So the sentence, 'The world is getting warmer', will count as constitutive of my conscious thought if it (together with my other beliefs and desires) causes my intention to walk to work, but *not* by virtue of first being translated into a non-imagistic event that carries the content, [that the world is getting warmer]. But is it even *possible* for an imaged sentence to occupy the causal role of an occurrent thought? The answer, surely, is 'Yes'—in at least three different ways.

*First*, it may well be that our *non*-conscious thinking *doesn't* involve natural language sentences, but rather consists in manipulations of sentences of Mentalese (or, alternatively, of activations in a connectionist network, as it might be). These non-conscious thoughts may also be used to generate imaged natural-language sentences, which are then processed in some sort of metarepresentational executive system, in such a way that we can say, not merely that the imaged sentence gives us *access* to the underlying thought, but that it *constitutes* a distinct (conscious) token of the *same* thought.[3] Such a description will be appropriate provided that the effects of the imaged sentence-token within the executive aren't mediated by the equivalent sentence of Mentalese. This will be the case if, for example (and as Dennett, 1991, has argued) there are certain kinds inference that one can learn to make amongst thoughts, that one can make *only* when those thoughts are tokened in the form of a natural-language sentence.[4]

*Second*, it may be that *all* propositional thoughts involve natural language representations of one sort or another (or, at least, that some significant sub-set of propositional thought-types do). Conscious thoughts might, as above, be constituted by imaged natural-language sentences, which interact with one another in the manner distinctive of occurrent thoughts. But non-conscious tokens of (some of) those same thought-types, too, might be constituted by some non-phonological natural-language representation, say a sentence of Chomsky's 'Logical Form' (LF), as it might be, in which sentences are regimented in such a way as to resolve scope-ambiguities and the like (May, 1985; Chomsky, 1995). On this picture, then, human cognition will involve computations on two sorts of natural-language representation—computations on phonological entities, in consciousness, and non-conscious computations on LF representations with the same contents.[5]

*Third*, there is the possibility developed by Frankish (2004), which builds on some early work of Dennett's on the difference between belief and opinion (Dennett, 1978c). The idea here isn't (as it was above) that imaged sentences are manipulated by the sub-personal mechanisms operative in some central executive system, but rather that they are objects of personal (rationally motivated)

---

[3] This is the weaker of the two hypotheses I explored in my 1996, ch. 8, where natural language sentences are constitutive, not of propositional thought *types*, but of the conscious *tokens* of those types.

[4] For evidence that there are tasks that can be solved only with concurrent verbalization, see Berry and Broadbent, 1984, 1987.

[5] This is the stronger of the two hypotheses explored in my 1996, ch. 8, according to which some propositional thoughts, as *types*, constitutively require natural-language representations.

*decision*. On this model, when the sentence, 'The world is getting warmer, so I must use less fuel', figures in consciousness, I may *decide* to accept it, thereby deciding to adopt a policy of using that sentence thereafter as a premise in my theoretical and practical reasoning. Since such decisions may then have many of the same effects as would the corresponding belief, they may be thought of as constituting a kind of *virtual belief*. And here, as before, the sentence-token in question is partly constitutive of the opinion thereby adopted.[6]

The only question remaining, then, in order for us to demonstrate the possible truth of 7, is whether our access to our own mental images has the kind of non-inferential character necessary for those images to count as conscious. And the answer, surely, is that it has. Our access to our own visual and auditory images, for example, seems to be part of the very paradigm of immediate, non-inferential, non-self-interpretative awareness. And similarly, then, with inner speech: we have immediate access to a particular phonological representation, together with its interpretation. The latter point is worth stressing: when I form an image of a natural-language sentence in a language that I understand, just as when I hear someone else speak in that language, what figures in consciousness is *not* just a phonological object standing in need of interpretation. Rather, what figures there is *already* interpreted—I *hear meaning* in the words, just as I hear the speaker's (or my own imagined) tone of voice.[7]

It might be questioned how the *content* of an imaged sentence *can* be an object of immediate awareness. For suppose that the contents of my sentences are determined, at least in part, by my inferential dispositions—perhaps by my dispositions to find certain inferences to and from the sentences in question *primitively compelling* (Peacocke, 1992). Then how could these dispositions be objects of immediate, non-inferential, awareness? There are really two issues here, however. First, how could I know *that* the sentence has a content for me? And second, how could I know *what* content the sentence has for me? And thus divided, the problem is easily conquered. I can know *that* the sentence is contentful by a kind of feeling of familiarity (or, more plausibly perhaps, by the absence of any feeling of *un*familiarity)—by means of a well-grounded confidence that I should know how to go on from it, for example. And I can know *what* content the sentence has, simply by *embedding* it in a content report. Given that I have just entertained the sentence, 'The world is getting warmer', and that it is contentful,

---

[6] Note that this possibility will then admit of both weaker and stronger variants corresponding to those canvassed above, depending upon whether ground-level, non-virtual, beliefs are carried by sentences of Mentalese—or perhaps patterns of activation in a connectionist network—on the one hand, or rather by natural language sentences—i.e. non-imagistic, LF representations—on the other.

[7] Note, however, that this claim about the phenomenology of inner speech isn't sufficient, by itself, to establish the truth of 7. If the phenomenally immediate content of a tokened sentence is to count as a conscious *thought*, then it must itself occupy the causal role distinctive of such a thought. So we would also need to endorse one or other of the three possibilities sketched in the paragraphs above.

I can then immediately and non-inferentially report that I have just thought *that the world is getting warmer*. The content of the initial sentence is automatically made available within the content of the embedding sentence which reports on that content.

It is worth noting that the claimed immediacy of our access to the forms and contents of our own mental images is (despite initial appearances to the contrary) fully consistent with recent neuropsychological work on the generation of images. In the model developed at length by Kosslyn (1994), for example, the same backwards-projecting neural pathways that are used in normal perception to direct visual search, are used in imagination to induce an appropriate stimulus in the primary visual cortex (area $V_1$), which is then processed by the visual system in the normal way, just as if it were a percept. So on this account, the generation of imagery will involve at least sub-personal computations and inferences in the visual system, just as perception does. But that does *not* mean that the image is only available to us by means of such inferences. It is the self-induced pattern of stimulation in $V_1$ that has to be interpreted by the visual system, on this account, *not* the image. Rather, the image is the *result of* such a process of interpretation. The image itself is the *output* of the visual system to central cognition, not the input. So it is entirely consistent with Kosslyn's account to say that our access to our own conscious images is wholly non-inferential (that is, that it doesn't even involve sub-personal computations of any sort).

## 4. IN DEFENSE OF PREMISE 1: ON CONSCIOUS THINKING

This first premise of the argument laid out in section 2 above stated that our mode of access to our own occurrent thoughts must be non-interpretative in character if those thoughts are to count as conscious ones. This claim is by no means wholly uncontroversial; but it is accessible to, and defensible from, a number of different perspectives on the nature of consciousness.

Many philosophers, for example—especially those writing within a broadly Wittgensteinian tradition—are apt to emphasize that we are *authoritative* about our own conscious mental states, in a way that we cannot be authoritative about the mental states of others (Malcolm, 1984; Shoemaker, 1988, 1990; Heal, 1994; see also Burge, 1996). If I sincerely claim to be in a particular mental state, then this provides sufficient grounds for others to say of me—and to say with justification—that I *am* in that state, in the absence of direct evidence to the contrary. Put otherwise, a sincere claim that I am in a particular mental state is self-licensing—perhaps because such claims are thought to be *constitutive* of the states thereby ascribed—in a way that sincere claims about the mental states of others are not.

Now, it is very hard indeed to see how we could possess this kind of epistemic authority in respect of our own occurrent thoughts if those thoughts were known of on the basis of some kind of self-interpretation. For there is nothing privileged about my standpoint as an interpreter of myself. Others, arguably, have essentially the same kind of interpretative access to my mental states as I do.[8] So believers in first-person authority should also accept premise 1, and maintain that our access to our own occurrent thoughts, when conscious, is of a non-inferential, non-interpretative, sort.

Premise 1 can also be adequately motivated from a variety of more cognitivist perspectives. On the sort of approach that I favor, a mental state becomes conscious when it is made available to a faculty of thought that has the power, not only to entertain thoughts about the *content* of that state (e.g. about an item in the world, perceptually represented), but also to entertain thoughts about the *occurrence* of that state (see my 1996, ch. 7). When I perceive a ripe tomato, for example, my perceptual state occurs in such a way as to make its content available to conceptual thought about the tomato, where some of those concepts may be deployed recognitionally (e.g. *red*, or *tomato* ). That state is then a conscious one if it also occurs in such a way as to be available to thoughts about *itself* (e.g. 'It looks to me like there is a tomato there', or 'I am now experiencing red')— where here, too, some of the concepts may be deployed recognitionally, so that I can judge, straight off, that I am experiencing red, say. On this account, then, a conscious thought will be one that is available to thoughts about the occurrence of that thought (e.g. 'Why did I think *that*?'), where the sense of *availability* in question is supposed to be non-inferential, but rather recognitional, or at least quasi-recognitional.

It is worth noting that this account is fully consistent with so-called 'theory-theory' approaches to our understanding of mental states and events (which I endorse). On such a view, our various mental concepts (*perceive, judge, fear, feel*, and so on) get their life and significance from their embedding in a substantive, more or less explicit, *theory* of the causal structure of the mind (Lewis, 1966; Churchland, 1981; Stich, 1983, Fodor, 1987). So to grasp the concept *percept of red*, for example, one has to know enough about the role of the corresponding state in our overall mental economy, such as that it tends to be caused by the presence of something red in one's line of vision, and tends to cause one to believe, in turn, that one is confronted with something red, and so on. It is perfectly consistent with such a view that these theoretical concepts should also

---

[8] Of course I shall, standardly, have available a good deal more data to interpret in my own case, and I can also generate further data at will, in a way that I cannot in connection with others—but this is a mere quantitative, rather than a qualitative difference.

admit of recognitional applications, in certain circumstances. And then one way of endorsing premise 1, is to say that a mental state counts as conscious only if it is available to a recognitional application of some corresponding mental concept.

Amongst those who should *deny* premise 1 will be some (but by no means all) of those who think of introspection on the model of outer perception (the difference, here, will then turn on how perception itself is conceived of, as will shortly emerge). For suppose that consciousness is mediated by the operation of some sort of internal self-scanning mechanism (Armstrong, 1968, 1984)—in that case it might seem obvious that our access to our own mental states isn't crucially different from our access to the mental states of other people, and that such access must at least be partly inferential, contrary to what is claimed in premise 1. This conclusion would be too hasty, however. For it is important to distinguish between personal-level inference, on the one hand, and subpersonal computation, on the other.

The sense of 'inference' that figures in premise 1 is not, of course, restricted to *conscious* inference; but it *is* restricted to person-level inference, in which a cognitive transition or process draws on the subject's current beliefs on the matters in hand. The claim is that we take our access to our conscious thoughts to be immediate, not necessarily in the sense that it depends upon no subpersonal computations, but rather in the sense that it doesn't depend for its operation upon any other particular *beliefs* of ours. In which case it will be possible for someone to think of the self-scanning mechanism as an isolated *module*, in the sense of Fodor (1983), which may well effect computations on its inputs, but which does so in a manner that is mandatory and hard-wired, and which is encapsulated from changes in background belief.

So, if someone conceives of introspection on the model of outer perception, then much may depend, for our purposes, on whether or not they have a *modular* conception of the latter. If so, then they should be happy to endorse premise 1, since the self-scanning mechanism that produces awareness of our conscious mental states will operate independently of background belief (even if it embodies, itself, some sort of implicit theory of the mind and its operations), and so will not be *inferential* or *self-interpretative* in the intended sense. If, on the other hand, they think that all perception is theory-laden, in the sense that it is partly determined by the subject's explicit beliefs and changes of belief, then they *may* be committed to a denial of premise 1, depending upon which kinds of belief are in question. Certainly, rejection of premise 1 isn't necessarily mandatory for such a person. For as we saw earlier, theory-theory accounts of our conception of the mental are consistent with premise 1, provided that the theory-imbued concepts can also be deployed recognitionally. So one could claim that our quasi-perceptual access to our own mental states is theory-laden, while also maintaining that the access in question is non-inferential in character.

What really *is* inconsistent with premise 1 is a view of our relation to our own mental states that makes the latter dependent upon our *particular* beliefs about our current environment or circumstances, or about our recently prior thoughts or other mental states. If my awareness that I am in some particular mental state depends, not just on recognitional deployment of theoretically embedded concepts, but also on inferences that draw upon my beliefs about the current physical or cognitive environment, then introspection really *will* be inferential in a manner that conflicts with premise 1. But it is, I claim, a presupposition of our common-sense conception of consciousness that our access to our conscious mental states is *not* inferential in this sense. Those who disagree can stop reading this chapter here, since I shall say nothing further to persuade them of the falsity of their view—and yet the remainder of the argument depends upon it being false. Or better (or better for me): they should read what follows, but read it as having the form of a conditional, to see what they *would* be committed to if they *didn't* hold their particular theory of the nature of introspection.

Some people might allege that I have subtly begged the question in favor of my conclusion by writing as if consciousness were a unitary phenomenon. They may, for example, be keen to stress the difference between *phenomenal* consciousness and *reflexive* (or higher-order) consciousness, claiming that some mental states are conscious in the former sense and some only in the latter (e.g. Davies, 1993; Block, 1995).[9] And then they may assert that the sort of immediacy of access to our conscious thoughts, which is claimed in premise 1, is really only appropriate in connection with phenomenally conscious states. In which case it is being taken for granted that conscious thoughts must be imagistically expressed, and the only remotely plausible candidates for the images in question, will be imaged natural-language sentences, or 'inner speech'. So premise 1 it may be said, just *assumes* that conscious propositional thought is conducted in natural language.

Let us grant the distinction between phenomenal consciousness and reflexive consciousness. Still, it would surely be a mistake to claim that the thesis of *immediacy*, expressed in premise 1, applies only to the former. If reflexive consciousness is genuinely to be a form of *consciousness*, indeed, then the sort of access in question must be non-inferential and non-interpretative. We surely believe, for example, that there is all the difference in the world between entertaining, *consciously*, a jealous thought (even allowing that such a thought may lack phenomenal properties), and realizing, by interpretation of one's current behavior, that one is acting out of jealousy. So, in insisting that we must have immediate knowledge of thoughts, too, if they are conscious, I am certainly not

---

[9] States are phenomenally conscious which have phenomenal properties, or *feels*, like pains and experiences of red. States are reflexively conscious which are *available* or *accessible* to be thought about by the subject.

*assuming* that such thoughts must, of their very nature, be phenomenally conscious.

Moreover, there is no good reason to think that if we do have self-knowledge of mental states that are reflexively conscious without being phenomenally conscious, then such knowledge would *have to be* inferential or interpretative. For it is easy to imagine a possible mechanism that would underpin the kind of immediate access that we take ourselves to have to our conscious occurrent thoughts, but without presupposing any sort of phenomenal consciousness. In particular, suppose that *thinking that P* were constituted by entertaining, in appropriate mode (that is: judgment, supposition, expression of desire, etc.), some Mentalese sentence 'S' that means that P. Then you could imagine a mechanism that operated by semantic ascent, in such a way that the occurrence of 'S' in the belief mode would automatically cause one to be disposed to entertain, in judgmental mode, the Mentalese equivalent of 'I have just thought that S' (where this would, by hypothesis, be the same as thinking that one has just entertained the thought that P). But this would happen without our having any awareness of, or mode of access to, the fact that the sentence 'S' was used in the expression of the original belief. That sentence would be *used* over again, embedded in the higher-order sentence that carried the content of the higher-order thought, but without the subject having any knowledge that it is so used. Such a mechanism would give us reliable non-inferential access to our own occurrent thoughts, without any sentences (let alone natural-language sentences) having to figure as objects of phenomenal awareness.

## 5. IN DEFENSE OF PREMISE 3: ON INTERPRETING ONE'S OWN INNER SPEECH

Suppose, then, that inner speech isn't constitutive of, but rather expressive of, propositional thinking. In that case the picture would be this: first a thought is entertained, in a manner that does *not* constitutively involve natural language (carried by a sentence of Mentalese, as it may be); and then that thought is encoded into a natural-language sentence with the same (or sufficiently similar) content, to be displayed in auditory or motor imagination. By virtue of the conscious status of the latter, we thereby gain access to the underlying thought. But this access is not, I claim, of the kind necessary for that thought to count as a conscious one.

One argument for this conclusion is that the imaged natural-language sentence can only give us access to the thought that caused it through a process of interpretation. In order for me to know *which* thought it is that I have just entertained, when the sentence, 'I just have time to get to the bank', figures in auditory imagination, that sentence needs to be interpreted, relying on cues provided by the context. These cues can presumably be both cognitive and non-cognitive in nature. What enables me to disambiguate the sentence may be other recent thoughts, or current goals, of mine; or it may be background knowledge of the circumstances, such as that there is no river near by. Not that this process of interpretation is characteristically a conscious one, of course; quite the contrary. In general, as emphasized in section 3, the sentences entertained in inner speech certainly don't *strike* one as standing in need of interpretation; their phenomenology is rather that they are objects that are *already* interpreted. But interpretation there must surely have been, nevertheless. An imaged sentence, just as much as a heard sentence, needs to be parsed and disambiguated in order to be understood. So what figures in consciousness, on this account, is not a thought, but rather a *representation of* a thought; and a representation constructed through a process of interpretation and inference. This is, I claim, sufficient to debar the thought represented from counting as a conscious one.

It might be objected that one doesn't *need* to interpret the imaged sentence in order to disambiguate it, since one *already* knows what one *meant* or *intended*. But this objection presupposes, surely, that we have non-inferential access to our own conscious, but non-verbalized, intentions. For if my only access to my own meaning-intentions were itself inferential, then it is very hard to see how their existence could help in any way to demonstrate that I have *non-inferential* access to the thoughts that I verbally articulate in inner speech. But as we shall see in section 6, there is every reason to think that our only access to our occurrent unverbalized thoughts *is* inferential, by means of swift self-interpretation.

Another, related, argument for the conclusion that verbalized thoughts aren't really conscious, if the thoughts themselves are distinct from their verbalizations, is this: in that case we would have essentially the same sort of access to our own occurrent thoughts as we have to the thoughts of other people when we hear them speak. In both cases the communicative conception of language would have it that an occurrent thought causes the production of a natural-language sentence, which is then represented and interpreted by the consumer of that sentence (another person, in the case of overt speech; the same person, in the case of inner speech). But in both cases the resulting representation of the content of the sentence (on this account, the underlying thought) strikes us, normally, with phenomenological immediacy.

It is true that we do sometimes have to pause to reflect, before settling on an interpretation of someone else's utterance, in a way that we don't have to reflect to understand our own inner speech. This is presumably because the cognitive factors necessary to cue the disambiguation of another person's utterance are often not available to guide the initial process of interpretation. And it is also true that there is scope for *mishearing* in connection with the utterances of another, in a way that appears to lack any analogue in the case of inner speech. But these differences appear insufficient to constitute a difference in the *kind* of access achieved in the two cases.

It might be objected against the line being argued here that, if sound, it must also undermine the position defended in section 3—the position, namely, that if imaged sentences occupy the causal roles of occurrent thoughts (and hence are constitutive of thinking), then those thoughts can count as conscious ones. For it may be said that interpretation will need to take place in any case. Whether an imaged sentence is constitutive of an occurrent thought of ours, or caused by the occurrence of a thought existing independently of it, that sentence must still be subject to a process of interpretation.

So far I agree. But the difference lies in whether or not the process of interpretation occurs *upstream* or *downstream* of the event that occupies the causal role of the thought. According to the communicative conception, the process of interpretation occurs downstream of the thought—first a thought is tokened, which is then used to generate a natural-language sentence in imagination, which is then interpreted; but the causal role of the initial thought, sufficient for it to qualify *as* that thought, is independent of what happens after it gets tokened. According to the cognitive conception, in contrast, it is quite the reverse. Here the hypothesis is that the causal role of the token thought in question is dependent upon its figuring as an interpreted image. It is the imaged (and interpreted) natural-language sentence itself that causes the further cognitive effects distinctive of entertaining the thought in question.

It might also be objected that all the arguments of this section share a common assumption: namely, that the mechanisms that generate a meaningful sentence of inner speech will involve some process of disambiguation and interpretation. But this assumption can be challenged. For why shouldn't the content of the sentence of inner speech be determined, *non*-inferentially, by the content of the thought that causes its production? Why shouldn't the sentence just drag its own interpretation with it, as it were—acquiring its content, not through any sort of process of inference, but simply by virtue of its causal connection with the underlying thought that it serves to express?

One sort of answer to this challenge is to point out that this doesn't seem to be how imagination, in general, works—at least if we take visual imagination as our model. As we noted in section 3, our best current theories of visual imagery would have it that images are generated by the production of an input to the visual system, which is then interpreted by that system in the normal way. I am not aware that any similar work has been done on the generation of inner speech. But if similar mechanisms are involved, then one would expect that inner speech operates by one's producing an input to the language system, which is then interpreted by that system (in a manner that involves processes of parsing and disambiguation) in exactly the way that it would set about interpreting the speech of another person.[10]

A more powerful answer to the above challenge is also available, however. For it is doubtful whether the assignment of content to sentences of inner speech *can*, even in principle, be determined in any other way than by means of a process of interpretation and disambiguation, drawing on the thinker's current beliefs. This is because the systems that produce, and those that consume, such sentences must be distinct. Of course it is true that the inner sentence in question *has* content, independently of any act of interpretation, by virtue of its causal connection with the thought that produced it—just as my utterances have content whether or not you succeed in interpreting them. But this is no good at all to the system (or person) who has to make use of the generated sentence, or who has to draw inferences from it. For, by hypothesis, the consumer system for the sentence (in the sense of Millikan, 1984) lacks access to the thought that caused the production of that sentence. (If it *did* have such access, then it wouldn't *need* inner speech, in order to gain access to the underlying thought.)

The idea of a sentence 'dragging its own interpretation with it' is surely incoherent, indeed. If the mere fact of having been caused by a certain thought were sufficient to confer an interpretation on it, from the perspective of the consumer system, then one might just as well say that the mere fact that my *spoken* utterance is caused by a particular thought of *mine* is sufficient for *you* to interpret it. But that would be absurd. So, in conclusion: if the sentences of inner speech are distinct items from the thoughts to which they give us access, then it must follow that the sort of access in question does *not* have the kind of non-inferential immediacy necessary for those thoughts to count as conscious ones.

## 6. IN DEFENSE OF PREMISE 4: AGAINST PURELY PROPOSITIONAL CONSCIOUS THINKING

Supposing, then, that 'inner speech' is neither constitutive of conscious thinking, nor gives us the kind of non-inferential access to the underlying thoughts that is necessary to render the latter conscious: is there any *other* way in which we might nevertheless have non-inferential access to our own occurrent thoughts? Many people believe so. They believe that we can entertain a thought and just know, immediately, that we have entertained it, without any sentence (or image) figuring in consciousness. Thus the introspection-sampling data provided by Hurlburt (1990, 1993) contains many reports of *purely propositional* thought,

---

[10] And indeed, there is evidence that *both* the language production area *and* the language comprehension area of the cortex are active when subjects engage in inner speech. See Paulescu *et al.*, 1993; Shergill *et al.*, 2002.

where subjects say that at the time of the beep they were thinking *that P*, but non-linguistically, without any sort of inner voice or inner speech.[11]

I propose to argue that we are subject to a systematic illusion here. What we take to be non-inferential access to purely propositional thought is, in reality, the result of a swift bit of self-interpretation, but one that takes place so smoothly and quickly that we do not know that that is what we are doing. This has been convincingly demonstrated by a rich body of data coming out of the social psychology literature, where it has been found that there are a wide variety of circumstances in which subjects will confabulate self-explanations that are manifestly false, but without realizing that this is what they are doing (Nisbett and Wilson, 1977; Nisbett and Ross, 1980; Wilson *et al.*, 1981; Wilson, 1985; Wilson and Stone, 1985). What follows are just a few salient examples.

First, when asked to select from a range of identical items (shirts, say), identically presented, people show a marked preference for items on the right-hand side of the display; but their explanations of their own choices never advert to position, but rather mention superior quality, appearance, color, and so on. These explanations are plainly confabulated. (Remember, there is really no difference at all between the items.) And note that people's explanations, here, can be offered within seconds of the original choice. So the problem is unlikely to be one of memory (contrary to the suggestion made by Ericsson and Simon, 1980). Moreover, although the explanations are in fact elicited by an experimenter's questioning, there is every reason to think that they could equally well have been spontaneously offered, had the circumstances required.

Second, people who have been paid to play with some sort of puzzle or game report less intrinsic interest in it than those who do so purely voluntarily; but these reports don't correlate with the extent to which they are observed to play with it in their free time. It seems that people assume that they must enjoy the puzzle less, since, knowing the facts of the situation, they interpret their behavior as motivated by payment rather than by enjoyment. But their explanations don't match their actual behavior.

Third, people are also very poor at knowing which factors in a situation influence their evaluations or decisions, such as which aspects of someone's behavior influenced their evaluation of his physical characteristics (appearance, etc.), or which aspects of a job-applicant's portfolio influenced their decision to call her for interview; and interestingly, observers merely *told about* these studies make exactly the same erroneous judgments as do the subjects *in* them. Moreover, both groups (participants and observers) tend to make correct judgments when, and only when, the influential factor is recognized as such within common-sense psychology.

---

[11] And recall that we saw in section 4 how there are conceivable Mentalese-involving mechanisms that would make such purely propositional conscious thinking possible.

The best explanation of these data (and the explanation offered by Nisbett and Wilson) is that subjects in such cases lack any form of conscious access to their true thought-processes. (See also Gopnik, 1993, for a range of developmental data that are used to argue for the same conclusion.) Rather, lacking immediate access to their reasons, what they do is engage in a swift bit of retrospective self-interpretation, attributing to themselves the thoughts and feelings that they think they *should* have in the circumstances, or in such a way as to make sense of their own behavior. And note, too, that in all but the first of the above examples, at least, the subjects do seem to act for reasons. So it is not open to us to say that subjects will confabulate self-explanations when, and only when, there aren't really any reasons for their actions for them to have access *to*. Who knows what cognitive mechanisms produce the bias for right-hand items in a display? But the other cases cited seem plainly to be caused by the subject's occurrent thoughts. And, indeed, in the third type of case it is possible to *discover* (or at least make reasonable inferences about) what those thoughts were, by correlating factors in the situation with subjects' choices across a range of studies.

It is important to emphasize that it doesn't *feel* to subjects in any of the above experiments as if they are engaging in self-interpretation. On the contrary, their self-attributions strike them with just the sort of phenomenological immediacy that one might expect of a conscious thought (that is, one that is immediately and non-inferentially available, but unverbalized). But then nor does it *feel as if* we are interpreting *other* agents much of the time, either—rather, we just *see* much of their behavior as intentional, and as imbued with certain thoughts. Indeed, our theory-of-mind faculty appears to have a number of the properties of a Fodorean module (Fodor, 1983): besides being at least partly innately specified (Baron-Cohen, 1995), its operation is both mandatory and fast. We often just *cannot help* seeing the behavior of an actor on the stage as displaying anger, or fear, or what-ever, despite the fact that we know him to be acting. And much of the time we aren't aware of ourselves as having to interpret his behavior, either, as being deceitful, or conciliatory, or whatever; rather, we just *see it that way*, immediately. So it is only to be expected that when people engage in self-interpretation, this will often take place extremely swiftly, and without self-awareness of what they are doing.

Now, it doesn't *follow from* the psychological data that there is no such thing as purely propositional conscious thinking. From the fact that we *sometimes* engage in unwitting self-interpretation, in attributing unverbalized thoughts to ourselves, it doesn't follow that we *always* do. But there is, surely, a sound inference to the best explanation to this conclusion. For, rather than believe that those of our occurrent propositional thoughts that aren't expressed in inner speech fall into two very different classes (that are nevertheless indistinguishable to intro-spection)—namely, those to which the subject has immediate non-inferential

access, and those that are self-ascribed on the basis of swift self-interpretation—
it is simpler to suppose that *all* such thoughts are only available through
interpretation. Indeed, in the absence of some definite proposal about what
might be the distinguishing characteristics of the two kinds of circumstances in
which we form beliefs about our unverbalized thoughts, the hypothesis that we
sometimes have non-inferential access to such thoughts, while sometimes
engaging in self-interpretation, is too unformed to constitute a real competitor.

In fact, looking across the full range of the experimental data available, the one
factor that seems to stand out as being common to all those cases where individuals confabulate false self-explanations is simply that in such cases the true
causes of the thoughts, feelings, or behavior in question are unknown to
common-sense psychology. The best explanation of the errors, then, is that in *all*
cases of unverbalized thought individuals are actually *employing* common-
sense psychology, relying on its principles and generalizations to attribute
mental states to themselves. The distinguishing feature of the cases where confabulation occurs is simply that in these instances common-sense psychology is
itself inadequate.

This account is also further supported by the neuropsychological data, in
particular the investigations of split-brain patients undertaken by Gazzaniga
and colleagues over many years (see Gazzaniga, 1994, for a review). For in these
cases self-attributions are made in a way that we *know* cannot involve access to
the thought-processes involved, but are made with exactly the same phenomenological immediacy as normal. And yet these self-attributions can involve the
most ordinary and everyday of thoughts, being erroneous in a way that mani-
festly does *not* depend upon the inadequacies of common-sense psychology, as
such, nor upon any special features of the case—rather, these are just cases in
which the psychology faculty lacks insufficient data to construct an accurate
interpretation. So, if unwitting self-interpretation can be involved here, it can be
involved anywhere. Let me briefly elaborate.

As is well known, in connection with split-brain, or commissurotomy,
patients, information can be presented to (and responses elicited from) each half-
brain independently. In the cases that concern us, both half-brains have some
comprehension of language, but only the left-brain has access to the language-
production system; the right-brain, however, is capable of initiating other forms
of activity. When an instruction, such as, 'Walk!', is flashed to the right-brain
alone, the subject may get up and begin to leave the room. When asked what he
is doing, he (that is: the left-brain) may reply, 'I am going to get a Coke from the
fridge.' This explanation is plainly confabulated, since the action was actually
initiated by the right-brain, for reasons to which, we know, the left-brain lacks
access. In fact these and similar phenomena lead Gazzaniga (1994) to postulate
that the left-brain houses a special-purpose cognitive sub-system, which he dubs

'the Interpreter', whose function is continually to construct rationalizing explanations for the behavior of oneself and other people. And it then seems reasonable to suppose that it is this same sub-system that is responsible for the confabulated self-explanations in the data from normal subjects discussed by Nisbett and Wilson. Indeed, it is reasonable to suppose that this sub-system is responsible for *all* of the access, or apparent access, that we have to our unverbalized thoughts.

I propose, then, that what are often described as purely propositional (non-verbal) thoughts, available to introspection (and hence conscious), are really the results of active self-interpretation. So even where the interpretations in question happen to be correct, and the thoughts are self-ascribed veridically, those thoughts are *not* conscious ones (at least, not on any of the various approaches to consciousness that entail a version of premise 1). So, given the truth of premises 1, 2, and 3 of the argument set out in section 2 above, it follows that we only ever engage in conscious propositional thinking at all if the cognitive conception of language is correct.

## 7. CONCLUSION

The arguments given in support of the three main premises of my initial argument (that is, the arguments given in sections 4, 5, and 6 in support of premises 1, 3, and 4) were non-demonstrative, of course—so there are various ways in which any conclusions might be resisted. But if those premises are taken as established, then the subsidiary conclusion, premise 5, follows: if we engage in conscious propositional thinking at all, then natural language sentences must be constitutively involved in such thinking. In which case our choices are either: to *deny* that we ever engage in conscious propositional thinking, and to become eliminativists about such thinking; or to accept that such thinking is conducted in natural language, and so to embrace at least a weak version of the cognitive conception of language. I propose that we should adopt the latter course. But for present purposes I shall be content if I have convinced my readers that there is a plausible case to be made for saying that they are faced with just this choice.[12]

---

[12] And note, too, that if we reject eliminativism, by accepting the cognitive conception of language, then this won't come cheap. For we shall then be committed to one or other of the three accounts of the causal role of inner speech that we sketched in section 3.

# CHAPTER 8

# Conscious Experience versus Conscious Thought

Are there different constraints on theories of conscious experience as against theories of conscious propositional thought? Is what is problematic or puzzling about each of these phenomena of the same, or of different, types? And to what extent is it plausible to think that either or both conscious experience and conscious thought involve some sort of self-reference? In pursuing these questions I shall also explore the prospects for a defensible form of eliminativism concerning conscious thinking, one that would leave the reality of conscious experience untouched. In the end, I shall argue that while there might be no such thing as conscious judging or conscious wanting, there *is* (or may well be) such a thing as conscious generic thinking.

## 1. THE DEMANDS ON THEORIES OF CONSCIOUS EXPERIENCE

What needs to be explained about conscious experience is its *what it is likeness*, together with a number of surrounding puzzles. The primary demand on a theory of conscious experience is that it should explain how conscious experiences come to possess their distinctive subjective dimension, and hence explain why there should be something that it is *like* for subjects to undergo them. Arguably, a good theory should also explain the distinction between conscious and *unconscious* perceptual states, accounting for the fact that the latter *aren't* conscious.[1] It should explain how we can come to form purely recognitional concepts for our conscious experiences.[2] And a successful theory ought also to explain why our conscious experiences should seem especially *ineffable* and private, why they

---

[1] Consider, for example, the kinds of visual percepts that one finds in blindsight (Weiskrantz, 1997), or in the online guidance of movement, if a 'two systems' account of vision is correct (Milner and Goodale, 1995; Jacob and Jeannerod, 2003).

[2] Such concepts are arguably at the bottom of inverted-qualia and zombie-style thought experiments. Possessing such concepts, there will be no incoherence in thinking, 'Someone might possess states with such-and-such functional role/intentional content while lacking *this* type of state'—where the indexical *this* expresses a concept that is purely recognitional, with no conceptual connections to causal-role concepts or intentional concepts. See Ch. 5.

should seem to possess intrinsic (non-relational and non-intentional) properties, and so on. (See Chapter 6 for more detailed discussion.)

Is it also a *desideratum* of a successful theory that conscious experiences should be shown to be somehow self-referential in character? While not in the usual catalog of things to be explained, it is arguable that the answer to this question is, 'Yes', in each of two distinct senses. First, it is plausible that the contents of perceptual experience contain an implicit reference to the self (Bermúdez, 1998). Objects are seen as being closer or further away, for example, or as being above or below. Closer to or further from what? Above or below what? The only available answer is: oneself. Equally, when one moves through the world there is a distinctive sort of 'visual flow' as objects approach, loom larger, and then disappear out of the periphery of the visual field. This experience of visual flow is normally apprehended as—that is, has as part of its intentional content—motion through a stationary (or independently moving) environment. Motion of what? Again the only available answer is: oneself.

There is also quite a different sense in which it can be argued that conscious experiences involve a sort of self-reference, however. This is not reference to the self (in the manner sketched above), but rather reference to the very same experience itself. For it seems that conscious experiences, in their distinctive subjectivity, somehow present *themselves* to us, as well as presenting whatever it is that they are experiences *of*. So conscious experiences, besides presenting or referring to items in and properties of the world (or of our own bodies), also present or make reference to themselves. On this sort of view, then, an experience of red, besides having the world-presenting content, *red over there*, will also have the self-referential content, *this is an experience of red over there*.[3]

How can these varying demands on a theory of conscious experience best be met? My own view is a version of higher-order representational account. This is developed and defended at length elsewhere (Carruthers, 2000, and Chapters 1, and 3 through 6 of the present volume); here there is space for just the barest sketch. What constitutes an experience as phenomenally conscious, in my view, is that it possesses a dual representational content: both world (or body) representing and experience representing. And experiences come to possess such a dual content by virtue of their availability to a higher-order thought faculty (which is capable of entertaining higher-order thoughts about those very experiences), and by virtue of the truth of some or other form of 'consumer semantic' account of intentional content.

There are a number of components that need to be set in place in order for this account to work. First, we need to accept that the intentional content of all

---

[3] According to Caston, 2002, this kind of dual-reference or dual-content view has a venerable history, stretching back at least to Aristotle.

perceptual states (whether conscious or unconscious) is non-conceptual, or at least *analog* or fine-grained, in character. Many in recent years have defended the reality of non-conceptual intentional content (Bermúdez, 1995; Tye, 1995, 2000; Kelly, 2001; Luntley, 2003). And even if one feels that these claims may go too far, and that the contents of perception are always to one degree or another *imbued with* concepts, still it needs to be recognized that perceptual experience is always *analog* in relation to any concepts that we can possess (Carruthers, 2000; Kelly, 2001). Our color experiences, for example, have a fineness of grain that far outstrips our capacity to conceptualize, recognize, and remember them. The same holds for movement and shape; and similar things are true in all other sense modalities.

The second necessary ingredient is acceptance of some or other form of consumer semantics. What all kinds of consumer semantics have in common is a commitment to the idea that the intentional content of a state depends in part on what the 'down-stream' consumer systems for that state are apt to do with it or infer from it.[4] (Teleo-semantics is one form of consumer semantics; see Millikan, 1984, 1989; Papineau, 1987, 1993. Functional or inferential role semantics is another; see Loar, 1981; Block, 1986; McGinn, 1989; Peacocke, 1992.) In fact the only kind of semantic theory that *isn't* a form of consumer semantics is pure input-side, causal co-variance, or 'informational' semantics (Fodor, 1990).

These two main ingredients then need to be put together with what many consider to be a plausible architecture for human cognition, in which perceptual contents are widely 'broadcast' and made available to a variety of down-stream consumer systems for conceptualizing and drawing inferences from those contents (Baars, 1988, 1997). Included amongst the latter will be a higher-order thought faculty capable of deploying concepts of experience. And then what we get is the account sketched above. Each perceptual representation with the analog content $red_a$,[5] for example, acquires the higher-order analog content $seems\text{-}red_a$ or $experience\text{-}of\text{-}red_a$, by virtue of its availability to a higher-order thought system capable of judging immediately and non-inferentially that one is experiencing red.[6]

---

[4] The metaphor comes from conceiving of cognition as a *stream* flowing from input (sensory stimulation) to output (action). Our perceptual systems are 'up-stream', constructing representations as output that are taken as input by (that are consumed by) a variety of 'down-stream' inferential systems, belief-forming systems, planning systems, and so forth. The latter in turn produce representations that are eventually consumed by the motor-control systems.

[5] Here and throughout this chapter I shall use a subscripted 'a' when referring to perceptual contents, to emphasize their fine-grained analog character.

[6] Note that not *any* form of consumer semantics can be endorsed if this account is to be plausible. Rather, we need claim that it is only the *immediate* further effects of a state that are determinants of its content. Otherwise, if distant inferences were determinants of content, we would face the implausible consequence that our perceptual experiences can have the contents, $ripens\text{-}in\text{-}July_a$, $is\text{-}Aunt\text{-}Anne's\text{-}favorite_a$, and so forth. It is fortunate, then, that consumer semantics is especially plausible in respect of the *immediate* inferences that consumer systems are apt to derive from a given state. For example, it

Such an account can meet all of the main demands made on a theory of conscious experience. First, it can explain how conscious experiences have a subjective dimension of *what it is likeness*. This is their higher-order analog content, in virtue of which they themselves (and not just the objects and properties that their first-order contents are *of*) are presented to us non-conceptually or in analog fashion. Second, the account can explain the distinction between experiences that are phenomenally conscious and those that aren't. This will be the distinction between perceptual states that are, and those that aren't, made available to our higher-order thought faculty, thereby acquiring a higher-order analog content. Third, the account can explain how we can have purely recognitional concepts of our experiences. These will be recognitional concepts whose application conditions are grounded in the higher-order analog content that attaches to those experiences (see Chapter 5). Fourth, the account can explain why our conscious experiences should seem especially ineffable. This is because the fine-grained character of our awareness of those experiences, mediated by their higher-order analog contents, will seem to 'slip through the gaps' of any of our attempts to describe them in conceptual terms. And so on. (For more extensive discussion, see Chapter 6.)

Notice that on this account there is an important respect in which conscious experiences turn out to be self-referential, in addition to the reference to the self that is implicit in their first-order intentional contents. This flows from the dual content that attaches to them. Conscious experiences of red, for example, aren't just targeted on the worldly property (redness) that is represented in analog fashion by their first-order contents. They are also targeted *on themselves*, via their higher-order analog contents of the form, *experience-of-red$_a$*. So we have a vindication of the intuition that conscious experiences don't just present the world (or our own bodies) to us, but also somehow present themselves to us. This 'presenting' is done via their higher-order analog contents, which represent, and replicate in 'seeming fashion', their first-order contents.

## 2. THE DEMANDS ON THEORIES OF CONSCIOUS THOUGHT

If the *desiderata* for theories of conscious experience and conscious thought were the same, then one would expect that people would need to converge on

---

seems that part of what fixes the content of '&' as *and*, is a disposition to move from 'P&Q' to 'P' and to 'Q'—but not necessarily any more elaborate disposition to derive '~ (P ⊃ ~Q)'. Thus someone could surely mean *P and Q* by 'P&Q', even though they lacked the inferential capacity to deduce from it '~ (P ⊃ ~Q)'.

theories of the same general type in respect of each. But this isn't so. While I myself endorse higher-order theories of both conscious experience and conscious thought, for example, such a combination of views is by no means mandatory. In particular, someone might sensibly combine some kind of first-order account of phenomenally conscious experience, with a higher-order account of the conscious status of thought (e.g. Kirk, 1994). This suggests that the demands on explanation, here, are distinct.[7]

If the *desiderata* for theories of conscious experience and theories of conscious thought were the same, indeed, then one would expect that those who endorse first-order representational theories of the former (Kirk, 1994; Dretske, 1995; Tye, 1995, 2000) should also endorse a purely first-order account of the latter. Not only isn't this the case (Dreske and Tye are silent on the nature of conscious thinking; Kirk endorses a higher-order account), but I suspect, moreover, that first-order accounts of conscious thinking aren't even defensible. This can be brought out by considering what first-order theorists might say in response to the widespread evidence of *un*conscious perception and *un*conscious thought (Baars, 1988, 1997; Milner and Goodale, 1995).

In the case of conscious experience the main *desideratum*, as we noted, is to explain the properties involved in *phenomenal* consciousness. And it is always then open to a first-order theorist to respond to alleged evidence of non-conscious experience (blindsight, dual-systems theories of vision, and so forth) by insisting that the experiential states in question are actually phenomenally conscious ones, despite not being *access* conscious. (That is, despite not being available for the subject to know of or report on directly. Tye, 1995, sometimes seems to endorse a view of this sort.) There is nothing incoherent in the idea of phenomenally conscious experiences that subjects aren't aware of themselves possessing (even if such a thing is rather hard to believe).

In the case of conscious thinking, however, there would seem to be no independent target of explanation. For in this case there doesn't seem to be any scope for someone to claim that the 'unconscious' thoughts investigated by psychologists are, really, conscious ones, despite being thoughts of which the subjects lack awareness. In the case of conscious thinking *the* phenomenon to be explained is the way that we (seem to have) immediate and non-inferential awareness of (some of) our own thought processes. And this is because thoughts aren't phenomenally conscious *per se*. Our thoughts aren't *like* anything, in the relevant sense, except to the extent that they might be associated with visual or

---

[7] Is it any argument against imposing different *desiderata* on theories of conscious experience and thought, that 'conscious' appears to be univocal when applied to experiences and thoughts? Not at all. For theories of consciousness aren't theories of the *concept* 'conscious'. The concept can very well be univocal while the phenomena picked out by that concept give rise to different explanatory problems.

other images or emotional feelings, which will be phenomenally conscious by virtue of their quasi-sensory status.[8]

There is, of course, *a* sense in which it is *like* something to entertain a conscious thought. This is that, depending on what one is thinking about, different aspects of the world thought about will loom into focus. As one's thoughts shift from one topic to another, so one's attention shifts from one aspect of the world to another. Siewert (1998) believes that this supports the view that non-imagistic thought is phenomenally conscious. But this is to conflate *worldly* subjectivity with *mental-state* subjectivity (see Chapter 3 of the present volume). Of course *the world* is *like* something to any perceiver and to any thinker, whether their states are phenomenally conscious or not. For any experience, and any thought, will involve a partial and partially subjective 'take' on the objects of experience/thought. What is crucial for phenomenal consciousness, however, is that there should be something that the subject's *own mental states* are *like*, for them. It is the mental states themselves that are subjective in character, that possess properties that are available to introspective recognition, and so on. With this distinction in place, there is no reason to believe that non-imagistic thoughts will be *like* anything.

The only remaining puzzle about conscious thinking, in fact (given that such thinkings aren't necessarily and intrinsically phenomenally conscious) is that we seem to have immediate and non-inferential awareness that we are doing it. So we might as well say that conscious thoughts *are*, then, the thoughts that we can be immediately aware of possessing. Or so, at any rate, I propose to assume in what follows. Our question will be: how is such non-inferential awareness of our own thought processes even so much as *possible*?[9] We will begin on this question shortly, in section 3.

Before we get to that, however, recall the familiar distinction between thoughts as standing states and thoughts as occurrent events (acts of thinking). What is it for beliefs and desires (qua standing states) to be conscious? One

---

[8] Admittedly, if 'inner speech' can be a kind of thought, as I am inclined to believe, and as we shall discuss briefly in section 6.2, then some thinking *will* have phenomenal properties. These will be the properties, namely, associated with the auditory images that constitute the stream of inner speech. But even in this case it won't be *qua* thoughts that the events in the stream are phenomenally conscious. Phenomenal consciousness will attach to the imaged *sounds* of the sentences in inner speech, not to the contents of those sentences, i.e. not to the thoughts that are thereby entertained.

[9] See Ch. 7 for discussion of the sense in which knowledge of our own thoughts has to be non-inferential and immediate, in order for those thoughts to qualify as conscious ones. I certainly don't mean to rule out *all* processes that one might describe as 'inferential' (c.f. the processing that takes place within the visual system). But certainly *conscious* inferences are ruled out. And so, too, are the sorts of unconscious inferences that one might engage in when interpreting another person, drawing on knowledge of the circumstances, behavior, and other mental states of that person. For it is surely part of our common-sense notion of conscious thought that there is an important asymmetry between our knowledge of our own thoughts and our knowledge of other people's.

proposal, that might seem to flow directly from the assumption we have just made, would be as follows. We might say that standing states are conscious provided that the subject has immediate non-inferential awareness of them. This won't do, however, for a variety of reasons. One (the only one I shall discuss) is that there exist a range of convincing counter-examples, drawn from both Freudian-style psychology and common sense (Lurz, 2005). These are cases where a standing-state belief or desire is the target of seemingly non-inferential higher-order awareness, but without thereby being conscious.

Suppose, for instance, that in a discussion of the merits and demerits of utilitarianism, someone points out to me that I have not only been putting forward utilitarian views, but that I have been speaking of utilitarians as 'we', and have felt threatened and become angry when utilitarian views as such are maligned. This might strike me with the force of self-discovery. Had I been asked whether I was a utilitarian previously, I would have denied it. I didn't *consciously* believe in the truth of utilitarianism. Yet my behavior suggests both that I *believe* utilitarianism to be the correct moral theory, and that I have second-order awareness of this belief (hence the fact that I feel threatened when utilitarian views are attacked).

A better answer to the question of what renders standing-state beliefs and desires conscious would be this: they are conscious just in case they are apt to emerge as conscious occurrent thinkings with the very same first-order content. This is why I didn't consciously believe in utilitarianism, in the example above: I wasn't disposed to think consciously and spontaneously, 'Utilitarianism is true', or something to that effect. This answer also fits neatly with what Gordon (1996) has defended as the 'question/check procedure' for self-ascribing beliefs.[10] If someone asks you whether or not you believe something, what do you do? You surely ask yourself, 'Is it true that P?', and you ascribe the belief to yourself just in case you find yourself inclined to answer, 'Yes, it is the case that P.' In effect, you use your conscious occurrent judgment with the first-order content *P* as the basis on which to ascribe to yourself the standing-state belief that P.

It is plausible that the conscious status of standing-state thoughts should be explained in terms of that of their occurrent counterparts, then. At any rate (again), this is what I propose to assume in what follows. So we will need to focus on what it is for an occurrent act of thinking to be conscious. Here is one very natural proposal: a conscious act of thinking is one whose occurrence and content the subject has immediate and non-inferential awareness of (Rosenthal, 1993;

---

[10] Note that endorsing this thesis needn't involve any commitment to Gordon's 'simulation theory' of the basis on which we ascribe mental states generally. Endorsing the 'question/check procedure' as the basis on which we have self-awareness of standing-state beliefs is perfectly consistent with some or other version of 'theory-theory' of the overall basis of mental-state ascription.

Carruthers, 1996).[11] The awareness in question surely has to be non-inferential, since otherwise judgments that I attribute to myself as a result of self-interpretation would count as conscious ones. While there is no doubt much that could be said in support of (or against) such a proposal, for present purposes I shall simply assume its correctness, and see what then follows concerning the likely reality of, and the self-referential status of, conscious thinking.

## 3. HOW IS CONSCIOUS THINKING POSSIBLE?

Can we describe a possible functional architecture that might serve to realize conscious occurrent judgment, in the sense explained above? What we need is that whenever a judgment of a certain type is being made (e.g. occurring at a particular stage in the stream of processing within the mind's executive or decision-making systems, say), then that judgment is disposed to cause or give rise to the higher-order judgment that just such a judgment is occurring. And such causation needs to be quite direct, in a way that doesn't count as inferential or self-interpretive.

How might such an architecture be possible? And how might it be realized? Suppose that there is a language of thought, or 'Mentalese'. Then when a sentence in this language, |P|,[12] is entertained at a particular point in processing, we can suppose that the system has been built in such a way that the subject is automatically disposed (if relevant, i.e. depending on what else is going on in the subject's mind) to token the sentence |I am thinking that P|. And provided that the different causal roles distinctive of belief, desire, and so forth are signaled explicitly by operators in the language of thought, then the very same sort of mechanism will also yield non-inferential awareness that I am judging (factively) that P, or that I have an activated desire for P, and so on.

In functional accounts of cognition, beliefs and desires are generally represented by distinct *boxes*. But even if something like this were literally true, it would still have to be the case that token activated beliefs and token activated desires can interact with one another within other systems, such as in practical reasoning. So they would have to be tagged somehow to indicate which 'box' they derive from. What we might have, then, is the belief that P realized by

---

[11] Note that a major difference between the two authors cited concerns the question whether the higher-order awareness has to be actual, or whether it can be merely dispositional. (There is a perfectly respectable sense in which I can be said to be aware that zebras in the wild don't wear overcoats, of course, or to be aware that ten million and one is larger than ten million, even if I have never explicitly considered and endorsed these propositions. I may be said to be aware of these things because I *would* immediately assent to them if I *were to* consider them.) I shall be assuming the latter in what follows.

[12] I shall use line-brackets when referring to sentences in the language of thought/Mentalese, using quote-marks when referring to natural-language sentences, and italics when referring to sentence contents.

a Mentalese representation |BEL- P| and the desire for P realized by |DES- P|, where the tags |BEL-| and |DES-| determine their causal roles as beliefs and desires respectively.[13] And then a mechanism can easily be imagined that would go immediately from the former to |BEL- I am entertaining the belief that P| and that would go immediately from the latter to |BEL- I am entertaining the desire that P|—where these would of course mean that I am aware that I am *judging* that P, and that I am aware that I am occurrently *wanting* that P, respectively.

Notice, too, that such an architecture (together with the truth of some version of consumer semantics of the sort appealed to in the explanation of phenomenal consciousness in section 1) might entail that conscious judgments, as well as conscious experiences, are events with a dual intentional content. For the availability of the judgment *P* to a consumer system apt to judge, immediately and non-inferentially, *I am judging that P*, might be sufficient for the initial first-order judgment to acquire a higher-order content. And then one and the same token act of thinking would possess the dual contents *P* and *I am judging that P*.

## 4. IS CONSCIOUS THINKING ACTUAL?

I have outlined an architecture that would vindicate the reality of conscious thinking, while at the same time entailing (given consumer semantics) that conscious thinkings are self-referential. The evidence suggests, however, that the human mind may contain no such architecture as the one just sketched above. For there is now widespread evidence that humans routinely *confabulate* explanations of their own behavior, as has emerged again and again over the last quarter century of social-psychological and neuropsychological research. (For recent reviews, see Gazzaniga, 1998; Wilson, 2002.) Such data are in tension with the existence of the sort of non-inferential thinking-attribution mechanism envisaged above. (Some attempts to render them consistent will be considered in a moment.)

Let me quickly sketch a couple of highlights from this body of research. In one of the classic experiments of Nisbett and Wilson (1977), subjects in a shopping mall were presented with an array of four sets of items (e.g. pairs of socks or pantyhose), and were asked to choose one of them as a free sample. (All four sets of items were actually identical.) Subjects displayed a marked tendency to select

---

[13] Note that the representation |BEL- P| isn't yet a higher-order one. It isn't a representation *that* the subject believes that P. Rather, it is *constitutive* of the subject believing that P. The tag |BEL-| *causes* other systems to *treat* the representation in the manner constitutive of belief (e.g. by feeding it to inferential systems, or by feeding it to the practical reasoning system to guide action). It doesn't *represent that* the representation in question is a belief. One way of seeing this is to note that a creature could have representations within which the tag |BEL-| has just the causal role described, but where the creature lacks any conception whatever of what a belief is.

the item from the right-hand end of the display. Yet no one mentioned this when they were asked to explain why they had chosen as they did. Rather, subjects produced plainly confabulated explanations, such as that the item they had chosen was softer, that it appeared to have been better made, or that it had a more attractive color.

As Nisbett and Wilson (1977) point out, what seems to happen in such cases is this. Subjects have a right-hand bias, leading them to spend a longer time attending to the right-most item. Their higher-order thought faculty, noticing and seeking to explain this behavior, proposes an explanation. For example: I am attending more to that item because I believe it to be the softest. And this explanatory higher-order belief is then the source of the subject's verbal report, as well as of the subject's choice.[14] But the subject has no access to the process of interpretative thinking that generated their higher-order belief; and that belief itself is without any foundation in the first-order facts—it certainly isn't produced by the sort of non-inferential ascent-mechanism envisaged in section 3.

The second example is reported in Gazzaniga (1998), concerning one of his 'split brain' patients. When the instruction, 'Walk!', was flashed up in the patient's left visual field (accessible to his right hemisphere, which had some capacity to comprehend simple forms of language, but no productive abilities), the patient got up and started to walk across the room. When asked what he was doing, he (his left hemisphere, which controls speech) replied, 'I want to get a Coke from the fridge.' This answer was plainly confabulated, generated by his higher-order thought faculty (which independent evidence suggests is located largely in the left hemisphere) in order to explain his own behavior. But the answer came to him with all of the obviousness and apparent indubitability that attaches to any of our ascriptions of occurrent thoughts to ourselves.

The thoughts that actually produced the subject's behavior, in this example, were presumably |DES- I comply with the experimenter's instruction| and |BEL- To comply with the instruction to walk, I must walk|. Whereas the higher-order thought faculty, being aware of the subject's own behavior and seeking to explain it, came up with the explanation |BEL- I am walking because I want to get a coke from the fridge| (perhaps noticing that the fridge lay in the direction that he was walking). And the higher-order attribution of desire, here, was plainly

---

[14] Here is an alternative explanation, which seems to involve no confabulation. (I owe this suggestion to Georges Rey.) Subjects have a right-hand bias, leading them to spend more time attending to the right-most item. While attending to that item, they notice that it is soft, and choose it because they want softness. So when they explain their own behavior in terms of their belief in, and desire for, softness, they explain correctly; they are merely ignorant of the underlying *cause* of their belief. One difficulty for this explanation, however, is that it doesn't explain the subject's attribution to themselves of a *comparative* belief—that the item chosen is *softer*, that it is *better* made (as opposed to *well* made), etc. Another is that the explanation doesn't generalize to other sorts of cases, whereas the confabulation explanation does.

an inference-produced product of self-interpretation, not resulting from the operations of some sort of ascent-mechanism.

This and similar data lead Gazzaniga (1998) to propose that the left hemisphere of the brain houses an 'interpreter' (a higher-order thought faculty), which has access to perceptual input, but not to the occurrent conceptual thoughts and decision-making processes occurring elsewhere in the brain. The interpreter is continually weaving an explanatory story for the agent's own actions. These stories may often be true ones, in familiar-enough cases and in cases where the interpreter does its job well. But they are still a product of inter-pretation, and not the result of any sort of non-inferential access to the subject's own thought processes. And in unusual or unexpected circumstances the subject may end up with stories that are confabulated (i.e. false).

If any such account is true, then a plausible abductive inference—in this case an application of Occam's razor—suggests that the human mind does *not* have the sort of non-inferential semantic-ascent architecture that we sketched in section 3. And it appears to follow, too (if these cases can be taken as representative) that there is no such thing as conscious thinking.

Can such a conclusion be ruled out of court immediately, rejected on the grounds that we can be *certain* that there is such a thing as conscious thinking? No, it can't. For we are assuming that conscious thinking requires non-inferential awareness of our own thought processes. But all we can be certain of—the most that introspection can deliver—is that we are sometimes aware of our own thought processes without engaging in any *conscious* inference. We can't be certain that our awareness of our own thought processes isn't grounded in a form of *un*conscious self-interpretation. And if Gazzaniga is right, it always is.

It is worth noting that Gazzaniga's proposal is consistent with, and to some degree receives independent support from, an overall architecture for cognition that has been receiving increasing support in recent decades (Baars, 1997; Carruthers, 2000 ch. 11, 2002). On this account the various sensory systems produce integrated analog representations of the environment (and body), which are then widely broadcast and made available to a range of down-stream concep-tual systems (for higher-order thought, for folk mechanics, for folk biology, and so on). These latter systems have quite limited access to one another, however. (They are to some degree 'encapsulated'.) And neither do they have access to what takes place even further down-stream, within practical reasoning. (See Figure 8.1.) So on this model, although the higher-order thought faculty would have access to per-ceptual and proprioceptive input (and hence to whatever the agent is physically doing), it won't have any direct access to the thought processes that cause our actions. I shall return to discuss this model at greater length in section 5.

One way in which it might be argued that the confabulation data are consistent with an architecture of the kind sketched in section 3, however, would

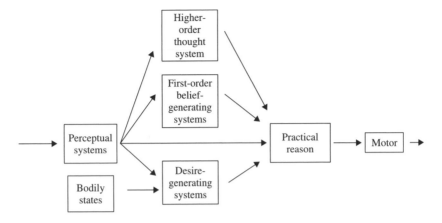

FIG 8.1  The place of higher-order thought in cognition.

be this. Perhaps the confabulated judgments are made too long after the event to be reliable, or for the semantic-ascent architecture envisaged in section 3 to operate. It is plausible enough that the decay-time for any given occurrent thought should be pretty brief. So if the token Mentalese sentence |P| doesn't give rise to |I am thinking that P| almost immediately, the subject will have no option but to self-interpret; which might lead, in the right circumstances, to confabulation. This reply doesn't really work, however. For a subject can be asked for an explanation immediately after she makes a choice (in the Nisbett and Wilson example), or while he is getting up out of his chair (in the Gazzaniga example). And the window for unrehearsed items to remain in working memory isn't generally reckoned to be *this* brief.

A related objection would be this. There are a range of experimental demonstrations that so-called 'think aloud protocols'—in which subjects verbalize their thinking out loud *while* reasoning to the solution of some problem—are really quite reliable in providing us with a window on the underlying sequences of thought in question (Ericsson and Simon, 1993). And how can this be possible unless those subjects have reliable (non-confabulated) awareness of the thoughts that they verbalize? But in fact, linguistic *expression* of a thought need not imply that the subject has higher-order awareness that they are entertaining that thought. And indeed, one of the central findings in this area is that subjects need to be induced *not* to report *on* their thoughts when they have them, since this is demonstrably *un*reliable (Ericsson and Simon, 1993).

Notice that the production sub-system of the language faculty will need to be situated down-stream of the various belief-forming and decision-making reasoning processes that figure in cognition, so that the results of those processes should be expressible in speech (Carruthers, 2002; see Figure 8.2). And although

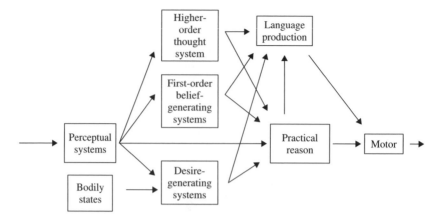

FIG 8.2 The place of language in cognition.

one of these systems that feeds input to the language faculty will be the higher-order thought faculty, there is no reason to assume that the language faculty can *only* receive higher-order thoughts as input. On the contrary, many of our first-order thoughts should be *directly* expressible in speech. This is sufficient to explain the Ericsson and Simon data. But then unless the linguistic expressions of thought are somehow constitutive of the thoughts being articulated, our awareness of what we are thinking will be derivative from our awareness of the sentences in which those thoughts are expressed—and it looks as if this won't, then, have the kind of immediacy required for those thoughts to count as conscious ones. (We return to some of these points in section 6.)

Another way in which someone might try to argue that the confabulation data are consistent with the required sort of semantic-ascent architecture would be this. Perhaps in the confabulation cases the thoughts in question don't occur in the right sub-system. Perhaps there are two distinct sub-systems in the mind in which thinking occurs, and which can generate behavior. But perhaps only one of these has the kind of direct access to the higher-order thought faculty that we envisaged earlier. So the thoughts in this sub-system would be conscious; whereas the confabulation behaviors are produced by the other sub-system, whose contents *aren't* conscious. However, it is hard to see any plausible way of drawing the sub-divisions here, that wouldn't simply be *ad hoc*.[15] For the confabulation examples seem pretty much like paradigmatic cases of (non-natural-language-based) judgment.

---

[15] One suggestion—which definitely isn't *ad hoc*, since it is supported by multiple lines of evidence— would be to claim that there are dual systems for thinking and reasoning, one of which is fast, implicit, and unconscious, and the other of which is slow, explicit, and conscious (Evans and Over, 1996; Stanovich, 1999). However if, as some have argued, the explicit system implicates natural-language sentences (Evans and Over, 1996; Frankish, 2004), then it won't exemplify the sort of Mentalese-based semantic-ascent architecture that is under discussion here. This point will be further explored in section 6.

It would appear then (if the problem of sub-divisions can't be overcome), that the confabulation evidence will show that we don't have the right kind on non-inferential access to our own acts of thinking for those acts to count as conscious ones. And nor will our acts of thinking have the right sort of self-referential content. For if the thought *P* isn't available to a higher-order thought faculty that is disposed to judge immediately that I am thinking that P, then the thought *P* won't at the same time bear the higher-order self-referential content *I am thinking that P*.

## 5. AN ALTERNATIVE MODEL OF THE HIGHER-ORDER THOUGHT FACULTY

Let us assume that the problem of subdivisions can be overcome, however. Assume that there is some non-arbitrary way of distinguishing between those reasoning systems whose processes are directly available to higher-order thought, and those that aren't. Then what we have on the table is an alternative model of the way in which a higher-order thought faculty could be embedded into the overall architecture of the mind, to be contrasted with the model deriving from Baars (1997) sketched above. According to the latter, the higher-order thought faculty has direct access *only* to those of our occurrent states that are perceptual, necessary to construct explanations and predictions of people's behavior.[16] Call this the 'mind-reading model'. According to the alternative now being suggested, the higher-order thought faculty *also* has direct access to some of the other reasoning processes taking place down-stream of perception, especially some of the processes that occur within *practical* reasoning. Call this the 'self-monitoring model'.

These two models correspond to two different accounts of what higher-order thought is *for*. According to the mind-reading model, higher-order thoughts are for interpreting and predicting behavior. The mind-reading faculty evolved in highly social creatures (such as our great-ape ancestors manifestly were) for purposes of manipulation, cooperation, and communication. This is the standard explanation that cognitive scientists offer of the evolution of our capacity for higher-order thought (e.g. Byrne and Whiten, 1988, 1998). And on this account, the application of higher-order thoughts to ourselves, and the dual-analog content that consequently comes to attach to our perceptual states, is an evolutionary spin-off.

---

[16] The higher-order thought faculty would also need access to (activations of) standing-state beliefs, of course, such as beliefs about the target-subject's long-term goals or idiosyncratic beliefs. But this wouldn't require it to have access to the processes within the agent that generate beliefs and decisions.

The self-monitoring model, in contrast, will claim that higher-order thought is *also* for monitoring our own processes of thinking and reasoning—enabling us to trouble-shoot in cases of difficulty or breakdown, and enabling us to reflect on and improve those processes themselves. (It could be claimed *either* that this is the *basic* function of our higher-order thought faculty, and that a capacity to predict and explain behavior came later, *or* that the mind-reading and self-monitoring functions of the faculty co-evolved.) Some cognitive scientists have begun to explore just such an hypothesis (e.g. Smith *et al.*, 2003).

There are some strong prima facie reasons for preferring the mind-reading model to the self-monitoring model, however. The most important is that the former appeals to what is, uncontroversially, a highly developed cognitive competence, whereas the latter doesn't. Everyone agrees that human beings are quite remarkably good at predicting and explaining the behavior of themselves and others through the attribution of mental states. And everyone agrees that this capacity forms part of our natural endowment, emerging in any normally developing member of the species. In contrast, it is *very* controversial to claim that humans have any natural competence in correcting and improving processes of reasoning. On the contrary, both common sense and cognitive science are agreed that naïve subjects are extremely *poor* at spotting errors in reasoning, and at seeing how to improve their own reasoning.[17]

These issues are too large to pursue in any detail here. (See Chapter 11 for further discussion.) And to the extent that they remain unresolved, the self-monitoring model (combined with the semantic-ascent architecture envisaged in section 3) holds out the hope that we may yet be shown to engage in conscious thinking independently of the use of sensory images. In what follows, however, I shall assume that the mind-reading model of our higher-order thought abilities is the correct one. This is partly because interesting questions then arise, concerning the extent to which sensory images could nevertheless underpin a kind of conscious propositional thinking. And it is partly because it is worth exploring what would follow if the self-monitoring model turns out to be false, since it may well turn out to *be* false. And in philosophy, of course, the conditional questions are often the most interesting and important ones.[18]

---

[17] People *can* monitor their own reasoning, of course, even if they aren't very good at improving it (although they can get better)—especially when their reasoning is verbally expressed. But this lends no support to the version of self-monitoring model under discussion here. For the best account of this capacity is that it is *realized in* cycles of operation of other systems (including language and mind-reading), and that it is—like Dennett's 1991 *Joycean machine*—heavily influenced by cultural learning (Carruthers, 2002; Frankish, 2004). By learning to verbalize our own thoughts we can learn to monitor and improve upon our own patterns of reasoning. But only if our verbalizations are constitutive of (a kind of) thinking will our access to our own thoughts count as immediate and non-inferential. (See the discussion in section 6.)

[18] As one of the characters in the Walt Disney movie *Hercules* remarks to another, 'If is good!'

## 6. DOES INNER SPEECH MAKE THINKING CONSCIOUS?

So far, then, the evidence looks as if it might point to the conclusion that there is strictly speaking no such thing as conscious thinking (at least, to the extent that thinking isn't expressed in natural language or other imagery). And some cognitive scientists have concluded just this (even if not in exactly these words; see Gopnik, 1993). But what of 'inner speech', however? Might this give us the kind of immediate awareness of our own thought processes to constitute some of the latter as conscious?

Our discussion of these questions now needs to proceed in two parts, corresponding to the contrast that I have drawn elsewhere between 'communicative' and 'cognitive' conceptions of the role of natural language in cognition (Carruthers, 1996, 2002). According to the communicative conception of language, the only real function of language is communication (whether with another or with oneself). Natural-language sentences *express* thought, but aren't *constitutive of* thought. According to the cognitive conception of language, on the other hand, at least some of our thinking takes place in natural language. So on this view, natural-language sentences are, at least sometimes, (partly) constitutive of acts of thinking. Let us take these possibilities in turn.

### 6.1. *Inner speech as expressive of thought*

Consider first, then, the traditional view that inner speech is *expressive* of thought, rather than directly (and partly) *constitutive of* it. On this account, thinking itself might be conducted in some sort of Mentalese. (Let us assume so.) But some of these Mentalese representations can be used to generate a representation of a natural language sentence in auditory imagination, creating the phenomenon of inner speech. Might this be sufficient to give us the sort of non-inferential awareness of the underlying thoughts that is required for the latter to count as conscious ones?

Suppose that the contents of the Mentalese acts of thinking and the contents of the natural-language sentences generated from them line up neatly one-for-one. Then thinking something carried by the Mentalese representation |BEL- P| will cause a suitable (indicative-mood) natural-language sentence 'P' to be imaged, where the contents of |P| and 'P' are the same. But we might suppose that the imaged sentence 'P' comes with its semantic properties somehow attached—for after all, when we form an image of a sentence, we don't just hear imaginary *sounds*, we also (as it were) hear *the meaning*, just as we do in normal speech comprehension.

Then suppose that I am disposed to move from the imaged sentence 'P' to the higher-order representation |I am thinking that P|, in which the content of the representation 'P' is extracted and reused within the content of the that-clause. It will then turn out that it is pretty much guaranteed that such self-attributions will be reliable. Moreover, the immediacy of the causal pathway involved could be sufficient for the higher-order item of awareness in question to count as non-inferentially produced; in which case the first-order thought that *P* could count as conscious. By the same token, too, that thought might qualify as having a dual content, making conscious thinking self-referential in something like the way that conscious experiences are (on my account).

There are two significant problems with this neat picture, however. The first is that, even if self-attributions of thought *contents* resulting from the use of inner speech are immediate (non-self-interpretative and non-inferential), self-attributions of thought *modes* (such as judging and wanting) surely aren't. This is because natural-language sentences don't wear their modes on their face.

An utterance of the indicative sentence, 'The door is open', can in suitable circumstances express the *belief* that the door is open, or ask a *question* as to whether or not the door is open, or issue a *command* to close the door, or merely express the *supposition* that the door is open for purposes of further inference, and so on. So whether or not an indicative-mood sentence in inner speech, 'P', is expressive of the subject's *judgment* (i.e. occurrent belief) that P, simply cannot be recovered from the sentence alone. It is always going to be a matter of self-interpretation to attribute to oneself a given judgment, on this sort of account. And that seems sufficient to disqualify such judgments from counting as conscious ones.

It might be replied that in spoken language, *mode* is often indicated by tone of voice; and this can be amongst the contents of the auditory images that figure in inner speech. So the basis for my knowledge that I am *judging* that P when I token the natural language sentence 'P' in auditory imagination, is the imagined tone of voice in which that sentence is 'heard'. This reply won't wash, however, for two distinct reasons. The first is that although the mode in which a sentence is meant *can* be marked by intonation, it needn't be—someone's delivery can be entirely neutral, or 'flat'. So this couldn't be a quite general solution to our problem. But the second, and more fundamental, reason is that tone of voice must in any case be *interpreted* to yield the intended mode. If someone says, 'The door is open', in a sharp, angry-sounding voice, for example, it requires interpretation to tell whether they are expressing a *belief* about something that they disapprove of, or are issuing a *command* to close the door. Telling which it is might require knowledge of our respective power/authority relations, among other things.

The second problem for the simple account sketched above is that natural-language sentence contents and the contents of the Mentalese sentences used to generate them will rarely line up one-for-one. Language routinely makes use of contextual factors in expressing meaning. The sentence, 'The door is open', leaves it to the context to determine which door is *the* door; it also leaves it to the context to determine the appropriate standard of openness (unlocked? open just a crack? wide open?); and so on. In contrast, the corresponding sentence of Mentalese must render such facts determinate. So again, one can't recover the underlying Mentalese thought from the natural-language sentence alone.

It might be argued that these problems can be overcome, however, if self-generated sentences (in inner-speech) can somehow carry with them the elements necessary for their interpretation. For then, provided that those same meaning-determining connections are also inherited by the higher-order Mentalese sentence that replicates the content of the first-order one within a that-clause, we may still have the sort of immediacy needed for conscious thinking.

Perhaps it works like this. The underlying assertoric thought with the content *P* is carried by the Mentalese expression |BEL- P|. This is then used to generate a natural-language sentence 'Q' in auditory imagination. But that sentence comes with the connections to |BEL- P| already attached. The imaged sentence 'Q', by virtue of being 'experienced', is a state of the right sort to be received as input by the mind-reading faculty, which can deploy the concept of occurrent belief. The mind-reading faculty detaches the Mentalese sentence |BEL- P| from the natural-language sentence received as input, and forms from it the Mentalese belief |BEL- I am judging that P|, in which the Mentalese sentence |P| is reused with the same content as the original. And the result might then count as non-inferential awareness of my own act of thinking.

I suspect that there may be a good many problems with this attempted vindication of the reality of conscious thinking. Let me focus on one. It is quite widely accepted that the language faculty is divided into two distinct sub-systems, one for production and one for comprehension (with perhaps each of these drawing off a single language-specific database; Chomsky, 1995). It will be the work of the production sub-system to create the natural-language sentence 'Q' from the Mentalese representation |BEL- P|. But in order for that sentence to be displayed in auditory imagination and received by the mind-reading faculty, it needs to be passed across to be received by the *comprehension* sub-system. (See Figure 8.3.) And there is good reason to think that the connections with the underlying thought, expressed by |BEL- P|, will thereby be severed.

One reason for this is that the comprehension sub-system simply isn't *built* to receive Mentalese thoughts as input, of the sort that might be taken as input by the language production sub-system, received from the various belief-generating systems (see Figure 7.3). Its job is rather to receive natural-language sentences as input and to construct interpretations of them, perhaps

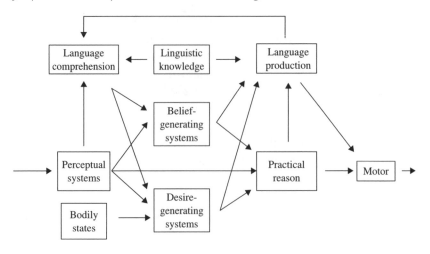

FIG 8.3 Inner speech.

in co-operation with other systems. Another reason is that 'inner speech' may well exploit the feed-back loops within the overall language faculty that are used during normal speech production for phonological and semantic monitoring and repair (Levelt, 1989). In normal speech production, the sentence 'Q', generated from the Mentalese message-to-be-communicated |BEL- P|, is passed to the consumer sub-system to check that the intended utterance will indeed convey the intended message. This can only work if the consumer system doesn't *already* have access to the message |BEL- P|. Otherwise it can't do an honest job of simulating how the sentence 'Q' would be interpreted by a naïve hearer.

## 6.2. *Inner speech as (partly) constitutive of thinking*

It appears, then, that if language is but a means of *expressing* thought, then there may be no such thing as conscious thinking. For although we come to be aware of our thoughts by consuming their internal expressions, in inner speech, the route from thought, to speech, to awareness of thought is too indirect and interpretative to constitute the thoughts in question as conscious ones. Everything may look a bit different if we switch to a version of the cognitive conception of language, however (Carruthers, 1996, 2002), according to which inner speech *is*, or is some-how constitutive of, thinking. To be plausible, such a view should only claim that representations of natural-language sentences in inner speech are *partly* consti-tutive of thinking. (This is because of the problems of indeterminacy attaching to natural-language sentences, *inter alia*, discussed in section 6.1.)

  Within the framework provided by a cognitive conception of language an account can be given of how we have non-inferential knowledge of the *contents* of some of our occurrent thoughts. The sentence 'Q', generated by the production sub-system, is tokened in inner speech and consumed by the comprehension sub-system. The result will be a representation of an interpreted sentence, carrying with it the connections to the Mentalese expressions, underlying data structures, perceptual experiences, or whatever else is necessary to make the meaning of 'Q' determinate. In the simplest case, if the interpretation process is a reliable one, then the meaning that gets attached to 'Q' might be the same as the content of the Mentalese sentence |P| that initiated the production of 'Q'. But this doesn't really matter in the present context. And it might not always happen. So let us work with an example in which it doesn't: let us imagine that the process of interpreting 'Q' attaches to it the Mentalese sentence |R|.

Now by hypothesis (if some version of the cognitive conception of language is correct) the pairing <'Q', |R|> has further consequences in cognition; and not just *any* consequences, but those that are distinctive of thinking. One way in which this might be the case is if the representation |R| is one that can *only* be formed via the construction of an appropriate natural-language sentence, as 'module-integration' accounts of the role of natural language in cognition suggest (Hermer-Vazquez *et al.*, 1999; Carruthers, 2002). Another way in which it might be true is if it is only by virtue of articulating the sentence 'Q' in auditory imagination, and hence making its content available to the various inference-systems that exist down-stream of perception and consume its products, that the subject comes to believe |R| for the first time. (See Figure 8.3.) The process of articulating 'Q' leads to |R| being evaluated and accepted, in a way that would not have happened otherwise.[19]

Now amongst the consumer-systems to which <'Q', |R|> is made available by the language comprehension sub-system will be the mind-reading faculty. Suppose that the latter is immediately disposed, whenever it receives such a pairing, to form the belief |I am thinking that R|. Then the result will be non-inferential awareness of what I am thinking. We can regard the immediacy and reliability of the connection between the higher-order thought and the thought thereby attributed as being sufficient both to render the act of thinking that R conscious, and to mean that the sentence 'Q' has both the first-order content *that R* and the higher-order content *I am thinking that R*. So now we have a single event (a token representation of the natural-language sentence 'Q' in inner speech) that has both a first-order and a higher-order content, similar to the case of experience.

Note that this 'immediacy' needn't be at all undermined by the fact that the comprehension process that generates an interpretation for 'Q' is an inferential

---

[19] This might happen if the subject *avows* 'Q', for example—where this means that they *commit themselves* to thinking and reasoning in future as if 'Q' were true (Frankish, 2004). If the subject thereafter remembers and executes this commitment, the effect will be that the underlying representation |R| will become the functional equivalent of |BEL- R|.

and interpretative one. For it is the product, rather than the initial cause, of the interpretative process that gets self-attributed. And this can be attributed to oneself *without* further interpretation or inference. According to the hypothesis that we are considering (the cognitive conception of language), the sentence 'Q' displayed (and interpreted) in inner speech is *itself* a thought, or is rather partly *constitutive of* a thought, given its causal role in the overall architecture of cognition. And it is *this* thought (the thought expressed by |R|) that gets reliably and non-inferentially attributed.

It would appear, therefore, that if the cognitive conception of language is correct, then we have a vindication of the reality of conscious thinking. For we can have immediate and non-inferential awareness of the contents of those acts of thinking that occur in inner speech, on this account. However, the point that awareness of attitude (as opposed to awareness of content) must always be inferential/interpretative remains in force. Even if the tokening of some natural language sentence 'Q' in auditory imagination is sometimes constitutive of thinking, still the fact that the entertaining of that sentence is an assertoric judgment, or a wondering-whether, or an act of supposition, or whatever, will be a matter of its larger causal role *beyond* the point at which interpretation occurs. (It will be a matter of the further causal role of |R|, indeed.) And that role just can't be read off from the sentence itself. It will have to be a matter of further self-interpretation.[20]

The upshot is that, while there might be such a thing as conscious (and self-referring) *thinking*, there might be no such thing as conscious assertoric *judging*, conscious (propositional) *wanting*, conscious *supposing*, and so forth. Put differently: although there are conscious episodic propositional *contents*, there might be no conscious episodic propositional *attitudes*.

What of the self-referential character of conscious thinking, on this conception? In what sense is it vindicated? As I presented the view above, I tacitly assumed that the higher-order thought generated from the sentence/thought pair $<$'Q', |R|$>$ would be |BEL- I am thinking that R|. That is, I assumed that the sort of self-reference here would be a reference *to the self*. But perhaps this was

[20] Will the conclusion here be any different if some of the sentences in inner or outer speech have the character of *avowals*? That is, does it matter if when making the utterance I thereby *commit* myself to thinking and reasoning in the future as if the thought expressed were true? Frankish (2004) claims that if certain of our utterances (whether inner or outer) have the character of commitments, then this can explain how we can be authoritative about the beliefs which are created by those commitments, thereby rendering those beliefs conscious. I grant the former point, but deny the latter. If I sincerely utter 'Q' and thereby commit myself to the truth of 'Q' for purposes of future thinking and acting, then my sincere utterance is conclusive in establishing that I believe that Q. So the utterance is authoritative. And I too (like my hearers if the utterance is a public one) am licensed to draw the conclusion that I believe Q— but *only*, note, if my utterance of 'Q' is sincere, and does express a commitment. Yet this isn't something that can be read off or recognized from the utterance itself. It is always going to be a matter of interpretation of the verbal behavior in the context. And this is enough to show that the attitude of believing, here, doesn't qualify as conscious.

unwarranted. One can just as well move directly from, <'Q', |R|> to |BEL- *That is an act of thinking that* R|. This suggests that (assuming the truth of some form of consumer semantics) the sentence 'Q' might have the dual contents R and *that is a thinking that* R, where the pronoun refers to the sentence 'Q' in question. In that case, conscious thoughts may be self-referential in exactly the same sort of way that conscious experiences are (as discussed in section 1).

## 6.3. *Conscious standing-state beliefs and desires?*[21]

What are the implications of the above discussion for the conscious status of standing-state thoughts? Recall the suggestion that for a standing-state belief or desire to be conscious, is for it to be apt to be activated as a conscious occurrent event (a conscious judgment, or a conscious act of desiring) with the same content. It is obvious, then, that if there is no such thing as conscious occurrent thinking, then there will be no such thing as conscious standing-state thoughts either. So the pessimistic conclusion of section 6.1 generalizes, to embrace standing-state thoughts as well as their occurrent counterparts.

What, though, are the implications of section 6.2? For similar reasons, the pessimistic conclusion regarding occurrent thought *modes* will extend to standing-state propositional attitude modes. If it is always a matter of self-interpretation to determine whether or not I am *judging* that P when I entertain in inner speech an indicative sentence that means *that P*, then it will equally be a matter of interpretation to know that I have a standing-state *belief* that P. The point is especially obvious in connection with standing-state desires, since the sentences in which we express our desires generally bear a somewhat complex and indirect relation to the desires themselves. This is because we rarely use *mood* as an indicator of desire. The desire for P is hardly ever expressed using the optative sentence, 'Would that P!' Rather we say (in indicative mood), 'I want it to be the case that P', or 'It would be good if P', or 'I must try to ensure that P', and so on.[22] So it is always going to require an inferential move or two to get from the interpreted sentence that figures in inner speech to the underlying desire-state that it expresses.

But what of the *content* of standing-state beliefs? Could they, at least, remain conscious if inner speech is (partly) constitutive of thinking? For we allowed that the contents of our occurrent thoughts could count as non-inferentially known, and hence be conscious, given that it is *interpreted* sentences in inner speech that are constitutive of the thinking in question. Here, though, the difference between the language-producer system and the language-consumer system kicks in with a vengeance. For the standing-state belief that P first has to be

---

[21] This sub-section has been newly written for the present volume.
[22] See Carruthers (2004) for some speculations as to why this should be the case, having to do with enabling an enhanced language-involving practical reasoning system to become *practical*.

activated as an occurrent Mentalese representation |BEL-P|, and then taken as input by the language production sub-system. The latter then generates a representation of the natural-language sentence 'Q' from it, which gets passed to the language-comprehension sub-system. Even if the latter should end up interpreting the sentence 'Q' to mean P (attaching to it the very same content with which we began), the connection is still going to be an interpretative, inferential, one. And this is surely sufficient to debar the underlying standing-state belief from counting as conscious.

The important point here is this. If language is constitutive of (some) thinking, it will be the post-interpretation pair <'Q', |P|> that occupies the causal role distinctive of thinking that P. So it doesn't matter that the process of interpretation that gave rise to this pairing in the first place was an inferential one. But the standing-state belief that P exists on the other side of the interpretation process. So even if the pairing in question is constitutive of thinking that P, and even if that thinking can count as conscious by virtue of the immediacy of our knowledge of the pairing (post-interpretation), our knowledge of the standing-state belief that gave rise to the sentence 'Q' in the first place *will* be a result of a process of interpretation. And that is enough to debar it from conscious status.

Suppose (as we suggested in section 5 above) that there is no such thing as non-linguistic conscious thinking, then. Then whether or not inner speech is constitutive of some forms of thinking, and whether or not some or all aspects of those acts of thinking count as conscious thereby; what emerges is that there are no such things as conscious standing-state beliefs or conscious standing-state desires. For here neither mode nor content can count as conscious. This is because both exist on the other side of a process of interpretation from the knowledge that we have of them.


## 7. CONCLUSION

I have sketched an account of phenomenally conscious experience according to which such experiences always have dual (and self-referential) analog contents. I have argued that the constraints placed on a theory of conscious thinking are different from those placed on a theory of conscious experience, since conscious thoughts aren't necessarily and intrinsically *phenomenal* in character. I have sketched some reasons for thinking that there might be no such thing as conscious thinking if natural language plays no direct role in our thoughts, since all self-attributions might then be inferential/self-interpretative ones. And I have argued that if language *does* play such a role, then the *contents* of our episodic thoughts might be conscious (and self-referential) even if the *attitudes* that we take to them aren't, and even if our standing-state attitudes aren't either.

# CHAPTER 9

## Sympathy and Subjectivity

This chapter shows that even if the mental states of non-human animals lack phenomenal properties, as some accounts of mental-state consciousness imply, this needn't prevent those states from being appropriate objects of sympathy and moral concern. The chapter argues that the most basic form of mental (as opposed to biological) harm lies in the existence of thwarted agency, or thwarted desire, rather than in anything phenomenological.

## 1. INTRODUCTION AND BACKGROUND ASSUMPTIONS

This chapter makes four main assumptions—two about consciousness and two about value—that together raise an important question concerning the possible scope of morality and moral concern. I shall make little attempt to defend these assumptions, beyond saying just enough to explain and motivate them. Each of them can be made to seem plausible, at least; and three have been defended at length elsewhere.[1] If these premises are granted, then fundamental questions are raised about the moral status of non-human animals. But even those who aren't prepared to grant one or more of my assumptions should take an interest in the questions that they generate, and in my proposed answers. For the discussion will lead us to look quite closely at the nature of psychological (as opposed to biological) *harm*,[2] and at the proper objects of sympathy, raising issues that have not, I think, been discussed before. Even if one or more of my assumptions are rejected, there will remain the question whether, and in what sense, sympathy is necessarily tied to subjectivity—which is not a question with quite the same practical import as the one that I address, admittedly, but an interesting one nonetheless.

---

[1] For detailed explanation and defense of Assumptions 1 and 2, see my 2000. For a classic defense of Assumption 3, see Mackie, 1977, Part One.
[2] Any living thing that can be *damaged* (including plants and micro-organisms) can be harmed in the biological sense; but it is doubtful whether this notion is of any direct moral significance. I assume in this paper that the proper object of sympathy is *psychological* harm, involving either pain or the frustration of desire.

## 1.1. *Assumptions about consciousness*

Here are the two main assumptions about consciousness laid out in summary form, together with the initial conclusion that they entail:

> *Assumption 1:* All of the mental states of non-human animals (with the possible exception of the great apes) are non-conscious ones.
>
> *Assumption 2:* Non-conscious mental states lack phenomenology, or subjective 'feel'.
>
> *Conclusion 1:* The mental states of non-human animals lack phenomenal feels (unless those animals are apes, perhaps—I drop this qualifier in what follows, for the sake of simplicity).

The conclusion C1 then generates, quite naturally, a further question. This is the main question to be answered in this chapter, and is as follows:

> *Question 1:* Given C1, ought we to conclude that sympathy (and other moral attitudes) towards the sufferings and disappointments of non-human animals is inappropriate?

In Carruthers (1992b, ch. 8) I argued tentatively for a positive answer to this question. But I am now not so sure. Indeed, the main burden of this chapter is to demonstrate that there is a powerful case for answering Q1 in the negative. (And this is a case that doesn't need to rely upon an objectionable realism about value—see A3 below.)

Why should we think that animals don't have conscious mental states? The short answer is that some or other form of higher-order thought (HOT) theory gives the best account of mental-state consciousness (Rosenthal, 1986, 1997; Carruthers, 1996, 2000).[3] And although there is vigorous debate about whether chimps and other apes are capable of HOTs (e.g. Byrne and Whiten, 1988; Povinelli, 2000), it is generally agreed that cats, dogs, sheep, pigs, etc. are *not* capable of HOTs. But then why should we accept a HOT account of phenomenal consciousness? First, HOT theory gives a good explanation of the difference between conscious and non-conscious experience (so my experiences now are phenomenally conscious because available to or targeted by HOTs; whereas experiences in blindsight, absent-minded driving, sleep-walking, and during mild epileptic seizure are not so targeted). Second, HOT theory can provide a satisfying *explanation* of the phenomenal properties of conscious experience; which gives us reason to think that phenomenology, or 'feel', just *is* perceptual information available to, or targeted by, higher-order recognition (Carruthers, 2000 and Chapter 6 of this volume).

---

[3] See also Dennett, 1991, who also endorses a higher-order thought account, only with linguistic descriptions substituted in place of thoughts.

C1 is highly controversial, of course, and I make no pretence to have defended it here. It also conflicts with a powerful common-sense intuition to the contrary. But I suggest that this intuition may well be illusory, and can easily be explained away. For notice that one important strategy we often adopt when attributing mental states to a subject is to try *imagining the world from the subject's point of view*, to see how things then seem. But when we do that, what we inevitably get are imaginings of *conscious* perceptions and thoughts, and of experiences with phenomenal feels to them. So of course we naturally assume that the experiences of a cat will be *like* something, once we have got to the point of accepting (correctly, in my view) that the cat does have experiences. But this may merely reflect the fact that imaginings of perceptual states are always imaginings of *conscious* perceptual states, that is all. It may go no deeper than the fact that we have no idea how to imagine a non-conscious perception.

Let me stress again that it won't matter very much, for the purposes of this chapter, whether or not A1 and A2 are accepted, or thought plausible. My main interest is in the *conditional* question Q1; and to assess this you don't need to believe in, or accept the plausibility of, the antecedent. Another way of raising essentially the same conditional question, in fact (although without the same practical import), is to ask whether those inventions of the philosophical imagination, *zombies*, would be appropriate objects of sympathy and concern. (A zombie is someone who is supposed to be functionally and intentionally isomorphic to a normal person, but who is completely lacking in phenomenal consciousness, or 'qualia'.) Again, it doesn't matter whether or not zombies are really possible. They just provide another way of raising the general theoretical issue that is the concern of this chapter: if we distinguish between the *feel* and the *functional role* of our sufferings and disappointments (which normally have both, of course) can we form a view about which (if not both) is the appropriate object of sympathy?

## 1.2. *Assumptions about value*

One route to a negative answer to Q1—that I want to close off with my third assumption—would be to endorse what Parfit (1984) calls an 'Objective List' theory of value, and to maintain that the sufferings and disappointments of non-human animals figure on this list, irrespective of questions of phenomenology. So it might be claimed that pleasure and desire-satisfaction are moral goods, and pain and desire-frustration moral evils, quite apart from the question whether or not these states possess phenomenal properties or 'feel'. [4] In which case we are morally

---

[4] Of course there is a question whether a state that lacked 'feel' could properly be described as 'pain'— see Kripke, 1972. But this semantic question is irrelevant to the main point at issue, which is whether a state with the functional and intentional/representational properties of pain, but without the distinctive phenomenology, could be an appropriate object of sympathy and concern.

obliged not to cause suffering to non-human animals, if we can help it, even if their mental states should prove to be lacking in phenomenology, as A1 and A2 entail.

The problem with an Objective List theory, however, is that it commits us to a form of metaphysical realism about value that is very hard to believe, as well as rendering ethical epistemology mysterious (Mackie, 1977). And there are a number of viable alternatives on the market. One would be to maintain, as Singer (1979) does, that moral value is grounded in rationalized sympathy. Another would be to claim, following Scanlon (1982), that moral values and requirements are those that no one could reasonably reject who shared the aim of reaching free and unforced agreement; and this approach, too, will arguably find a central place for sympathy, embedded at the heart of the moral virtue of beneficence (to be contrasted with justice) (see my 1992b). I therefore make the following assumption:

> A3: Metaphysical realism about moral values is false; rather, such values are somehow *constructed* from a basis in human attitudes, or human reason, or both.

The issues surrounding A3, and the lines of argument available in its support, are broadly familiar if not universally accepted. I therefore feel justified in leaving A3 as just that—an *assumption* of the chapter, without requiring anything further in the way of elaboration and comment.

It might be felt that there is another position that could accord moral standing to animals without becoming entangled in questions of phenomenology. This would focus on the idea of an *interest*, claiming that things that go against an animal's interests are appropriate objects of sympathy and moral concern, irrespective of issues to do with animal subjectivity. I believe that this position faces a dilemma: either it conceives of interests as being fixed, and as obtaining their value, independently of us—in which case it collapses into the sort of realism rejected in A3; or the moral significance of interests depends upon the mental states of the creatures in question—in which case we don't have a real competitor for the idea that *psychological harm* is the most basic object of sympathy and concern. This then gives me my fourth assumption:

> A4: Attempts to ground sympathy in *interests* either collapse into a form of moral realism, or covertly appeal to the more basic importance of psychological harm.

This assumption raises large issues, to which I cannot hope to do justice within the scope of this chapter. But I can say just a few words to motivate it.

Consider the claim that good health is in my best interests. What might this mean, and how might such a claim be grounded? It might, in the first place, be a claim about the intrinsic value of health, independent of my attitudes, feelings, and goals, both now and in the future. This would be a very strong claim to make. And it is hard to see how it could be defended without commitment to the idea that *health* figures on some 'objective list' of goods. And the claim is, in any case, counter-intuitive in its own right. Of course it is generally true that poor health has a bad impact on the lives of people, even in cases where it is caused by the satisfaction of powerful desires, like desires for nicotine or for chocolate. But it is possible to conceive of cases where—unusually—someone's life-goals positively *require* poor health, in which case it is no longer true that good health is in their interests, it seems to me. A range of examples might be considered here. But imagine someone living in a country with a system of conscription of the healthy into the armed services, where that country is fighting a bitter and bloody (and, let us stipulate, unjust) war. Is it really in this person's best interests to be completely healthy in these circumstances if that will mean, almost inevitably, severe psychological distress, together with a significant chance of painful injury and death?

It is true, of course, that interests are independent of *present* desires. It is familiar that health can be in my best interests even though I don't presently desire it. But in these cases, I think, the source of our concern derives from the belief that loss of good health will be seriously *regretted* in the future, or will otherwise have a negative impact upon my psychological life. That is to say, it derives from a belief in the psychological harm that poor health will bring in its train. But then this is no longer a competitor to the idea to be explored in this chapter, that the proper object of sympathy is some sort of psychological harm. And the same question arises, as to whether such harm, in order to be an appropriate object of sympathy, must involve some kind of subjective phenomenology.

## 2. HARM AND THE FRUSTRATION OF DESIRE

In this section I shall defend two further assumptions, this time about the nature of psychological harm. The first is that the most basic form of such harm consists in the frustration of desire; the second is that only frustrations of desire that are *subjective* (in a sense to be explained) should count as harms.

I should stress that my focus throughout will be on present-tensed harm, rather than on the sort of harm that consists in longer-term psychological damage. For it is obvious that the former is the more fundamental phenomenon—if things could not be bad for me *at* a time, abstracting from any future effects on my life, then they could never be bad for me *over* time either; indeed, it seems plain that the most basic way in which an event can be bad for me in the longer term is by causing present-tensed harms at each of a number of later times. This is fully in accord with common-sense belief, I think. If I suffer intense pain for a short period of time, then everyone would allow that I am harmed psychologically, and that my state is an appropriate object of sympathy and preventative action, even if I am caused to forget about the occurrence of that pain immediately it finishes, and even if it has no further detrimental effects on my life.

I should also stress that a full account of the phenomenon of psychological harm is likely to be a complex business, the elucidation of which would take me well beyond the scope of this chapter. To mention just one issue: we think that someone can be harmed, not just by being caused to suffer, but also if their life is caused to go less well, psychologically speaking, than it would have done otherwise.[5] So sometimes, at least, judgments of harm can involve cross-world comparisons of psychological goods and evils. But again it should be plain that the basic notion, on which I concentrate here, is the one that needs to be fed into such comparisons—namely, that of the goodness or badness of a psychological state for a subject *in* a given world.

## 2.1. *Sensation versus frustration*

First, let us consider what is the most basic form of psychological harm. Is it the sensations characteristic of suffering (paradigmatically pain)? Or is it, rather, frustrations or thwartings of desire? Two considerations demonstrate that the correct answer to this question is the latter, I believe. The first derives from the existence (or at least possible existence) of pure masochism. While most of us shun pain, the masochist welcomes it. In *im*pure forms of masochism, sensations of pain are welcomed, not for their own sake, but rather for their consequences, or because of their causally indispensable position in a desirable package of desires and other sensations (of sexual excitement, say). In such cases we may say that the sensation of pain is itself unwanted, but is welcomed in context—somewhat as one might, in context, welcome the pain involved in the lancing of a boil: it is unwanted in itself, but it forms an indispensable part of a welcome event.

In cases of *pure* masochism, however, sensations of pain are themselves welcomed.[6] This need not mean that the pure masochist welcomes each and every pain, of course, irrespective of context and circumstances. A pure masochist

[5] It is arguable that this idea can explain some of the intuitions that might otherwise seem to support the Objective List theory of value. For example, consider Rawls's man who just wants to count the blades of grass in various lawns, rather than become a mathematician (discussed in Parfit, 1984). Although his only actual desire is satisfied, we might naturally think of that desire as itself standing in the way of a more worthwhile (in the sense of psychologically satisfying) life for the man.

[6] Some might then wonder whether the state that the pure masochist welcomes is properly describable as 'pain'. Here, as before, the semantic issue is beside the point—which is that what the pure masochist welcomes has the characteristic phenomenology, of felt characteristics, of pain.

need not be someone who enjoys toothache, or the pain of a gouty toe. Rather, it may only be pains surrounded by certain other sensations and satisfactions that are welcome. For example, it may be that only pains that are deliberately inflicted by another person in the context of sexual activity are welcomed. But in these cases, the sensations of pain aren't just *tolerated*, as they are by the impure masochist, as being an indispensable part of a package that is worthwhile overall. Rather, they make a further addition to the satisfactoriness of the overall set of sensations and satisfactions. The pure masochist wouldn't wish the sensations of pain away, even if everything else in their circumstances and sensations could remain the same.

I believe that there probably are some pure masochists in the world (Warren, 1985). But I don't need to argue for this here. It is enough that pure masochism seems plainly conceivable, or conceptually possible. For what this then shows is that it isn't the *sensation* of pain (that is, its phenomenology, or felt quality) that is bad, in the normal case. It is rather that most of us want very much not to *have* that sensation. So it is the frustration of this desire that constitutes the harm, not the experience of the sensation itself.[7] This gives us the following claim:

> *A5:* Pains (and other sensations characteristic of suffering) only count as harms to the agent to the extent that they are unwanted by that agent; and the most basic form of psychological harm consists in frustrations or thwartings of desire.

This claim can be further defended in the light of the effects of certain types of analgesic, as Dennett once pointed out.[8] People under the influence of certain types of morphine report that the *sensation* of pain remains exactly the same, but that they no longer *care*. They say that the felt qualities of their pains remain just as they were before they were given the morphine, but that the presence of these qualities no longer bothers them. Such reactions are by no means arbitrary, inexplicable, or insane. On the contrary, they are predictable from, and explicable in terms of, the physiology of pain perception.

As is now widely known, pain perception is mediated by two distinct nervous pathways—there is the *old path*, which is slow and projects primarily to the sub-cortical limbic system of the brain, and which seems to be responsible for pain *motivation*, underlying aversion to pain; and there is the *new path*, which is faster and which projects to a number of different cortical centers, and which seems to underlie fine discrimination, location, and feel (Young, 1986). What

---

[7] What about the suggestion that it is really a frustration-sensation *pair* that constitutes the harm? This hasn't strictly been ruled out. But since in other cases—where the desire is not for the presence, or absence, of a sensation—frustration of desire alone can constitute a harm, it is simplest to suppose that this is so in the case of pain too. The question whether such frustration must itself have phenomenological properties is the main topic of the remainder of the chapter.

[8] See Dennett, 1978b. This is the second of the considerations in support of A5 that I spoke of above.

some types of morphine can do is suppress the old path, while leaving the new path fully functional. So pain *perception*, in the sense of discrimination and feel, is unaffected, while pain *aversion* is suppressed. In such circumstances it seems plain that there is nothing bad, or harmful to the agent, in undergoing a mere pain sensation. Indeed, it really does seem appropriate to regard such types of morphine as an analgesic, removing pain in the sense in which pain *matters* to the agent.[9]

## 2.2. *Objective versus subjective frustrations*

While the two considerations presented above seem sufficient to establish A5, it should be noticed that A5 itself contains an ambiguity, depending upon how desire frustration is conceived of. For we can distinguish between *objective* and *subjective* frustrations of desire. The first occurs whenever the desired state of affairs fails to obtain or come about, *whether or not this is known of by the agent.* The second occurs whenever the agent *believes* that the desired state of affairs fails to obtain or come about, whether or not this is actually the case.

Everyone will allow, I think, that subjective frustrations of desire are a species of psychological harm. Everyone will grant that it is bad for agents, *ceteris paribus*, to think that things that they desire have failed to occur. But some maintain that it is *also* a harm when an agent's desires are *objectively* frustrated, whether or not they are also subjectively thwarted (Feinberg, 1977; Nagel, 1979). If we held that objective frustrations of desire were a species of harm, and hence that such frustrations are worthy of sympathy and moral concern, then the answer to Q1 should obviously be negative. For then what makes frustrations of desire an appropriate object of concern would have nothing to do with phenomenology or feel. It would be the mere objective fact that an animal is in an unwanted state (e.g. pain) that is bad, irrespective of whether there is any phenomenology associated with the thwarting of its desire for the absence of the pain, and irrespective of whether or not the animal knows that it is in pain, or that its desire is being frustrated. Similarly, *mutatis mutandis,* for the case where an animal is starved of food or water—it would be the mere fact that its desires for these things are objectively thwarted that constitutes the existence of a psychological harm to the animal, irrespective of anything subjective.

---

[9] Note that the existence of a *new path* in many species of mammal isn't immediately sufficient to establish that these species have pains that possess phenomenological properties. For it is one thing to *perceive* or to *discriminate* states of the world or of the organism's own body—which is what the presence of a new path strictly establishes—and it is quite another thing for these states of perception, or these discriminations, to be conscious ones—which is what is necessary for them to *feel like* anything, I maintain. According to the HOT theory of mental-state consciousness that lies behind A1 and A2, perceptual states only get to feel like anything when they are present to a conceptual system that is capable of classifying these states *as such*—as opposed to classifying the states of the world, or of the body, represented by those states.

However, I believe that objective frustrations of desire are *not* a species of harm. I propose, in fact, to defend the following claim:

*A6:* Only subjective frustrations or thwartings of desire count as psychological harms, and are appropriate objects of sympathetic concern.

But this will require some setting up, beginning with a small detour through the falsity of philosophical hedonism.

The hedonist's focus is primarily on the satisfaction rather than the frustration of desire, but it carries obvious implications for the latter. For the hedonist claims that every desire aims at its own subjective satisfaction—normally interpreted to mean the *feelings* of satisfaction to be gained from achieving the overt object of the desire. For well-known reasons this is false (Feinberg, 1985). Most desires aim at objective states of affairs—eating an apple, gaining a degree, or whatever—where knowledge that those states of affairs have been realized may characteristically *cause* certain feelings of satisfaction, but where those feelings were not what were desired in the first place. This then suggests that what is a benefit or a psychological good—from the perspective of the agent—about the satisfaction of desire is *achieving the goal of the desire*, not the subjective phenomenology of desire-satisfaction.

Indeed, in the case of many desires (e.g. the desire that my children should grow up healthy, or the desire that my latest book should be well thought of ) what I desire is the existence of a certain objective state of affairs *whether or not I ever come to learn of it*. So this then suggests that it is *objective* satisfactions of desire that constitute the primary form of psychological good. And then by parity of reasoning we might expect that what would be bad about the frustration of desire would be, not the phenomenology of frustration, or the knowledge that a desired state of affairs has failed to materialize, but rather the objective failure to achieve a goal.

This argument moves too swiftly, however. For it conflates the question of what is good or bad *from the perspective of the agent*—that is, in the light of the content of agent's desires and goals—with the question of what is good or bad *for* the agent, or a harm *to* the agent. The former notion of *good from the perspective of an agent* can be constructed—very roughly—by listing the contents of the agent's major goals (which may or may not mention the agent's own subjective states). But the latter notion is distinguished by its ties with beneficence and sympathy—to act beneficently towards someone is to do something that is good *for* them; and sympathy for someone's state is only appropriate for something that is bad *for* them, or a harm *to* them.

So it would be perfectly consistent with the fact that my desires *aim at* objective states of affairs to claim that the satisfaction of those desires should only count as a benefit, from the perspective of a beneficent observer, when I come to learn that the states of affairs in question have been realized. Similarly, it would be consistent with allowing that it is the objective failure of my goals that is bad from my perspective, to claim nevertheless that the frustration of those desires should only count as a harm, from the perspective of a sympathetic observer, when their failure is known to me. [10] Not only would such claims be consistent, but they have a good deal of intuitive support. It is very hard indeed to see how anything could be good or bad *for* agents, or be a harm *to* them, without having any impact upon the (subjective psychology of) the agents themselves.

Admittedly, there are cases that can make it seem plausible that objectively frustrated desires are bad for—or constitute harm to—an agent, irrespective of their impact upon the subjectivity of the subject. Consider, for example, the case of the unknowingly cuckolded husband. Suppose that I love my wife, and want her to be faithful to me. Then what I want is that she should *be* faithful, not merely that I should continue to believe that she is faithful; and this is what constitutes the good, from my perspective. But now suppose that, unknown to me, she has an affair, which in no way affects our relationship. Some people have the intuition that I am harmed, and that I am, in the circumstances, an appropriate object of sympathy. But one possible confounding factor here is that what my wife does exposes me to is *risk* of subjective harm (in addition to being *wrong*, involving breach of trust and evincing a failure of friendship), since her infidelity may one day be found out; and it may be that this itself is a harm.

In fact I doubt whether exposure to risk of harm is itself a harm. For consider the matter after the fact: when I finally die, having never found out my wife's infidelity, and having lived happily with her throughout, I think it would be a mistake to say that her actions had harmed me. For the risk never materialized. But even if risk of harm *is* itself a harm, it is plainly one that is parasitic upon the possibility of subjective harming. So a creature that is incapable of being subjectively harmed will be incapable of being exposed to risk of harm either. And then just the same questions concerning the moral status of animals will arise if animal mental states are lacking in subjective phenomenology.

When we consider examples where factors such as wrong-doing and risk of harm are controlled for, I believe that any temptation to say that objective frustrations of desire should be counted as harms is dissipated. We can imagine a case, for example, where a woman has left Earth forever on a space-rocket, which lacks any means of radio communication (hence, what now happens on Earth can

---

[10] The standpoint of a sympathetic observer (which is the standpoint of beneficence) should be distinguished from that of a friend or lover. To love someone is, in part and to a degree, to be prepared to enter into and adopt their goals as your own. So my friends may feel an impulse to assist in the realization of my goals even if I will never know of the achievement of those goals, and so even if my failure to achieve those goals wouldn't be a psychological harm to me.

never be known to her). One of her deepest desires is that her late husband should be suitably honored on Earth, and to this end she had commissioned a magnificent public statue of him to stand in a city square. But some months after her departure from Earth the statue is struck by lightning and destroyed. It seems plain that this event doesn't constitute any sort of harm to her—although it leads to the objective frustration of an important desire—and that sympathy for her situation is inappropriate. It seems equally plain that I don't act benevolently towards her if I see to it that the statue is rebuilt.[11]

Some readers may wonder whether these examples only *seem* to work because they are, in some sense, 'non-serious'; and may suggest that our intuitions will be different in cases where the objective frustration of a desire is of fundamental importance to the subject. To test this, imagine that the woman had left Earth on a space-rocket, not from choice (she is very distressed at having to leave), but because this is the only way she can earn enough money to pay for her children's education (she lives in an unenlightened land with no public education system, has no other realistic source of income; etc.—the example can be fleshed out). But then soon after her departure, her children are killed accidentally in a house-fire. Should we not feel sympathy for her, despite the fact that she will never know?

Here, however, the confounding factor is that her children's deaths make her own sacrifice *unnecessary*; and it may be for this reason that our sympathy is engaged. This hypothesis can be confirmed. For we can switch the example so that she does not leave Earth *in order to* provide for her children, but for independent reasons, because she cannot stand to remain amongst the ungodly (or whatever). In such circumstances we no longer feel sympathy for her when her children are killed, I think, even though we know that she would have been devastated had she known.

I conclude, therefore, that only subjective frustrations of desire—frustrations that have a subjective impact upon their subject—count as harms, and are worthy of moral concern. This certainly makes it sound as if frustrations of desire that are lacking any phenomenology may therefore be *in*appropriate objects of concern. For what is it for a frustration to be *subjective* except that it possesses a phenomenology? In which case frustrations of desire that are non-conscious, and so which lack any phenomenology, will be *non-subjective* frustrations; and so, by A6, they will be inappropriate objects of concern.

---

[11] Matters may be different if I am, not a stranger, but rather the woman's friend or lover. Here I might well feel an obligation to see the statue rebuilt. For as I noted above, to love someone involves a preparedness to take on their goals as your own. This explains, I think, the attitude characteristic of bereaved people towards the desires of the deceased. That we regard fulfilling the wishes of the dead as a way on honouring them, shows not that objective satisfactions of desire are a moral good, but rather that love may involve an identification with the loved one's goals.

## 2.3. *Two kinds of subjective frustration*

However, the sense of 'subjective' in A6 need not be—or not without further argument, at least—that of possessing phenomenal properties. Rather, the sense can be that of being *believed in by the subject*. On this account, a desire counts as being subjectively frustrated, in the relevant sense, if the subject *believes* that it has been frustrated, or *believes* that the desired state of affairs has not (and/or will not) come about. Then there would be nothing to stop a phenomenology-less frustration of desire from counting as subjective, and from constituting an appropriate object of moral concern. So we have a question:

> Q2: Which is the appropriate notion of *subjective* to render A6 true?—
> (a) possessing phenomenology? or (b) being believed in by the subject?

If the answer to Q2 is (a), then animal frustrations and pains, in lacking phenomenology by C1, won't be appropriate objects of sympathy or concern. This would then require us to answer Q1 in the affirmative, and animals would, necessarily, be beyond the moral pale. However, if the answer to Q2 is (b), then there will be nothing in C1 and A6 together to rule out the appropriateness of moral concern for animals; and we shall then have answered Q1 in the negative.[12]

It is important to see that desire-frustration can be characterized in a purely first-order way, without introducing into the account any higher-order belief concerning the existence of that desire. For it is primarily the absence of such higher-order beliefs in the case of non-human animals that constitutes the ground for denying that their mental states are conscious ones, as we saw in section 1.1 above. So, suppose that an animal has a strong desire to eat, and that this desire is now activated; suppose, too, that the animal is aware that it is *not* now eating; then that seems sufficient for its desire to be subjectively frustrated, despite the fact that the animal may be incapable of higher-order belief.

In fact there is no more reason for insisting that desire-frustration requires awareness that one *has* that desire, than there is for claiming that *surprise* (in the sense of belief-violation) requires awareness that one has that belief.[13] In both cases the co-occurrence, in one and the same agent at one and the same time, of two activated first-order states with directly contradictory contents is sufficient to account for the phenomenon. In the case of surprise, what one has is an activated belief with the content *that P* combined with a perception, say, with the content *that not P*. In the case of desire-frustration, what one has is an active desire with the content *that P* combined with an activated belief with the content *that not P*.

---

[12] Which is not to say, of course, that such concern is necessarily *required* of us, either. That issue is moot, and needs to be debated in another forum. For my own view, see my 1992b, ch. 7.

[13] Of course, Davidson (1975) has famously maintained that belief requires the concept of belief, in part on the grounds that surprise presupposes an awareness, on the part of the subject, of what one had previously believed. For a brief critique, see my 1992b, ch. 6.

Let me emphasize that it is the *co-activation* of a first-order desire and a first-order belief with contradictory contents that is sufficient for subjective desire-frustration in the sense of Q2(b), not necessarily co-*consciousness* or anything involving higher-order thoughts about the creature's own states. Of course someone may desire *that P* and come to believe *not-P* without their desire being subjectively frustrated if they never put the two things together. (For example, the desire may be dormant at the time when they acquire the belief; and the belief may remain dormant on the next occasion when the desire becomes active.) What is sufficient for subjective frustration is that a desire and a belief with directly contradictory contents should both be active together in the creature's practical reasoning system.

## 3. SYMPATHY AND SUBJECTIVITY

How should Q2 be addressed? If we try to enter sympathetically into the mind of someone whose sufferings and frustrations are non-conscious ones, what we draw, of course, is a complete blank. We simply have no idea how to imagine, from the inside, a mental state that is non-conscious. Since to imagine undergoing a mental state is to imagine what that state *is like*, and since only conscious mental states are *like* anything, in the relevant sense, it follows that only conscious mental states can be imagined. This certainly makes it seem as if animal sufferings and disappointments, in being non-phenomenal by C1, cannot be appropriate objects of sympathy or concern. At any rate, this is what I argued in my 1992b (ch. 8).

But it may be that this conclusion is too hasty. It may be that *sympathy* and *imagination* can, and should, be pulled apart. That they *can* be pulled apart is obvious, I think. Sympathy can surely be grounded in a purely third-personal understanding of someone's situation and/or mental states; and certainly a *desire to help* need not be preceded by any sort of imaginative identification. To decide whether they *should* be pulled apart, what we need to ask is: What is bad about the frustration of a desire, from the perspective of a sympathetic observer? The phenomenology of frustration? Or the fact of coming to know that the desired state of affairs has failed to materialize? For the latter sort of frustration can certainly be undergone, in some form, by non-human animals. So putting A6 and Q2 together, in effect, we have the question:

Q3: What is bad or harmful, from the point of view of a sympathetic observer, about the frustration or thwarting of desire? (a) The phenomenology associated with desire-frustration? Or (b) the fact of learning that the object of desire has not been achieved?

Another way of putting the point is this: we should concede that whenever we *enter sympathetically into* the frustrations and disappointments of another creature we always, and inevitably, imagine mental states with phenomenology. But it may be that this has more to do with imagination than with morals. It may be that imagination, as a conscious activity, can only represent from the inside mental states that are conscious, and so that possess phenomenological properties. But this may have nothing to do with what properly grounds sympathy. It may be, indeed, that what makes sympathy appropriate has nothing to do with phenomenology, just as answer Q3(b) envisages.

## 3.1. An (unsuccessful) argument from subjective importance

One argument in support of Q3(a)—that it is the phenomenology associated with desire-frustration that constitutes the harm to an agent—can be constructed as follows. Surely not *all* thwartings of desire constitute present-tensed psychological harm, and are appropriate objects of sympathy and moral concern. In particular, the thwartings of *trivial* desires, or mere whims, are not. But then how are these to be distinguished, except in terms of subjective phenomenology? It appears that our *important* desires are those whose frustration gives rise to more or less intense feelings of disappointment, whereas a trivial desire is one whose known frustration gives rise to no such feelings. In which case it is only those thwartings of desire that are accompanied by a certain characteristic phenomenology that are worthy of sympathy.

If it is only the thwartings of important (or, at any rate, non-trivial) desires that constitute a form of psychological harm; and if what marks out a desire as important (or, at any rate, non-trivial) is something to do with the phenomenology associated with its frustration, then it will turn out that it is the phenomenology associated with desire-frustration that is psychologically harmful, just as answer Q3(a) envisages. And then it will follow, if C1 is correct, that the pains and frustrations of non-human animals will not be appropriate objects of sympathy and concern, because lacking in the relevant sort of importance.

It is surely false, however, that the only way to distinguish those desires that are important (rather than trivial) for an organism is in terms of some sort of subjective phenomenology. It may be that such phenomenology is used as evidence of importance in the human case, but it is doubtful whether it is constitutive of such importance. In the case of human beings, it is true, we often rely upon the extent of felt disappointment, or psychological devastation, in gauging the importance of a desire, but it is doubtful whether such feelings are what importance really consists in. At any rate, it seems easy enough to carve out a notion of *importance* that isn't phenomenological, but for the application of which phenomenology might be evidential.

If desires can be ranked in terms of *strength*—where strength is defined, not phenomenologically, but rather in terms of which of its desires an agent would choose to satisfy first, *ceteris paribus*, or at what cost—then we can characterize those desires that are important as those that are stronger than most, or something of the sort. This would then give us a notion of *importance* of desire that would be applicable to non-human animals, whether or not such animals are subjects of phenomenology. And I think it is plausible that we humans use felt disappointment as evidence of importance, so defined. At any rate, unless this can be shown not to be the case, we lack any argument in support of Q3(a).

## 3.2. An (unsuccessful) argument from the case of Penelope

One attempt at answering Q3 has failed. We need to try a different tack. What we need to do, in fact, is to devise some thought-experiments to peel apart the respective contributions of known (or believed) failure of achievement, on the one hand, and phenomenological frustration, on the other, in our beliefs about psychological harm. Of course, many doubt the value of thought-experiments; and some maintain that a good theory is worth a thousand intuitions. But it is hard to see any other way forward in the present case. For the notion of sympathy that is our target isn't itself a moral one (rather, it is something that *feeds into* moral theory, rather than being *constructed by* it); so we cannot resolve the question that concerns us through considerations of moral theory. And in all the real-world cases involving humans where our sympathies are aroused, the two distinct notions of 'subjective frustration' that are separated in Q3 are co-instantiated; whereas in real-world cases involving non-human animals it may be that our sympathies are driven by false beliefs (given C1) about animal phenomenology. We have no option, then, but to engage in thought-experiments—albeit experiments that are supplemented and constrained, wherever possible, by arguments.

What kind of thought-experiment do we require? One possibility would be to consider cases in which one and the same agent has both conscious and non-conscious desires, asking whether the frustration of the latter constitutes any psychological harm *to him*. This was the kind of line I took in my 1992b (ch. 8), where I imagined the case of Penelope, who is unusual in only ever having non-conscious pains in her legs.[14] These pains cause her to rub the offended part, and in severe cases to scream and cry out, but all without any *conscious* awareness of

---

[14] Of course, we can again raise the (semantic) question whether what she has is properly described as 'pain'. But, as before, this is not to the point. Our question is whether a state that is at least *like* pain in respect of its functional role and intentional content, but which lacks any surroundings of subjective phenomenology, is an appropriate object of concern.

pain on her part. I suggested that these pains are not appropriate objects of sympathy and concern, largely because Penelope herself is not bothered by them—she may find it inconvenient when she cannot walk properly on a broken ankle (and we may feel sympathy for her inconvenience), but she isn't consciously distressed by her pains, and doesn't seek our assistance (other than physical assistance) or sympathy. In similar spirit, we could imagine someone who only ever has non-conscious desires, in some domain, suggesting that it is doubtful whether we should feel sympathy when these desires are thwarted, since such thwartings are of no concern to the (conscious) agent.

I now maintain, however, that it isn't really appropriate to consider thought-experiments of this type. This is because conscious subjects are apt only to identify with, and regard as their own, desires that are conscious. This is so for essentially the reason that makes it difficult for *us* to identify with those desires—there is no such thing as imagining, from the inside, what it is like to entertain such a desire; and subjects themselves can only ever know that they *possess* such desires by self-interpretation, just as we know of them by other-interpretation. So from the perspective of the conscious agent, non-conscious desires will seem to be *outside of* themselves. Such subjects could, then, quite easily be mistaken in denying that the frustration of a non-conscious desire constitutes any harm to them. In fact, they are in no better position to express a judgment on this matter than we are.

How, then, are we to peel apart thwarted agency from phenomenology in our beliefs about psychological harm? The way forward, I believe, is to consider, not examples in which one and the same agent has both conscious and non-conscious desires; but rather an example in which an agent has conscious desires, but where satisfactions and frustrations of those desires are lacking in any of the usual phenomenology. This is the example of Phenumb.

## 3.3. The case of Phenumb

Let us imagine, then, an example of a conscious, language-using, agent—I call him 'Phenumb'—who is unusual only in that satisfactions and frustrations of his conscious desires take place without the normal sorts of distinctive phenomenology.[15] So when he achieves a goal he doesn't experience any warm glow of success, or any feelings of satisfaction. And when he believes that he has failed to achieve a goal, he doesn't experience any pangs of regret or feelings of depression. Nevertheless, Phenumb has the full range of attitudes characteristic of conscious desire-achievement and desire-frustration. So when Phenumb

---

[15] Science fiction fans might identify Phenumb with Mr Spock from the early television series *Star Trek*; or perhaps better, with some pure-blooded Vulcan.

achieves a goal he often comes to have the conscious belief that his desire has been satisfied, and he knows that the desire itself has been extinguished; moreover, he often believes (and asserts) that it was worthwhile for him to attempt to achieve that goal, and that the goal was a valuable one to have obtained. Similarly, when Phenumb *fails* to achieve a goal he often comes to believe that his desire has been frustrated, while he knows that the desire itself continues to exist (now in the form of a wish); and he often believes (and asserts) that it would have been worthwhile to achieve that goal, and that something valuable to him has now failed to come about.

Notice that Phenumb is not (or need not be) a zombie. That is, he need not be entirely lacking in phenomenal consciousness. On the contrary, his visual, auditory, and other experiences can have just the same phenomenological richness as our own; and his pains, too, can have felt qualities. What he *lacks* are just the phenomenal feelings associated with the satisfaction and frustration of desire. Perhaps this is because he is unable to perceive the effects of changed adrenaline levels on his nervous system, or something of the sort.

Is Phenumb an appropriate object of moral concern? I think it is obvious that he is. While it may be hard to imagine what it is *like* to be Phenumb, we have no difficulty identifying his goals and values, or in determining which of his projects are most important to him—after all, we can ask him! When Phenumb has been struggling to achieve a goal and fails, it seems appropriate to feel sympathy: not for what he now *feels*—since by hypothesis he feels nothing, or nothing relevant to sympathy—but rather for the intentional state that he now occupies, of dissatisfied desire. Similarly, when Phenumb is engaged in some project that he cannot complete alone, and begs our help, it seems appropriate that we should feel some impulse to assist him: not in order that he might experience any feeling of satisfaction—for we know by hypothesis that he will feel none—but simply that he might achieve a goal that is of importance to him. What the example reveals is that the psychological harmfulness of desire-frustration has nothing (or not much—see the next paragraph) to do with phenomenology, and everything (or almost everything) to do with thwarted agency.

The qualifications just expressed are necessary, because feelings of satisfaction are themselves often welcomed, and feelings of dissatisfaction are themselves usually unwanted. Since the feelings associated with desire-frustration are themselves usually unpleasant, there will, so to speak, be *more* desire-frustration taking place in a normal person than in Phenumb in any given case. For the normal person will have had frustrated *both* their world-directed desire *and* their desire for the absence of unpleasant feelings of dissatisfaction. But it remains true that the most basic, most fundamental, way in which desire-frustration is bad for, or harmful to, the agent has nothing to do with phenomenology.

## 3.4. *Does consciousness make a difference?*

If the example is accepted, then the case of Phenumb is successful in showing that the thwarting of at least a *conscious* desire can be bad for an agent in the absence of any phenomenology of frustration, as seen from the perspective of a sympathetic observer. We now need to ask whether this subjective badness has anything to do with the fact that the desire is a conscious one. Or would the frustration of a non-conscious desire, too—such as non-human animals only have, by A1—be equally bad for the agent? In fact it is hard to see why consciousness, here, should make any difference.[16]

There are just two things that distinguish Phenumb's case from that of an animal, in fact (on the assumption that A1 and A2 are true). The first is that Phenumb has higher-order *beliefs* about (or knowledge of) the existence of his first-order desires, and their frustration, whereas by hypothesis an animal does not. The second is that Phenumb has higher-order *preferences* between, and evaluations of the significance of, his first-order desires, whereas again an animal will not. So we need to consider whether either of these differences can be used to block the inference from the fact that sympathy is appropriate for Phenumb, to the conclusion that it can be appropriate for the desire-frustrations of an animal. (And recall from section 2.3 above that desire-frustration can be characterized in an entirely first-order way.)

It is very hard to see how it could be the presence of a higher-order belief, in the case of Phenumb, that makes sympathy for his desire-frustrations appropriate. What is bad for Phenumb, surely, is that his desire is co-active with the knowledge that the object of his desire hasn't been achieved. It doesn't seem relevant that he knows that this was his goal—i.e. that he has a higher-order belief about his own state of desire. For what gets frustrated is the first-order desire. Of course, in the normal case, the presence of the higher-order belief may be sufficient to cause the feelings of disappointment that are normally consequent on the frustration of a desire. But we have already shown that it isn't these that are relevant. Once we have taken the phenomenology of desire-frustration out of the picture, in fact, it becomes plain that the first-person badness of desire-frustration has nothing to do with the fact that the agent *believes* that he has that desire, and so comes to believe that a desire of his has been frustrated. The badness consists in the frustration, not the higher-order belief.[17]

---

[16] Note that consciousness *may* make all the difference if the question is whether sympathy is morally *demanded* of us. For it may be that consciousness is a necessary condition of full moral personhood, and that only moral persons (and those of the same species as moral persons) can morally *command* our sympathy in and of their own right—see my 1992b, chs. 5–7. This is not to the point here. The issue in the text is whether non-conscious frustrations of desire count as psychological harms *from the perspective of a sympathetic observer*. So what is at issue is, at most, whether such frustrations are *possible* objects of sympathy, not whether sympathy for them is morally *required* of us.

[17] Of course it might be maintained that what is relevant for sympathy is a higher-order belief and first-order frustrated-desire *pair*. But it is very hard to see what could motivate such a view.

It is more plausible that it might be Phenumb's possession of second-order desires or preferences that makes the relevant difference. For this at least is something conative as opposed to cognitive. But consider an ordinary case where someone's first-order and second-order desires are in conflict. Suppose that Mary is trying to give up smoking and wants very much (first-order) to have a cigarette right now while also wishing (second-order) that this desire should not be satisfied. It is surely appropriate that one might feel sympathy for Mary's unsatisfied first-order craving. But we have already established that what makes this sympathy appropriate cannot be the *phenomenology* of first-order desire-frustration. And in this case it plainly cannot be the frustration of any second-order desire that might warrant our sympathy, because Mary has no such desire. So all that is left is that it is the bare first-order frustration that forms the object of our sympathy. And then we get a conclusion that will transfer to the case of animals.

## 4. CONCLUSIONS

If my assumptions A3 and A4 are granted, then the main point is (at least tentatively) established: the most basic form of psychological harm, from the perspective of a sympathetic observer, consists in the known or believed frustration of first-order desires (which need not require that agents have knowledge that they *have* those desires—just knowledge of what states of affairs have come about). That is to say, the answer to Q3 is (b). So the proper object of sympathy, when we sympathize with what has happened to an agent, is the known (or believed) frustration of first-order desire. And it follows, then, that the desires of non-human animals (which are non-conscious given A1 and A2) are at least *possible*, or *appropriate*, objects of moral sympathy and concern. (Whether they *should* then be objects of such concern is a further—distinctively moral—question, to be answered by considerations pertaining to ethical theory rather than to philosophical psychology.)[18] And it emerges that the complete absence of phenomenology from the lives of most non-human animals, derived in C1, is of little or no direct relevance to ethics.

What emerges from the discussions of this chapter is that we may easily fall prey to a cognitive illusion when considering the question of the harmfulness to an agent of non-conscious frustrations of desire. In fact, it is essentially the *same* cognitive illusion that makes it difficult for people to accept an account of mental-state consciousness that withholds conscious mental states from non-human animals. In both cases the illusion arises because we cannot consciously

[18] For my own hedged-about-negative (or heavily qualified positive) answer, see my 1992b, ch. 7.

imagine a mental state that is *un*conscious and lacking any phenomenology. When we imagine the mental states of non-human animals we are necessarily led to imagine states that are phenomenological; this leads us to assert (falsely, if C1 is true) that if non-human animals have any mental states at all (as they surely do), then their mental states must be phenomenological ones. In the same way, when we try to allow the thought of non-phenomenological frustrations of desire to engage our sympathy we initially fail, precisely because any state that we can imagine, to form the content of the sympathy, is necessarily phenomenological; this leads us (again falsely, if the arguments of this paper have been sound), to assert that if non-human animals *do* have only non-conscious mental states, then their states must be lacking in moral significance.

In both cases what goes wrong is that we mistake what is an essential feature of (conscious) *imagination* for something else—an essential feature of its *objects*, in the one case (hence claiming that animal mental states must be phenomenological); or for a necessary condition of the appropriateness of activities that normally *employ* imagination, in the other case (hence claiming that sympathy for non-conscious frustrations is necessarily *in*appropriate). Once these illusions have been eradicated, we see that there is nothing to stand in the way of the belief that the mental states of non-human animals are non-conscious ones, lacking in phenomenology. And we see that this conclusion is perfectly consistent with according full moral standing to the sufferings and disappointments of non-human animals.

# CHAPTER 10

# Suffering without Subjectivity

This chapter argues that it is possible for suffering to occur in the absence of phenomenal consciousness—in the absence of a certain sort of experiential *subjectivity*, that is. ('Phenomenal' consciousness is the property that some mental states possess, when it is *like* something to undergo them, or when they have subjective *feels*, or possess *qualia*.) So even if theories of phenomenal consciousness that would withhold such consciousness from most species of non-human animal are correct, this needn't mean that those animals don't suffer, and aren't appropriate objects of sympathy and concern.

## 1. INTRODUCTION

What sense can be made of the idea of *suffering*—pain and/or grief and disappointed desire—in the absence of phenomenal consciousness? More generally, can we understand the idea of a subjective harm whose harmfulness doesn't consist in or involve the subject's possession of phenomenally conscious mental states? (By a 'subjective' harm I mean an event whose harmfulness in one way or another derives from its causal impact upon the subject's ongoing mental life, as opposed to such things as objective damage to health, or the merely objective frustration of desire. I shall say more about this below.)

I have argued in Chapter 9 that the most basic kind of subjective harm is the first-order (non-phenomenal) frustration of desire. The fundamental form of harm, on this view, consists in the co-activation within a creature's practical reasoning system of a first-order desire together with the first-order belief that the state of affairs that is the object of the desire doesn't obtain. (Example: an animal that currently wants to drink, and believes that it isn't presently drinking.) The argument to this conclusion deployed two lemmas: first, that the harm of unpleasant sensations like pain consists, not in the sensation itself, but in the frustration of the subject's desire to be rid of that sensation; and second, that a creature that experienced no felt disappointment when its desires were frustrated would still be an appropriate object of sympathy and concern. Each of these two lemmas is controversial, and would be resisted by many. And the sort of harm in question is an extremely *thin* one, being confined to the bare frustration of desire, independent of any resulting emotion of disappointment.

The goal of the present chapter is to find an alternative route to the same overall conclusion. (The conclusion, namely, that there could well be subjective harms in the absence of phenomenal consciousness, sufficient to warrant sympathy.) But our focus, here, will be on harms like pain and grief that certainly deserve to be described as kinds of *suffering*. I shall be arguing that we can make sense of the idea that suffering, too, can occur in the absence of phenomenal consciousness.

These questions are of theoretical interest in their own right. For what is at issue is the way in which subjective harms and the appropriate objects of sympathy should properly be understood and characterized. But our questions also possess some practical bite. This is because there are theories of the nature of phenomenal consciousness that might withhold phenomenal consciousness from many species of non-human animal, as we shall see in the section that follows. Before we come on to that, however, something more needs to be said to delimit our overall target: subjective harm.

There is a perfectly respectable sense in which plants can be harmed, of course. Lack of water or sunshine will generally harm them, as will the application of a herbicide to their foliage. While it can be appropriate to feel a kind of *concern* at harms resulting to a plant (if one cares about the plant's health and flourishing) it would seem that *sympathy* is out of place here. While people do sometimes express sympathy for harm done to a plant ('Oh, you poor thing, your leaves are all withered!'), this seems most plausibly interpreted as mere anthropomorphic whimsy. Only a being that is a subject of mental states is an appropriate object of sympathy, surely. I propose to say, then, that a subjective harm is a harm that has some sort of impact upon the mental life of a subject.[1]

What *sort* of impact must something have on the mental life of a subject in order to count as a subjective harm, however? Here we can distinguish two possibilities: causal and a-causal. On the causal account, subjective harms are events that either cause a creature's goals to be subjectively frustrated (this is the thin sense of 'harm' at issue in Chapter 9), or that in one way or another cause a creature to *suffer*, either by causing it pain, or by causing it to undergo negative emotional states such as terror, grief, or disappointment. On the a-causal account, the mere fact that the things that an animal desires don't occur (as a matter of objective fact and independently of the animal's beliefs) is sufficient to constitute harm. Thus many have claimed that what one might call 'objective frustrations of desire' are a species of harm (Feinberg, 1977; Nagel, 1979). On this view, I am harmed if my wife cheats on me behind my back, for example, even if I never know and nothing in our

---

[1] Animals and humans can *also* be harmed in the same physical/biological sense that is applicable to plants, of course. Animals, too, can be deprived of what is necessary for normal growth, health, and physical flourishing. But such harms will, almost inevitably, have an impact on the animal's mental life as well. A sick animal—in contrast with a sickly plant—is generally a suffering animal, or an animal that cannot achieve some of the things that it wants, either now or in the future. When we feel sympathy at an animal's sickness, it is really these further effects that we have in mind, I suggest.

relationship ever suffers as a result. For my desire that she should be faithful to me has not, as a matter of fact, been fulfilled (even if I continue to believe that it has).

This is a debate that I don't propose to enter into here, important as it is for our understanding of the appropriate objects of sympathy. One reason is that I have discussed it at some length elsewhere (Carruthers, 1992b, and Chapter 9 of the present volume), arguing that only things that in one way or another have a negative impact on a creature's mental life (whether directly or indirectly, immediately or in the long run) should count as harm. But more importantly, if we were to opt for the a-causal construal of harm and the appropriate objects of sympathy, then our question about the implications of an absence of phenomenal consciousness for sympathy would immediately be foreclosed. For even if a creature lacks phenomenally conscious mental states, provided that it nevertheless has desires, then those desires will be capable of being objectively frustrated. And then it would be appropriate to feel sympathy for the frustrated desires of an animal, whether or not that animal is ever phenomenally conscious.

In what follows I propose to take for granted that subjective harm to an animal requires some sort of causal impact upon that animal's mental life, because making such an assumption is necessary to get my topic started. If this assumption should prove false, then that will just mean that there is yet another reason for thinking that sympathy for animals in the absence of phenomenal consciousness can be appropriate, that is all. More narrowly, I shall be assuming that harm to a subject (in the sense relevant to sympathy and moral concern) means causing the subject to *suffer*. My question is whether there can be states of suffering that aren't phenomenally conscious ones; and if there can, whether creatures that possess such states are appropriate objects of sympathy.

## 2. HIGHER-ORDER THEORIES OF PHENOMENAL CONSCIOUSNESS

Representationalist theories claim that phenomenal consciousness can and should be reductively explained in terms of some or other form of *access* consciousness. (An intentional state is access-conscious when it is available to, or is having the right kinds of impact upon, other mental states of the subject of the required sort; see Block, 1995.) *First-order* theories of the kind defended by Dretske (1995) and Tye (1995, 2000) claim that phenomenal consciousness consists in a certain sort of intentional content (*analog*, or *non-conceptual*)[2] being available to the

---

[2] *Analog* content is intentional content that is more fine-grained than any concepts we could possess (think of the fine shades of color that we can distinguish, but not remember), even if it is nevertheless imbued with, or shaped by, concepts. *Non-conceptual* content is intentional content that is not only fine-grained but independent of, and prior to, concept-deployment. See my 2000, ch. 5, for discussion.

belief-forming and decision-making systems of the creature in question. Some higher-order theories claim, in contrast, that phenomenal consciousness consists in the targeting of analog first-order perceptual states by *higher-order* states— either by higher-order thoughts (Rosenthal, 1997), or by higher-order experiences (Lycan, 1996).

In the version of higher-order account developed and defended by Carruthers (2000), perceptual states (and more generally, all states with analog content such as mental images, bodily sensations, and emotions) become phenomenally conscious when they are available to a faculty of higher-order thought that is capable of framing beliefs about those very states. Because of such availability, and in virtue of the truth of some or other version of 'consumer semantics', the states in question acquire a dual analog content. (All forms of consumer semantics claim that the intentional content of a state depends, in part, on what the 'downstream' systems that consume the state are capable of doing with it or inferring from it. Teleo-semantics is one form of consumer semantics; see Millikan, 1984, 1989; Papineau, 1987, 1993. Functional or inferential role semantics is another; see Loar, 1981; Block, 1986; McGinn, 1989; Peacocke, 1992.) Thus one and the same percept is *both* an analog representation with the content *red*, say, *and* an analog representation of *seeming red* or *experience of red*.[3]

Carruthers (2000) claims that such an account is warranted, because it can successfully explain all of the various supposedly puzzling features of phenomenal consciousness. Briefly (and by way of motivation for the discussion that follows), the account can explain how phenomenally conscious experiences have a *subjective aspect* to them; this is their higher-order analog content. These higher-order contents are the *mode of presentation of* our own experiences to us, rendering the latter subjective in something like the way that worldly properties acquire a subjective dimension via the modes of presentation inherent in our first-order perceptual contents.

The account can also explain how phenomenally conscious experiences can be available to us for introspective recognition, since their higher-order contents will present them to us in much the same sort of way that our first-order perceptions present to us a world of colors and shapes. And it can explain how we can come to have *purely* recognitional concepts of our phenomenally conscious experiences. These will be recognitional concepts grounded in the higher-order analog contents of our experiences, similar to the way that first-order recognitional concepts of color, say, are grounded in the first-order analog content of perception, only without any of the surrounding beliefs about the mechanisms by means of which such

---

[3] Note the awkwardness that we face, here and throughout this chapter, in having to describe intentional contents that are analog and/or non-conceptual in character using non-analog (or 'digital') concepts like *red* or *experience of red*. Although an analog content can't be *expressed* in language, however (in the way that a propositional/conceptual content can), it can still be talked about and referred to.

recognitions are effected. Moreover, the account can explain why phenomenally conscious properties should seem especially *ineffable*. For when we deploy purely recognitional concepts of them they cannot be further described, and—unlike public colors and textures—they cannot be exhibited to others. And it also explains why there should seem to be a pervasive *explanatory gap* between the higher-order account itself and the qualities of our phenomenal experiences—again, the blame falls squarely on our purely recognitional concepts. (See Carruthers, 2000, and Chapter 6 of the present volume for extended discussion.)

If some or other first-order account of phenomenal consciousness is correct, then this kind of consciousness will be widespread in the animal kingdom, and will perhaps even be present in insects (Tye, 1997). If the above form of higher-order account is acceptable, in contrast, then it seems unlikely that many animals besides ourselves will count as undergoing phenomenally conscious experiences. It is still hotly debated whether chimpanzees are capable of higher-order thought, for example, and powerful arguments can be adduced to the contrary (Povinelli, 2000). And if chimpanzees *aren't* so capable, then probably *no* animals besides ourselves are phenomenally conscious if a higher-order thought account of phenomenal consciousness is correct. I should stress, however, that I have no axe to grind here. If chimpanzees or other animals should turn out to have higher-order thoughts, then all well and good; they will turn out to be phenomenally conscious also. The point is just that for a higher-order thought theorist, the capacity for phenomenal consciousness is conditional on a capacity for higher-order thinking; and the latter capacity is unlikely to be widespread amongst non-human animals.

This is the background theoretical framework that gives the practical bite to our question whether suffering is possible without phenomenal consciousness. For on the answer to this question might turn the appropriateness of sympathy for non-human animals. I should emphasize that my goal in the present chapter isn't to *defend* a higher-order account of phenomenal consciousness, however. It is rather to explore what room might be left by such an account for forms of suffering that aren't phenomenally conscious in character.

## 3. EXPLAINING COLOR EXPERIENCE

My goal over the next four sections will be to approach the question whether pains that aren't phenomenally conscious might nevertheless be appropriate objects of sympathy and concern. In this discussion I shall set to one side the suggestion (made in Chapter 9) that what really makes pain bad is the subject's frustrated desire to be rid of the pain. So we may as well assume that pains are somehow intrinsically aversive, from the perspective of the subject. I need to approach my goal in stages, however, beginning with discussion of a more neutral case: that of color perception.

To a first approximation, color percepts are analog first-order representations of the surface properties of distal objects. Such perceptual states are analog in the sense of being fine-grained—our perceptions of color are characteristically much finer grained, admitting of many more distinctions amongst hues, than any concepts that we can form and recall. This is widely, if not universally, agreed upon.[4] But quite how the intentional content of our color perceptions should be characterized is very much in dispute. On the sort of externalist view championed by Tye (1995), color percepts are analog representations of the physical reflectance-determining properties of surfaces. However, it is also possible to defend an internalist account, according to which the content of the percept is to be characterized in abstraction from its normal worldly causes, as well as one that is non-reductive, where we would characterize the content of a percept of red, say, by saying that it represents *this* property (exhibiting a red surface).[5]

These disputes needn't detain us here. For present purposes, the point is just that there is nothing in the notion of a color percept, thus characterized, that requires such perceptions to be intrinsically phenomenally conscious. This is all to the good, since there is widespread evidence of non-conscious visual perceptions in general, and of non-conscious color perceptions in particular (Milner and Goodale, 1995; Weiskrantz, 1997). And of course a first-order theorist, too, will want to allow for the possibility of color percepts that aren't phenomenally conscious, where these would be representations with the right sort of analog content, but that aren't available to the required kinds of belief-forming and decision-making processes. Similarly, a higher-order theorist such as myself will claim that color percepts are only phenomenally conscious when they are non-inferentially available to a faculty of higher-order thought, and hence acquire at the same time a higher-order analog content of *seeming color* (Carruthers, 2000).

Many mammals and birds are capable of color perception, of course. But according to higher-order accounts of phenomenal consciousness, their percepts of color are unlikely to be phenomenally conscious ones. For if animals lack a capacity for higher-order thought, then their color percepts won't (of course) be *available to* higher-order thought. And consequently those percepts won't possess a dual analog content (e.g. both analog *red* and analog *seeming red*) in the way that our human color percepts do. What is it *like* to undergo a non-conscious perception of red? In the relevant sense, it isn't *like* anything. Nor, of course, can we reflectively *imagine* such a color percept. For any image that we form in this

---

[4] For the competing views, see on the one side Bermúdez, 1995, Tye, 1995, 2000, Carruthers, 2000, and Kelly, 2001; and on the other side McDowell, 1994.

[5] For discussion of these and other options, see my 2000, ch. 5.

way will itself be phenomenally conscious, and hence will be quite inappropriate for representing the content of the animal's experience.[6]

Color percepts that aren't phenomenally conscious will nevertheless have many of the same causal roles as color percepts that are, on a higher-order account. Thus a fruit-eating monkey might reach out for a particular piece of fruit because she *sees* that the fruit is red, *believes* that red fruit of that type is ripe, and *desires* to eat ripe fruit. Nothing here requires that the percept of red in question should be a phenomenally conscious one. Percepts of color that are merely first-order and non-phenomenal can perfectly well figure in many normal processes of belief formation and practical reasoning. And indeed, while a human in the same situation *would* enjoy a phenomenally conscious experience of red, it won't normally be *because* it is phenomenally conscious that the person acts as she does—that is, it won't be the higher-order analog content *seeming red*, but rather the first-order analog content *red*, that figures in the causation of her action.[7]

The monkey chooses as she does because she has learned that redness is a sign of ripeness, and because she values ripeness. But there may well be species that are 'hard-wired' to prefer, or to shun, certain colors—like the male sticklebacks who are inflamed to rage (in the breeding season) by the sight of anything red. So there might be creatures for whom redness is intrinsically attractive, or intrinsically repellant. And of course this, too, can all take place at a purely first-order level, independent of phenomenal consciousness. There are morals here to be drawn for the case of pain, as we shall see shortly.

## 4. PAIN AS A PERCEIVED SECONDARY QUALITY OF THE BODY

Tye (1995) argues that feelings of pain are best understood on the model of color perception, but in this case as percepts of secondary qualities of one's own body (see also Martin, 1995; Crane, 1998). A number of considerations lend support to

---

[6] In my view, this is one of the sources of our temptation to think that animals *must*, somehow, be phenomenally conscious. For we have no idea how to imagine an experience that *isn't* phenomenally conscious. See Carruthers, 2000, and Ch. 11 of the present volume. But of course imagination is a notoriously fallible guide to possibility. And in the present case we have to hand an explanation of *why* reflective/conscious imagination should be of no use in representing the perceptual states of non-human animals, given that those states are non-conscious ones. (Note that I can allow that non-conscious images are possible, and that such images would be of the right sort for representing non-conscious experiences. But we can't form and direct the content of such images at will, in such a way as to provide ourselves with an answer to the question of what the non-phenomenally conscious experiences of an animal might be like.)

[7] See Ch. 11 for extended defense of these claims. All that we need for present purposes is that they *make sense*, and that they are *permitted by* a higher-order thought-theory of phenomenal consciousness. For recall that our goal is just to explore what room *might* be left by such higher-order theories for non-phenomenal forms of suffering.

this sort of view. One is that pains are experienced as intrinsically located in space, in something like the way that colors are. Colors are generally perceived as located in particular positions in space, on the surfaces of surrounding objects. (Sometimes they can be perceived as 'free floating', independent of any perceived object, as when one has a red after-image. But even in these cases colors are experienced as being external to oneself, even if one knows that they aren't.) In a similar way, pains are perceived as located in one's own body—either within it, or on a region of its surface. Just as color percepts seem to have something like the content, '*That* [analog] property covers *that* region of that object', so pain percepts seem to have a content along the lines of, '*That* [analog] property is located in/on *that* region of my body.'

Another supporting consideration is that the sub-personal processes that generate pain sensations have just the same sort of constructive, interpretative character as one finds in connection with perception generally (Ramachandran and Blakeslee, 1998). This is demonstrated by, among other things, the fact that phantom-limb pains can be made to disappear by providing people with appropriate visual feedback. For example, a patient whose phantom hand was locked into a fist, with the nails felt as digging painfully into the palm, was temporarily cured by inserting his good hand—initially also closed in a fist—into a box divided by a mirror, arranging himself so that his phantom was *felt as* positioned in the place represented by the mirror-image of his good hand. When he opened his real hand, and so by looking at the reflection watched 'both' his hands open, the patient also *felt* his phantom hand opening, and the pain disappeared (Ramachandran *et al.*, 1995).

In claiming that pains *should* be understood as secondary qualities of the body, I am not saying that they are understood in this way by our common-sense psychology. One significant difference between pain and vision, for example, is that we ordinary folk have a proto-theory of the mechanisms that mediate vision. (We know that what we see depends upon the direction of our gaze, and that seeing requires light, for example.) In contrast, we have very little idea of how experiences of pain are caused. Partly for this reason, and partly because pains aren't intersubjectively available in the way that colors are, we don't have much use for the idea of an unfelt pain, in the way that we are perfectly comfortable with the idea of unperceived colors. Likewise we speak of 'having' or 'feeling' our pains, rather than perceiving them; whereas we talk about perceiving, rather than 'having', colors. And so on. None of this alters the fact that pain experiences are representational, however, nor the fact that such experiences are very similar in their structure and their type of content to color experiences. Both involve analog representations of a certain sort of secondary quality, distributed over a particular region of space.[8]

---

[8] I should stress that what is in question here is the character of our *experience* of pain, not the character of our *concept* of pain. There is no doubt that our folk concept of pain works rather differently from our concept of color. Consider cases of hallucination, for example. We say that people suffering

Given such a construal of pain experiences (as perceptions of secondary qualities of the body) then essentially the same range of options open up regarding their phenomenally conscious status. A first-order theorist such as Tye (1995) will say that all pain perceptions are phenomenally conscious, provided that they are available to the belief-forming and decision-making processes of the creature in question. My sort of higher-order theorist will say, in contrast, that pain perceptions are only phenomenally conscious when they are available to a higher-order thought faculty, and hence acquire a dual analog content (Carruthers, 2000). On this latter view, a feeling of pain is only phenomenally conscious when it acquires the higher-order analog content *feeling of pain* (in addition to the first-order analog content *pain*), in just the same way that a perception of red is only phenomenally conscious when it acquires the higher-order analog content *experience of red* in addition to the first-order analog content *red*. And it is the higher-order analog content that confers on the states in question their distinctive subjective aspect, and gives them the kinds of qualia or *feel* required for phenomenal consciousness.[9]

## 5. THE AVERSIVENESS OF PAIN

A great many kinds of non-human animal will be capable of feeling pain, of course, in the sense of perceiving the relevant quality as located in some specific region of their body. But on a higher-order account, it could well be the case that no animals except human beings undergo pains that are phenomenally conscious. Since it is possible that humans are unique in possessing a faculty of higher-order thought, it may be that we are the only creatures to undergo perceptual states with dual analog content, whether those states are percepts of color or of pain. But none of this seems relevant to the aversiveness—the awfulness—of pain. For animals plainly find their pains aversive; and it may be that such aversiveness is intrinsic to the perception of those states. In the way that some animals might be wired up to find certain colors intrinsically aversive or attractive (when perceived), so it may be that all animals are wired up to find the pains that they feel intrinsically aversive.

phantom limb pains are still—and are genuinely—in pain; whereas when someone hallucinates the presence of a pink elephant we say that they aren't really seeing anything pink. Thus our concept of pain seems to tie pains themselves to the experience of pain, in a way that our concept of color doesn't tie colors to our experience of color (Aydede and Güzeldere, 2005). Yet is it perfectly consistent with these differences that the experiential states in question should share essentially the same sort of character—they both have just the same sorts of spatially-locating secondary-quality-representing intentional contents, indeed.

[9] Pain-states that aren't phenomenally conscious are still *felt*, of course. This is just to say that the pain (the secondary quality of the body) is perceived. But pains that are felt can nevertheless lack *feel* in the quasi-technical philosophical sense of possessing the distinctive sort of subjectivity that constitutes a mental state as a phenomenally conscious one.

It should be emphasized that terms like 'aversive' and 'awful', here, can be given a fully cognitive (in the sense of 'mentalistic') characterization. To say that animals find their pain-properties awful, isn't just to say that they tend to *behave* in such a way as to avoid or ameliorate those properties. Rather, it is to say that animals very much *want* their pains to go away. Only a theory like that of Searle (1992)—which ties the very notions of 'belief' and 'desire' to a capacity for phenomenal consciousness—would need to deny this (on the assumption that animals lack states that are phenomenally conscious). And there are, in any case, many good reasons for thinking Searlean theories to be false, which we needn't pause to detail here. (In brief: non-phenomenal uses of 'belief' and 'desire' are *rife* throughout cognitive science.) So there are good reasons to allow that many non-human animals can be subjects of belief and desire, even if higher-order thought accounts of phenomenal consciousness are correct. Indeed, there is a case for thinking that beliefs and desires are *very* widely distributed throughout the animal kingdom, being possessed even by ants, bees, and other navigating insects (Tye, 1997, and the present volume, Chapter 12).

It should also be stressed that there is nothing tacitly higher-order involved when we say that animals *find their pains to be awful*. Granted, *to find* X *to be* Y might involve coming to *believe* that X is Y, in general. And so if an animal finds its own pains awful, we can allow that it must *believe* that its pains are awful. So it has a belief *about* its pain. But this isn't a higher-order belief, any more than beliefs about colors are higher-order. What the animal finds to be awful is the property that its perceptual state represents as being present in some region of its body (the pain), not its own perception of that property. And the animal's corresponding belief concerns that represented property, rather than its own state of *representing* that property. In short, the intentional object of the *awfulness* attribution is pain itself (when perceived), not the perception of pain.

So there seems nothing to prevent animals from finding their pains awful, even if their pain experiences aren't phenomenally conscious ones. Just as importantly, the awfulness of pain for human beings is unlikely to have anything much to do with its phenomenally conscious properties, on this account. What causes us to think and behave as we do when we are in pain will be the first-order perception of a secondary quality of the body, just as happens in other animals. The difference is merely that, because of the availability of the states in question to a faculty of higher-order thought, those states will *also* have acquired a higher-order analog content, paralleling and representing their first-order analog contents. But it is the first-order content that will carry the intrinsic awfulness of pain, if intrinsically awful it is.

One way of seeing this point is to reflect that the very same intentional law, or nomic generalization, will apply to both humans and other animals, even given the truth of a higher-order account of phenomenal consciousness. The generalization will be something along the lines of this:

> When perceiving a state of that sort (pain) as occurring in its body, the subject is strongly motivated to do things that might remove or minimize the property perceived.

This lawlike generalization is entirely first-order in character, and can remain true and applicable even when the perceptual state in question (the feeling of pain) *also* possesses a higher-order analog content. Another way of seeing the same point is to notice that, from the perspective of a higher-order theory of phenomenal consciousness, it is likely that a subject who is undergoing a phenomenally conscious pain would *still* have behaved in many of the same ways even if the state in question *hadn't* been phenomenally conscious (e.g. because the subject had failed to possess, or had lost, its capacity for higher-order thought).

Reflecting on the phenomenology of our own pain perceptions is yet another way of appreciating that it is the first-order content of pain-states that carry their intrinsic awfulness. Suppose that you have just been stung by a bee while walking barefoot across the grass, and that you are feeling an intense sharp pain between two of your toes. How would you characterize what it is that you want to cease, or to go away, in such a case? A naïve subject would surely say, 'I want *that* to go away [gesturing towards their foot, meaning to indicate the pain].' What is wanted is that *that property*—the one that you feel between your toes—should cease. The object of your desire, and the focus of your attention, is the property that is *represented* as being present in your foot, not the mental state of *representing* that property. And this would have been the very same even if your pain-state had lacked a higher-order analog content, and hence hadn't been a phenomenally conscious one (for a higher-order theorist).

Of course, a more sophisticated subject who knows about pain receptors, and who knows that analgesics work by blocking the signals generated by those receptors from reaching the brain, might say, 'I don't care whether you get rid of *that* [pointing to her foot and meaning to indicate the pain perceived], what I want is that you should get rid of the *feeling* of pain.' And this would indeed be a second-order judgment, comparable to saying that I want you to remove, not the redness of an object, but my *perception* of the redness. But this surely isn't the basic case. In the basic case, the object of aversion is the pain represented. And such aversions can be entirely first-order in character.

The awfulness of pain on this account, then, has nothing much to do with its phenomenally conscious properties. What is found awful is that the relevant secondary quality (pain) is perceived as occurring in one's body, and this can be a purely first-order (non-phenomenally-conscious) affair. Feelings of pain are perceptual states that we share with many other animals, who seem to find the properties perceived just as aversive as we do. Of course, here as in the case of color, we have no idea how to *imagine* what a pain might be like that isn't phenomenally conscious. Any pain that we reflectively imagine is *ipso facto* going to be a phenomenally conscious one. But given the right theoretical background, this needn't prevent us from recognizing that non-phenomenally conscious pains exist (indeed, are extremely common, if the pains of all non-human animals have this status). Nor should it prevent us from recognizing that non-phenomenally conscious pains are experienced as awful in essentially the same sort of way that we experience our own pains as awful.

## 6. FIRST-ORDER PAIN-STATES AS APPROPRIATE OBJECTS OF SYMPATHY

Given that pains that aren't phenomenally conscious are nevertheless found awful by those who possess them, it is prima facie plausible that the subjects of such pains are appropriate objects of sympathy and concern, despite the absence of phenomenal consciousness from their lives.[10] But is it really so obvious that pain-states that aren't phenomenally conscious are appropriate objects of sympathy, however? And how is such an intuition to be grounded? For doesn't Carruthers (1989) rely on the contrary intuition when arguing that non-conscious pains *aren't* appropriate objects of sympathy? Is there really anything more here than a clash of equally unwarranted intuitions?

Carruthers (1989) imagines the case of Mary, who is unusual in that she only ever has pains in her legs that are non-conscious. These pains cause her to rub the offended part, and in severe cases to scream and cry out, but all without any *conscious* awareness of pain on her part. It is suggested that these pains aren't appropriate objects of sympathy and concern, largely because Mary herself isn't bothered by them—she may find it inconvenient when she can't walk properly on a broken ankle (and we may feel sympathy for her inconvenience), but she isn't consciously distressed by her pains, and she doesn't seek our assistance (other than physical assistance) or sympathy.

The example of Mary goes much further than is appropriate as a test of the question whether pains that aren't phenomenally conscious are appropriate objects of sympathy, however. This is because Mary's reactions to her broken ankle don't appear to be cognitively mediated ones—i.e. they aren't mediated by her beliefs and desires, but are in some sense purely behavioral. (She appears not even to know that she *has* a pain in her ankle, except by inference from her own

---

[10] Whether we are *required* to feel sympathy for (or otherwise to take account of) the pains of non-human animals, however, is another, and in my view distinctively moral, question. It is a question that needs to be answered by considerations of moral theory rather than philosophical psychology. See my 1992b, chs. 2–7.

behavior.) Or at any rate, if her reactions *are* cognitively mediated, we can say that the cognitions in question aren't available in anything like the normal way to inform speech and to guide practical reasoning.

We can set Carruthers (1989) a dilemma, in fact. *Either* Mary's behavior isn't cognitively mediated, in which case, whatever it is that is causing her behavior, it isn't a state that intrinsically gives rise to *aversion* (i.e. to a desire that the represented property should cease). But in that case what causes her behavior isn't *pain* in the sense that we are discussing. *Or* Mary's behavior *is* cognitively mediated by a representation of a pain-property in her ankle together with an aversion to the presence of that property. But these states are unusual in not being available to inform her speech (e.g. leading her to say, 'There is a pain in my ankle'—note, *not* a second-order statement), nor to guide her practical reasoning (e.g. leading her to seek help in satisfying her desire for the pain to cease). But on this horn of the dilemma, we have no reason to trust Mary's own assessment of her situation. For if Mary *does* have a strong desire for her pain to cease, but something is blocking the expression of this desire in speech and action, then she surely *is* an appropriate object of sympathy.

The real point (and what really grounds the claim that pain-states that aren't phenomenally conscious can be appropriate objects of sympathy) is that there is good reason to think that *in our own case* it is the first-order property represented (the pain) that is the object of aversion, not the mental state of representing that property (the perception of the pain). The aversiveness of pain in our own case is primarily a first-order affair. So if sympathy is appropriate for our own pains, it is equally appropriate in the case of pain-states that aren't accompanied by higher-order analog contents representing that the pain in question is being perceived. Hence sympathy is equally appropriate in connection with states that aren't phenomenally conscious, given a higher-order thought account of phenomenal consciousness.

I have been arguing that there can perfectly well be aversive pain-states that aren't phenomenally conscious, and that such states are nevertheless appropriate objects of sympathy. But some philosophers will be inclined to object that the very *idea* of a pain-state that isn't phenomenally conscious makes no sense. They will insist that the idea of *pain* is the idea of a state with a certain distinctive introspectible *feel* to it. So a state that lacked *feel* (that wasn't phenomenally conscious) just couldn't be a pain. But equally, of course, philosophers were once inclined to object just as strongly to the idea of a non-conscious visual percept. Yet the last twenty years of psychological research has now convinced most of us that the idea of non-conscious visual experience does make sense after all.

The more general point is that there can be states that are similar to phenomenally conscious visual experiences, or similar to phenomenally conscious pains, in almost all respects *except* that of possessing an introspectible *feel*. In particular, there can be states that possess just the same sorts of (first-order) intentional contents, and that have many of the same functional roles, as their phenomenally conscious counterparts.[11] In which case it is surely well motivated to treat them as states of the same mental kind. Anyone is free to stipulate that the term 'pain', or the term 'visual percept', should be reserved for states that are phenomenally conscious, of course. But in that case all of our discussion could be couched in terms of states that are in other respects *similar to* pains, or *similar to* visual percepts. And then just the same issues would arise, concerning whether these pain-*like* states are appropriate objects of sympathy and concern.

## 7. EMOTION AS INVOLVING SOMASENSORY PERCEPTION

I have argued that, in the case of bodily pain at least, there can be suffering without subjectivity. But what of the forms of suffering characteristic of negative emotional states like grief? And can there be feelings of frustration without phenomenal consciousness? For example, can a creature experience *disappointment* at a lost opportunity for mating or predating without undergoing mental states that are phenomenally conscious ones? And can a creature feel anything like grief at the loss of a partner or offspring in the absence of such consciousness? I propose now (in this section and the one following) to sketch reasons for positive answers to these questions. Since most of the groundwork has already been laid, our discussion can be comparatively brisk.

Before we begin, however, we need to recall that our task is to investigate whether there can be forms of *suffering* that are worthy of sympathy in the absence of phenomenal consciousness, not whether sympathy might be warranted on other grounds. Chapter 9 argues that creatures whose desires are frustrated in a thinner sense than this (not involving anything naturally described as 'suffering') could be appropriate objects of sympathy—e.g. a creature that *wants* to drink but *believes* that it isn't presently drinking. Our present task is to see whether we can make sense of the idea that a creature can suffer emotionally in the absence of phenomenal consciousness, and whether such a creature would be an appropriate object of sympathy on that ground alone.

---

[11] In the case of visual experiences, what we have actually discovered is that there are *no* states that play all of the roles that common sense assigns to visual experiences; namely, leading to the formation of belief, feeding into planning in relation to the perceived environment ('I'll go *that* way'), and guiding the details of our bodily movements on-line, as well as possessing a distinctive *feel*. Rather, it turns out that there is one visual system realized in the temporal lobes that is concerned to provide inputs to conceptual thought and planning (and whose outputs are conscious), and another visual system realized in the parietal lobes that provides on-line guidance of movement, but whose outputs aren't conscious (Milner and Goodale, 1995; Clark, 2002). It seems better to say that *both* of these kinds of state are types of vision, rather than to say that neither is.

The main claim underlying a positive answer to these questions is that feelings of frustration, like feelings of pain and emotional states more generally, are best understood in terms of perceptions of secondary qualities of the body. As is now well known, emotional states like frustration, anger, and grief give rise to a variety of kinds of distinctive physical and physiological effects, such as changes in heartbeat, breathing, muscle tension, and bodily posture, as well as changes within the chemistry of the blood, such as its levels of adrenalin (Damasio, 1994; Rolls, 1999). When we are in such a state, we will be aware (via somasensory perception) of a complex bodily *gestalt*. And it is the content of this percept that gives rise to the distinctive phenomenology of emotion (Prinz, 2004).

Of course one doesn't need to know anything about hearts, or about breathing, or about bodily postures in order to experience these states of the body. One can still have analog perceptual representations of the various changes involved. And just as the contents of our color percepts take the form, '*This* surface has *this* [analog] property', and the contents of feelings of pain take the form, '*This* region of my body has *this* [analog] property', so too the contents of the somasensory percepts distinctive of emotional states take the form, '*These* regions of my body are undergoing *these* [analog] changes.' And just as pain properties are experienced as intrinsically aversive, so it may be that many of these somasensory *gestalts* are experienced as aversive or attractive.

It is important to realize that there is a sense in which the phenomenology of frustration is peripheral to the main motivational roles of desire and frustration of desire, however. When I am hungry, for example, I am in a state that is focused outwards on gaining access to and ingesting food, rather than inwards on the removal of an aversive sensation. I might sometimes feel such sensations, of course—such as a tightening of the stomach and feelings of bodily weakness— and I may believe that eating will remove them, thus providing myself with an additional motive to eat. But it is possible to desire food without ever experiencing such feelings. (Rats, for example, will work for food even if they have never experienced hunger. See Dickinson and Balleine, 2000.) And such feelings plainly aren't, in any case, the *primary* motivation to eat—the *desire to eat* itself provides that.

Similarly (to take a different example), when I drive to the airport to collect a loved one, my goal is to be in the presence of the loved person once again, rather than to remove some unpleasant feeling or sensation. And the disappointment that I feel when her flight is cancelled (the sinking in my stomach, the tightening in my chest, and so forth), consists in a set of states *caused by* the frustration of my desire, rather than being constitutive of it.

What, then, is the role of somasensory feeling in our lives if these feelings aren't part-and-parcel of desiring as such? According to the model of human practical reasoning proposed and elaborated by Damasio (1994), we continually monitor our bodily states via somasensory perception while contemplating envisaged options and outcomes. The thought of a fearful event makes us a bit afraid, and thinking about the loss of a loved one makes us somewhat bereft. We sense the resulting changes in ourselves, and use these as cues to the desirability or otherwise of the envisaged state of affairs. In effect, the functional role of these somasensory percepts (whether positive or aversive) lies in the mental rehearsal of action, rather than primarily in action itself.[12]

Given the correctness of some such account as this, it seems unlikely that the aversiveness of disappointment is as 'primitive' and widespread within the animal kingdom as is the aversion to pain. For as we noted above, the most basic kinds of desire-based and emotion-based attraction and aversion are directed outwards to objects and states of affairs in the world, rather than towards properties of our own bodies. A creature that is afraid of a nearby predator, say, has an aversion to remaining in the presence of the fearful thing. And although the creature's state of fear will give rise to a set of physiological changes, one wouldn't necessarily expect the animal's perceptions of these changes to be aversive in their own right. For why would this be needed, given that the animal *already* has an aversion to the fearful object? Somasensory properties probably only began to be aversive or attractive in and of themselves when animals started to engage in mental rehearsal of various sorts. For they would then have needed some way of determining the desirability or otherwise of an envisaged scenario. And it would appear, from the human case at least, that the monitoring of somasensory responses is what emerged as the solution to this problem.

While the aversiveness of some emotional states is probably by no means universal amongst animals, it may still be quite widespread amongst mammals, at least. For there is good reason to think that mental rehearsal isn't unique to humans. For example, much of the evidence that has been cited (controversially) in support of the higher-order thought abilities of chimpanzees can also be used (much *less* controversially) to support the claim that this species of great ape, at least, engages in mental rehearsal. For example: a subordinate ape knows the location of some food hidden within an enclosure, and from previous experience expects to be followed by a dominant who will then take the food. So the subordinate heads off in another direction and begins to dig. When the dominant pushes her aside and takes over the spot, she doubles back and retrieves and quickly eats the food.

Such examples are generally discussed as providing evidence that chimps can engage in genuine (higher-order thought involving) *deception*—that is, as showing that the subordinate chimp is intending to induce a false belief in the

---

[12] Of course, many of the bodily changes that we perceive will themselves have functional roles relevant to action. Consider, for example, the collection of changes constitutive of the 'flight-or-fight' response.

mind of another (Byrne and Whiten, 1988; Byrne, 1995)—whereas critics have responded that chimpanzees may just be very smart behaviorists (Smith, 1996; Povinelli, 2000). But either way, it seems that the chimp must engage in mental rehearsal, predicting the effects of walking in the wrong direction and beginning to dig (the dominant will follow and take over the digging), and discerning the opportunities for hunger-satisfaction that will then be afforded.

The suffering that arises from desire-frustration, then, and that is involved in other similar sorts of negative emotional state such as grief and terror, lies in the somasensory perception of a distinctive bodily *gestalt*, which is caused by the state in question, and which is experienced as aversive or intrinsically unwelcome. The question, now, is whether such suffering can exist in the absence of phenomenal consciousness.

## 8. THE HARM OF FELT FRUSTRATION WITHOUT PHENOMENAL CONSCIOUSNESS

Notice that the results of somasensory monitoring to produce bodily *gestalts*, just like percepts of pain, are first-order analog representations of secondary qualities of the body. So on any higher-order approach to phenomenal consciousness, such states won't be intrinsically phenomenally conscious ones. On the contrary, according to my own account, it will only be in cases where those states are available to a higher-order thought faculty capable of entertaining thoughts about those very states, that the percepts in question will acquire a dual analog content (both first-order and higher-order), and will hence come to have the kind of subjectivity that is distinctive of phenomenal consciousness.

Moreover (and again like percepts of pain) it seems likely that the causal roles of bodily *gestalts* (and particularly their aversiveness) are attached to their first-order, rather than to their higher-order, contents. It is the perception of increased heart-rate, dry mouth, and so forth distinctive of fear that is aversive in the first instance. Such states would very likely have been aversive prior to the evolution of a higher-order thought faculty if (as seems plausible) mental rehearsal was also available earlier. And they seem likely to remain aversive in the absence of such a mechanism (e.g. in severe autism).[13]

Thus there may well be animals that are capable of experiencing grief, for example, in the absence of phenomenal consciousness. These animals will perceive in themselves a complex bodily *gestalt* (physical lassitude and so forth) caused by the knowledge that a mate or infant is dead or lost, say. And they will

---

[13] Autism admits of a very wide spectrum of severity, of course, and not all autistic people are wholly lacking in a capacity for higher-order thought.

experience this bodily state as intrinsically aversive. But all of this can be purely first-order in character. The feelings, and the aversion to their objects, can exist in the absence of a capacity for higher-order thought, and so without the states in question having the dual-level analog content distinctive of phenomenal consciousness. And insofar as we realize that this is so, it seems perfectly appropriate to feel sympathy for the animal's state, even if we cannot imagine what such a state might be like.[14]

Of course, some philosophers will wish to object (as they did in the case of pain) that they can make no sense of the idea of states of disappointment, or of grief, that aren't phenomenally conscious ones. But the reply is essentially the same, too. People can give whatever stipulative definitions they want. But then the same issues can be raised concerning states that are in many respects *similar to* the targets in question (disappointment, grief). And it seems undeniable, moreover, that such states *can* exist, and very probably *do* exist given the correctness of some or other higher-order account of phenomenal consciousness.

## 9. CONCLUSION: SUFFERING WITHOUT SUBJECTIVITY

The conclusion of this chapter is the one that I advertised at the beginning: even if the pains and disappointments experienced by non-human animals are never phenomenally conscious, they can still be appropriate objects of sympathy and concern. In the relevant sense, there can be suffering without subjectivity. I want to emphasize, however, that the conclusion isn't (yet) that concern for the sufferings of non-human animals is morally required of us. That is a distinctively moral question, to be answered via considerations of moral theory (see my 1992b, chs. 1–7). All that has been established here is that sufferings that aren't phenomenally conscious can be *appropriate* objects of sympathy, not that such sympathy is morally mandatory. I also want to emphasize that the assumptions made (and sometimes sketchily defended) in the course of this paper (e.g. a higher-order thought account of phenomenal consciousness, and secondary-quality accounts of pain and disappointment) are for the most part just that: assumptions. My goal has only been to demonstrate that suffering without subjectivity is *possible*, or *makes sense*; not to show that it is ever actual.

---

[14] Here, as in the case of pain, any attempt at reflective imagination aimed at answering our own question will inevitably involve images that are phenomenally conscious, and hence inappropriate to represent the mental state of the animal.

# CHAPTER 11

# Why the Question of Animal Consciousness Might not Matter Very Much

According to higher-order thought accounts of phenomenal consciousness (e.g. Carruthers, 2000) it is unlikely that many non-human animals undergo phenomenally conscious experiences. Many people believe that this result would have deep and far-reaching consequences. More specifically, they believe that the absence of phenomenal consciousness from the rest of the animal kingdom must mark a radical and theoretically significant divide between ourselves and other animals, with important implications for comparative psychology. I shall argue that this belief is mistaken. Since phenomenal consciousness might be *almost* epiphenomenal in its functioning within human cognition, its absence in animals may signify only relatively trivial differences in cognitive architecture. Our temptation to think otherwise arises partly as a side-effect of imaginative identification with animal experiences, and partly from mistaken beliefs concerning the aspects of common-sense psychology that carry the main explanatory burden, whether applied to humans or to non-human animals.

## 1. INTRODUCTION

As is now familiar, a number of distinct kinds of consciousness can be distinguished (Rosenthal, 1986; Block, 1995; Lycan, 1996), and in many of these senses it isn't problematic that consciousness should be attributed to animals. Many animals are sometimes conscious (awake as opposed to asleep or comatose); and many animals are conscious *of* things in their environment. (Even insects perceive things and believe things, I would argue; see Tye, 1997, and Chapter 12 of the present volume.) But our concern, here, is with *phenomenal* consciousness. Phenomenally conscious states are states that are *like something* to undergo; they are states with a distinctive subjective *feel* or phenomenology; and they are states that each of us can immediately recognize in ourselves, 'straight off', without having to engage in any kind of self-interpretative inference. And in addition, phenomenal consciousness is supposed to constitute the 'hard problem' for cognitive science to explain (Chalmers, 1996).

Not everyone agrees that the problem is all that hard, however. Representationalist theories, in particular, claim that phenomenal consciousness can be reductively explained in terms of some combination of intentional content and functional role. *First-order* theories of the sort defended by Dretske (1995) and Tye (1995, 2000) claim that phenomenal consciousness consists in a certain sort of intentional content (*analog*, or *non-conceptual*)[1] being available to the belief-forming and decision-making systems of the creature in question. Higher-order theories claim, in contrast, that phenomenal consciousness consists in the targeting of analog first-order perceptual states by *higher-order* states—either by higher-order thoughts (Rosenthal, 1997), or by higher-order percepts (Lycan, 1996).

In the version of higher-order thought account developed and defended by Carruthers (2000), perceptual states (and more generally, all states with analog content such as images and emotions) become phenomenally conscious when they are available to a faculty of higher-order thought (HOT), which is capable of framing beliefs about those very states. Because of such availability, and in virtue of the truth of some or other version of 'consumer semantics',[2] the states in question acquire a dual analog content. One and the same percept is *both* an analog representation of *green*, say, *and* an analog representation of *seeming green* or *experience of green*. And it is claimed that such an account can successfully explain all of the various supposedly puzzling features of phenomenal consciousness.[3]

---

[1] *Analog* content is intentional content that is more fine-grained than any concepts we could possess (think of the fine shades of color that we can distinguish, but not remember), even if it is nevertheless imbued with, or shaped by, concepts. *Non-conceptual* content is intentional content that is not only fine-grained but independent of, and prior to, concept-deployment. See Carruthers (2000, ch. 5) for discussion.

[2] All forms of consumer semantics claim that the intentional content of a state depends, in part, on what the 'down-stream' systems that consume the state are capable of doing with it or inferring from it. Teleo-semantics is one form of consumer semantics (Millikan, 1984, 1989; Papineau, 1987, 1993). Functional or inferential role semantics is another (Loar, 1981; Block, 1986; McGinn, 1989; Peacocke, 1992).

[3] *Inter alia* the account can explain: how phenomenally conscious experiences have a *subjective aspect* to them (their higher-order analog content); how they can be available to us for introspective recognition (their higher-order contents will present them to us in much the same sort of way that our first-order perceptions present to us a world of colors and shapes); how we can come to have *purely* recognitional concepts of our phenomenally conscious experiences (these will be recognitional concepts grounded in the higher-order analog contents of our experiences, in something like the way that first-order recognitional concepts of color, say, are grounded in the first-order analog content of perception, only without any of the surrounding beliefs about the mechanisms by means of which such recognitions are effected); why phenomenally conscious properties should seem especially *ineffable* (when we deploy purely recognitional concepts of them they cannot be further described, and—unlike public colors and textures—they cannot be exhibited to others); and why there should seem to be a pervasive *explanatory gap* between the higher-order account itself and the qualities of our phenomenal experiences (again, the blame falls squarely on our purely recognitional concepts). See Carruthers (2000) and Ch. 6 of the present volume for extended discussion.

If some or other first-order account of phenomenal consciousness is correct, then such a form of consciousness will be widespread in the animal kingdom, and will perhaps even be present in insects (Tye, 1997). If some form of higher-order thought account is correct, in contrast, then it seems unlikely that many animals besides ourselves will count as undergoing phenomenally conscious experiences. It is still hotly debated whether chimpanzees are capable of higher-order thought, for example, and powerful arguments can be adduced to the contrary (Povinelli, 2000). And if chimpanzees aren't so capable, then probably *no* animals besides ourselves are phenomenally conscious, according to a higher-order theorist. I should stress, however, that I have no axe to grind here. If chimpanzees (or dolphins, or whatever) should turn out to have higher-order thoughts, then all well and good—they will turn out to be phenomenally conscious also. The point is just that for a higher-order thought theorist, the capacity for phenomenal consciousness is conditional on a capacity for higher-order thinking; and the latter capacity is unlikely to be widespread amongst non-human animals.

In what ways do these debates about phenomenal consciousness matter? Obviously they are of deep theoretical significance. For what is at issue is how best to solve the 'hard problem' of consciousness. But do they matter practically, for our treatment of non-human animals? And do they matter for psychology, having a bearing on the extent to which we can see continuities between the mental processes of ourselves and other animals? I claim not, in response to both of these questions. Although the issue of animal consciousness might be of deep importance for those of us trying to construct reductive theories of phenomenal consciousness, it has little bearing on anything else of significance.

Some people will resist the conclusion that most non-human animals lack phenomenally conscious states, on the grounds that this must then mean that the lives and sufferings of such animals are of no direct moral importance. Believing that the sufferings of a dog, or a cat, or a chicken are deserving of our sympathy and moral concern, such people will reject accounts of phenomenal consciousness that (they think) suggest otherwise. However, while it may *seem* inevitable that it can't be appropriate to feel sympathy for creatures that are incapable of phenomenal consciousness, this may just be because we have a difficult time imagining pains and disappointments that aren't phenomenally conscious ones. Indeed, it is arguable that the moral landscape can remain unchanged, no matter whether first-order or higher-order accounts of phenomenal consciousness should turn out to be correct.

I have developed these points at some length elsewhere (see Chapters 9 and 10 of the present volume), and so will not pursue them here. The focus of the present chapter will be entirely on the second of the questions raised above: does the thesis that non-human animals lack phenomenally conscious states have important implications for comparative psychology? I shall begin by considering the implications for common-sense psychology, turning to discuss the alleged implications for scientific psychology in later sections.

## 2. CONSCIOUSNESS AND COMMON SENSE

The thesis that few if any non-human animals are phenomenally conscious conflicts with common-sense belief, of course. Most of us believe that many of the species of animal around us enjoy phenomenally conscious experiences. But what, if anything, serves to ground this belief? It is hard to see what evidence we could have to support it. Indeed, Carruthers (2000) argues that the belief in question is merely the product of a kind of cognitive illusion (see also Chapter 9 of the present volume). Rightly believing that non-human animals are subject to perceptual states, and wondering what those states are like, we naturally represent them to ourselves in imagination 'from the inside'. But in doing so we inevitably find ourselves representing a state that has all of the features of phenomenal consciousness, because *the images* that we form have those properties. Since we have no idea how to imagine, from the inside, a perceptual state that *isn't* phenomenally conscious, the fact that we find ourselves thinking that the mental states of non-human animals must be phenomenally conscious ones is little to be wondered at.

Our belief that non-human animals enjoy phenomenally conscious states may actually be quite groundless, then. It may merely be a product of a cognitive illusion. In which case the fact that higher-order thought theories of phenomenal consciousness are in conflict with this belief won't really count against the acceptability of those theories. And it will cost us little or nothing to alter our common-sense attitudes accordingly, if one of those theories should be accepted as successful, explaining what needs to be explained about the character of our experience.

Lurz (2002) argues, however, that there is more to our attitudes towards animals than mere illusion, or the effects of over-extended imagination. He thinks that our real reason for believing that non-human animals enjoy phenomenally conscious experiences goes something like this. When we make use of our common-sense psychology, we deploy attributions of phenomenally conscious experiences to other people when explaining their behavior. And this doesn't just happen when we explain people's verbal behavior, either, or their higher-order beliefs about their own experiences. On the contrary, we also use such attributions when explaining the sorts of behavior that we share with non-human animals. When I explain why someone picked out one tomato from the vegetable rack rather than another, for example, I might believe that this happened because she was subject to a phenomenally conscious experience of the luscious red color. And when I explain why someone froze in fear when meeting a grizzly bear in the woods, I might believe that this happened because she had a phenomenally conscious perception of the bear's ferocious aspect.

Similarly, then, when explaining why an animal picks out one object rather than another when foraging, or when explaining an animal's fear when confronting a predator—I should attribute phenomenally conscious experiences to the animal to do the explanatory work. And then I have much the same sort of reason to ascribe phenomenally conscious states to animals as I have for attributing them to other people. And a theory of phenomenal consciousness that required us to think otherwise would be deeply revisionary of our folk-psychological practice. Or so Lurz (2002) argues.

There is another kind of illusion at work here, however, which one might call 'the *in virtue of* illusion'. Granted, when someone picks out a tomato by its colour, she will generally have a phenomenally conscious experience of red. But it is another matter to claim that she chooses as she does *in virtue of* the phenomenally conscious properties of her experience. While we cite experiences that are, *de facto*, phenomenally conscious ones when explaining other people's behavior, it is quite another matter to believe that phenomenal consciousness plays any essential role in those explanations. Indeed, this is just what a higher-order theorist should deny. And doing so doesn't force any deep revision of folk psychology. It just requires us to be somewhat clearer about the properties in virtue of which our explanations are successful.

It isn't just common-sense practice that is vulnerable to the *in virtue of* illusion, either. The sorts of functional-role accounts of phenomenal consciousness constructed by psychologists can run into the same problem. Consider the 'global workspace' model of consciousness proposed by Baars (1988, 1997), for example. On this account, phenomenally conscious mental events serve the function of broadcasting their contents to a wide range of other cognitive systems. And it is indeed true that phenomenally conscious events in humans are *de facto* widely available. However, it is another matter to claim that those events are thus available *in virtue of* being phenomenally conscious; and a higher-order thought theorist will deny that this is so. On the contrary, animals lacking a capacity for higher-order thought may well have states that are globally broadcast. And such states only come to have the distinctive properties of phenomenal consciousness when embedded in an architecture that contains, in addition, a faculty of higher-order thought to which those states are available.

All of this requires some setting up to become convincing, however. In what follows I shall first present and discuss the 'dual visual systems' hypothesis of Milner and Goodale (1995). I shall then use this as a springboard from which to explain the *in virtue of* illusion, before discussing a couple of case-studies from the comparative psychology literature. I shall then close by considering the implications of two different accounts of our faculty of higher-order thought. The overall conclusion will be as advertised: very little of significance turns on the question whether or not non-human animals undergo phenomenally conscious experiences.

## 3. DUAL VISUAL SYSTEMS AND PHENOMENAL CONSCIOUSNESS

According to Milner and Goodale (1995), the human mind/brain contains two visual systems that are functionally and anatomically distinct; and indeed, there is now a wealth of evidence that this is so (Jacob and Jeannerod, 2003). The dorsal system is located in the parietal lobes and is concerned with the online detailed guidance of movement. The ventral system is located in the temporal lobes and serves to underpin conceptual thought and planning in relation to the perceived environment. Each receives its primary input from area V1 at the posterior of the cortex, although the dorsal system also receives significant projections from other sites. The dorsal system operates with a set of body-centered or limb-centered spatial co-ordinates, it is fast, and it has a memory window of just two seconds. The ventral system uses allocentric or object-centered spatial co-ordinates, it is slower, and it gives rise to both medium and long-term memories. Importantly for our purposes, the outputs of the dorsal system are unconscious, while those of the ventral system are phenomenally conscious (in humans). Finally, homologous systems are widespread in the animal kingdom, being common to all mammals, at least.

On this account, the phenomenally conscious experiences that I enjoy when acting are *not* the percepts that guide the details of my movements on-line.[4] Rather, the phenomenally conscious percepts produced by the ventral system are the ones that give rise to my beliefs about my immediate environment, that ground my desires for perceived items ('I want *that* one'), and that figure in my plans in respect of my environment ('I'll go *that* way and pick up *that* one'). But my planning only guides my actions indirectly, by selecting from amongst a database of action schemata. The latter then directly cause my movements, with the detailed execution of those movements being guided by the percepts generated by the dorsal system. The basic two-systems arrangement is depicted in Figure 11.1.

---

[4] This is already enough to show us that common sense is vulnerable to the *in virtue of* illusion, since ordinary folk surely believe that the precise movements of my hand and fingers when I grasp a cup occur as they do in virtue of the phenomenally conscious experiences that I undergo at the time. But according to the dual visual systems hypothesis, this isn't so. Those movements are guided by the outputs of the dorsal system, which aren't conscious ones (although the *planning* and *monitoring* of the action is informed by the outputs of the ventral system, which *are* conscious).

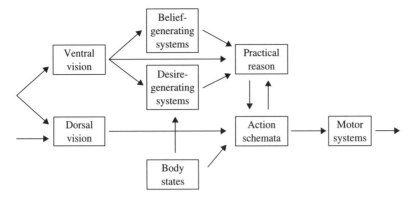

FIG 11.1 A mind with dual-visual systems (but lacking a HOT faculty).

The dual visual systems hypothesis provides the grounds for one of the main arguments against first-order accounts of phenomenal consciousness (of the sort defended by Dretske, 1995, and Tye, 1995), and in support of some sort of higher-order approach (Carruthers, 2000). For looking just at the architecture depicted in Figure 11.1, it is quite mysterious why the outputs of the dorsal system should be unconscious while those of the ventral system are conscious. Both generate analog intentional contents that represent the world as being a certain way to us. Admittedly, only the outputs of the ventral system are available for belief-formation and planning. But it remains unclear why this should make a difference. Why should such availability serve to confer on those (and only those) visual percepts a dimension of *subjectivity*?[5]

A version of higher-order thought theory can provide the necessary explanation, in contrast (Carruthers, 2000, and Chapter 6 of the present volume). Consciousness results because the ventral percepts are *also* available to a faculty of higher-order thought (HOT), as depicted in Figure 11.2. By virtue of their availability to higher-order thought (and because of the truth of some or other version of consumer semantics), the perceptual outputs of the ventral system acquire a *dual* analog intentional content. At the same time as representing (in analog fashion) worldly redness, greenness, and so on, they *also* represent *seeming* redness, *experienced* greenness, and so forth (also analog), thus acquiring their distinctive subjective aspect.

For our purposes here, the point to stress is that a Figure 11.1 architecture might be quite widespread in the animal kingdom. It may be common to all animals that are capable of thought, but that lack a faculty of higher-order thought (hence being

---

[5] See Ch. 6 of the present volume for extended development of the argument against first-order theories sketched here.

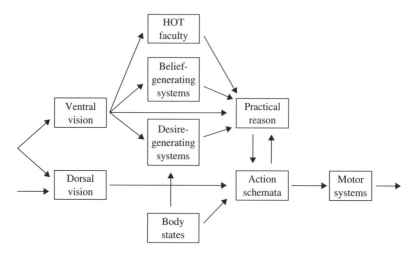

FIG 11.2 A mind with dual-visual systems and possessing a HOT faculty.

incapable of phenomenal consciousness, for a higher-order theorist). In fact, the addition of a HOT faculty to the basic mammalian cognitive architecture might be the only relevant difference between ourselves and other animals.[6] In which case the correct explanation for the behavior that we share with other animals will be exactly the same—this will be behavior underpinned by first-order perceptual contents. The fact that those perceptual states *also* happen to be phenomenally conscious ones in the case of humans will be irrelevant to the explanation.

Consider the human who selects a tomato from the vegetable rack because of its luscious red color, then; and consider a monkey or any other fruit-eating color-sighted mammal making a similar choice. Although the experience of the human is phenomenally conscious, whereas the experience of the monkey probably isn't (according to a higher-order thought account), the explanations for their respective actions can be (and is) exactly the same. Each chooses as she does because she *sees* the luscious red color of the fruit, and judges in consequence that the fruit is ripe. The content of the *seeing* here, in so far as it is relevant to the explanation of the action, is entirely first-order in character. It is because the human sees the redness of the surface of the tomato (and hence enjoys a first-order analog content representing worldly redness), *not* because her percept also has the higher-order analog content *seeming redness*, that she chooses as she does.[7] Likewise with the monkey.

[6] Of course humans are also distinctive in possessing a language faculty, but this isn't relevant to issues concerned with phenomenal consciousness, I claim. See Carruthers, 2000, ch. 10.

[7] Let me stress that according to my sort of dual-content account of phenomenal consciousness, it is one and the same perceptual state that has *both* the first-order analog content *red* and the higher-order analog content *seems red*. So when the human chooses as she does, her choice is actually caused by a phenomenally conscious mental state. But her choice isn't caused *in virtue of* the phenomenally conscious status of that state (i.e. in virtue of the content *seems red*), but rather in virtue of its first-order content.

What determines explanatory relevance, in general? And what makes it the case that the first-order analog content *red*, rather than the higher-order analog content *seeming red*, is what explains the human's behavior? The answer is that genuine explanations fall under laws, or nomic generalizations; and they should also generate true counterfactuals. The relevant psychological generalization, in this case, is surely something like this:

> Seeing a red fruit, and believing that redness is a sign of ripeness, and wanting ripe fruit, one will choose the red one.

The acts of both human and monkey fall under this first-order intentional law; and it is reasonable to believe that if the redness of the tomato had *not* been perceived, then neither human nor monkey would have acted as she did. In contrast, it seems reasonable to suppose that even if the human's percept had *lacked* the higher-order analog content *seeming red* (perhaps because the human had lacked a higher-order thought faculty), she would still have chosen and acted just as she did.[8]

Recall Lurz's (2002) argument. Since we explain the actions of humans by attributing phenomenally conscious experiences to them, and since non-human animals perform many of the same actions, he says that we have good reasons for believing that such animals, too, undergo phenomenally conscious experiences. The error in the argument is now plain to see. Granted, I explain the actions of a human by attributing to her experiences that are, *de facto*, phenomenally conscious ones. But on a higher-order thought account of phenomenal consciousness, their phenomenally conscious status will actually play no explanatory role (in most cases, at least; see below). Rather, the explanatory burden is carried by the purely first-order, not necessarily phenomenally conscious, character of those states. And these are just the sorts of perceptual states that non-human animals can share. So the cross-species explanations can be the very same, just as Lurz claims, but consistent with the truth of a higher-order theory that withholds phenomenal consciousness from most species of animal.

Similar points can now be made in respect of Baars' (1988, 1997) 'global work-space model' of phenomenal consciousness. Granted, the phenomenally

---

[8] We don't have any theory-independent evidence for the truth of this counterfactual, of course. To the extent that it is warranted, it is supported by (a) the two visual systems hypothesis, together with (b) the reasons that there are for accepting the dispositional higher-order thought account of phenomenal consciousness. Note, however, that if both of these assumptions are granted, and it is also true that autism is characterized by an incapacity for higher-order thought (Baron-Cohen, 1995), then an autistic person selecting a fruit on the basis of its color will be a true instance of the counterfactual—this would be a case of someone lacking phenomenally conscious experiences, whose choices are nevertheless guided by color information, just as ours are. (But of course we can't verify that this is so by *asking* the autistic person whether or not they are phenomenally blind; for lacking a capacity for higher-order thought, they will be incapable of understanding the question. And note, too, that autism is a syndrome admitting of a wide spectrum of degrees and kinds of severity, so any claim about the absence of phenomenal consciousness in autism would in any case have to be suitably nuanced.)

conscious outputs of ventral vision, in Figure 11.2, are available to a wide range of cognitive systems (belief-generating systems, memory systems, desire-generating systems, and practical reasoning). But on a higher-order thought account it isn't by virtue of being so available that those outputs are phenomenally conscious. On the contrary, the outputs of the ventral visual system in other mammals, too, will be almost as widely available (see Figure 11.1). But because they aren't available to a higher-order thought faculty, they will lack a dimension of subjectivity, and so will fail to be phenomenally conscious.

Is phenomenal consciousness epiphenomenal, then? Do phenomenally conscious properties play *no* role in explaining human actions? Of course not. Phenomenal consciousness is intrinsically involved when we think *about* our experiences, as such, or when we *describe* our experiences to others. And phenomenal consciousness is implicated whenever we draw a distinction between the way things *are* and the way they *seem* or *appear*. So phenomenally conscious properties will have a genuine explanatory role whenever our actions manifest higher-order thought about our experiences, or whenever they depend upon the distinction between *is* and *seems*. But there is no argument from this to the phenomenal consciousness of non-human animals. For if such animals are incapable of higher-order thought, then by hypothesis they won't be engaging in the relevant behavior either.

The upshot of this section is that very little of significance for comparative psychology need follow from the fact that phenomenal consciousness is denied to many non-human animals by higher-order thought theories of consciousness. All types of first-order experience, first-order cognitive state, and first-order cognitive process can be shared across (many) species, and can be common to humans and other animals. The only predicted differences would concern thoughts and behavior that in one way or another depend upon higher-order thought processes. Certainly there is no radical Cartesian divide here, between genuinely minded humans and mere mindless automatons, or anything of that sort. On the contrary, non-human animals can be full subjects of (first-order) mindedness (see also Chapter 12 of the present volume).

I shall now reinforce and elaborate upon these points by discussing two case-studies: one concerning blindsight in monkeys, and the other concerning alleged meta-cognitive behavior in other species besides ourselves.

## 4. CASE-STUDY (1): BLINDSIGHT IN MONKEYS

One of the things that can be explained within the framework of the two visual systems hypothesis is the striking phenomenon of *blindsight*. As is now familiar to most, these are cases involving people who have had a region of the primary visual projection area, V1, damaged, and who consequently become blind in a portion of their visual field (at least as regards conscious experience). While they are aware of seeing nothing within that region, however, they prove remarkably good at *guessing* the orientation of an illuminated grating, at tracing the movement of a light across a screen within their blind field, or at reaching out to grasp an object on their blind side (Weiskrantz, 1986, 1997; Marcel, 1998).

The explanation of these findings is as follows. Besides the main projection from the retina to V1 (via the lateral geniculate nucleus in the thalamus), there is also a substantial, and phylogenetically older, projection to the superior colliculus in the mid-brain. (In fact this sub-cortical pathway alone is as large as the whole of the auditory nerve.) And from the superior colliculus there are substantial projections, not only to motor and pre-motor neurons in the brainstem and spinal cord, but also to the parietal cortex, which is the hypothesized site of the dorsal pathway (charged with the control of movement). Yet there are no projections to the temporal cortex, which is the hypothesized site of the ventral system (and which is intimately connected with conscious experience). So even with cortical area V1 completely removed, substantial quantities of visual information should be available in parietal cortex for the control of movement.[9]

Now, it has been known for some time that monkeys who have had area V1 of visual cortex surgically removed are nevertheless capable of a range of visual discriminations, and a range of visually-guided actions. But what Cowie and Stoerig have shown is that the results are analogous to human blindsight, at least in the sense that stimuli in the blind field are judged by the monkey not to be present (Cowie and Stoerig, 1995; Stoerig and Cowie, 1997). A monkey with one half of area V1 missing can be trained, first, to press a button following a warning tone if a light does *not* illuminate on a screen presented to her sighted field. When a light or a bright moving stimulus is then presented to her blind field, she presses for 'not seen', thus indicating that she lacks awareness of the stimulus—and this despite it being one that she can be shown to discriminate in other conditions.

Does the discovery of blindsight in monkeys show that monkey visual experiences are, normally, phenomenally conscious? Many people seem to assume so. For, like Dretske (1995), they use evidence of the residual capacities of blindsighted monkeys when speculating about the function that phenomenal consciousness may have. They assume that blindsighted monkeys must have lost whatever blindsighted humans have lost, and therefore that normally sighted monkeys must be phenomenally conscious, given that blindsighted humans

---

[9] How, then, does such information enable patients, not only to point and grasp appropriately, but also to answer questions concerning the orientation of a grating? Milner and Goodale (1995) suggest that such patients may be influenced by subtle behavioral and motor-programming cues of which they lack conscious awareness, e.g. to begin tracing out the line of orientation of the grating with a hand or with the eyes.

have lost their capacity for phenomenally conscious visual experience. But this is a mistake. Despite the common presence of (at least) two functionally distinct visual pathways in monkeys and humans, there are other differences between the species that may be sufficient to make a difference in phenomenal consciousness. In particular, humans exemplify the architecture depicted in Figure 11.2, whereas monkeys (probably) only exemplify the architecture of Figure 11.1.[10]

The point is that when monkeys press the key for 'not seen' they are, more strictly, only signaling that *a light* isn't present in front of them. There isn't really any reason for claiming that they are making a higher-order comment on their lack of *awareness* of a light. And conversely, when a monkey omits to press a key because a light *is* seen, it is strictly only expressing a judgment that a light is present, not that it is currently *experiencing* a light. So there is nothing in the data that can't be explained in purely first-order terms, by deploying the architecture shown in Figure 11.1. And so from the perspective of a higher-order thought account of phenomenal consciousness, too, there is nothing in the data to suggest that monkeys are, normally, phenomenally conscious.

## 5. CASE-STUDY (2): META-COGNITIVE PROCESSES IN ANIMALS?

One of the morals of our discussion so far has been that the denial of consciousness to animals needn't imply any sort of Cartesian divide between humans and the rest of the animal kingdom; and nor, therefore, need it have significant consequences for comparative psychology. In the present section I shall argue that the cognitive divide between humans and other animals might be even smaller than might appear thus far. For even processes of thinking and reasoning in humans that we are strongly disposed to describe in meta-cognitive terms (that is, in such a way as to involve higher-order thought, and hence phenomenal consciousness where those processes also involve experiential states), may actually be so described erroneously. The underlying thought processes may really be first-order ones, shared with other animals. They may merely be given a meta-cognitive gloss by the human self-interpretation system (our higher-order thought faculty).

Consider some of the evidence of uncertainty monitoring in other species of animal, recently discussed at length by Smith *et al.* (2003). The authors show how some animals in a state of uncertainty in a forced-choice situation (the pattern is dense/the pattern isn't dense; the tone is a high one/the tone isn't high) will choose adaptively in favor of some third alternative when given the chance

---

[10] Let me reiterate that I have no axe to grind here. I am happy to let the facts concerning higher-order thought in monkeys and apes fall where they may.

(e.g. opting to move on to another trial without a time-out). They show how the response profiles of monkeys and dolphins in such circumstances closely parallel those of humans (even displaying similar degrees of individual variation in strategy). And they note that in these sorts of situations humans will explain their own behavior as resulting from their awareness of their own state of uncertainty (i.e. humans will couch their self-explanations in meta-cognitive terms). Since uncertainty behavior in humans display both higher-order thought and phenomenal consciousness, Smith *et al.* (2003) argue, it is likely that similar states are present in monkeys and dolphins in such circumstances.

Uncertainty monitoring can be explained without resort to attributions of meta-cognitive processes, however. Suppose, first, that beliefs come in *degrees*. Just as desires can be more or less strong or powerful, so something can be believed with greater or lesser confidence. This assumption is routinely made by philosophers, at least.[11] So both animals and humans in the described experimental situations will have a particular *degree* of belief that a tone is high, or that a pattern is dense, say.

Nothing meta-cognitive is required for degrees of belief and desire. Having a strong desire doesn't mean that the animal believes *of* itself that it has a desire with a certain strength. Rather, it has a desire that is apt to beat out other desires in the competition to control behavior, and which is also apt to have further cognitive and physiological effects of a distinctive sort (e.g. increased heart-rate). Equally, having a strong belief doesn't mean that the animal believes itself to have a belief with a certain high degree of warrant. Rather, the animal has a belief on which it is more likely to act, all else being equal (and especially given equal strengths of competing desires). And degrees of belief might be realized in different levels of activation in the appropriate neural network, for example.

Suppose, second, that in circumstances in which an animal has conflicting desires of roughly equal strength (to get a food pellet now; to avoid *not* getting a food pellet now—i.e. to avoid a time-out), and where it also has conflicting beliefs of equal strength (the pattern is dense; the pattern isn't dense), the animal will (a) be in a state of some anxiety, resulting in a bodily *gestalt* that will be experienced as aversive (see Chapter 10 of the present volume), and (b) will be disposed to

---

[11] Some people also claim, however, that there is a distinct kind of ungraded 'flat-out' belief, which may be dependent upon language, and which consists in an explicit *commitment* to assent to a sentence/proposition and to think and reason as if that proposition were true. These states are variously called 'opinions' or 'acceptances' and belong within so-called 'dual-process' models of human cognition (Dennett, 1978c; Cohen, 1993; Evans and Over, 1996; Frankish, 1998, 2004). Note that dual-process models imply that a capacity for *opinion* is dependent upon a capacity for higher-order thought, which is also what is responsible for phenomenal consciousness, according to higher-order theories of the latter. So creatures incapable of higher-order thought will not only lack phenomenal consciousness, but will also be incapable of opinions. And then to the extent that dual-process models are necessary and important for describing human behavior, to that extent there will be significant differences between the psychologies of humans and other animals.

engage in behavior of a sort that tends to eradicate such conflicts of belief (e.g. by attending more closely, by moving to change its angle of view by shifting its head from side to side in the way that the dolphins in the experiments reported by Smith *et al.* did, and so on). Call such a state 'an uncertainty state'.

Again, nothing meta-cognitive need be involved. A state of uncertainty is a state that is caused when the animal is equally disposed to act in two contrary ways, and which has a variety of characteristic further effects of cognitive, affective, physiological, and behavioral sorts (e.g. engaging in information-seeking behavior). And that an animal engages in behavior designed (by evolution or by learning) to elicit new information doesn't mean that the animal represents itself as lacking a sufficient degree of belief. It just means that this behavior is one that has been sculpted to issue in changed degrees of belief (changes that are apt, in turn, to diminish an aversive state of anxiety).

What is an animal to do when in a state of conflict, and when information-seeking behavior is failing to resolve that conflict? Plainly it needs some heuristic to enable it to reach a decision and move on, or (like Buridan's ass) it will remain perpetually frozen. The simplest such heuristic is: *when in a state of that sort, choose at random.* It seems that this is a heuristic that many animals (and some humans) employ. A more complex heuristic is: *when in a state of that sort, opt for a less-favored third alternative if you can.* This seems to be the heuristic adopted by some monkeys, dolphins, and humans. Why is this heuristic more complex? Because it requires the animal to represent and to factor into its decision-making, not just the two alternatives between which it faces the initial choice, but also a third option. But what would explain the individual differences in the use of this heuristic? Perhaps differing degrees of risk-aversion.[12]

Once again, nothing meta-cognitive is required in order for these heuristics to operate. Granted, the animal needs to have some way of telling when it is in a state of the required sort. (That is, it needs a way of telling when it is in the uncertainty state that is the trigger for the heuristic to apply, picked out by the antecedent clauses in the conditionals above.) But this doesn't mean that the animal has to conceptualize the state *as* a state of uncertainty, or as a state in which a conflict of belief remains unresolved. Rather, it just has to have some way of reliably picking out a state that *is* a state of uncertainty. And here its continuing state of anxiety and/or its awareness of its own distinctive information-seeking behavior (e.g. its side-to-side head movements) would be sufficient.

But how is it, then, that humans will describe these situations in meta-cognitive terms if nothing meta-cognitive is involved in the decision-making process?

---

[12] Amongst human subjects, males are more likely to choose randomly when uncertain, females are more likely to opt for a new trial without any penalty (or reward). See Smith *et al.*, 2003.

One answer is that humans are chronically self-interpretative creatures, by virtue of possessing a faculty of higher-order thought. (Another weaker answer will be considered in section 6 below.) Humans will correctly conceptualize the state that they are in as one of uncertainty—i.e. as one in which they lack sufficient information to adjudicate between two conflicting beliefs. And they generally interpret themselves to be choosing as they do *because* they are *aware* that they are in a state of uncertainty. But from the fact that their explanations of their feelings and behavior are meta-cognitive, it doesn't follow that the decision-making process itself is a meta-cognitive one. And indeed, there is good reason to think that much of the self-interpretative cognition of humans is *merely* interpretative, not reflective of an underlying meta-cognitive decision-making process. (For recent reviews of the evidence, see Gazzaniga, 1998; Wilson, 2002.)

A quarter century of research, beginning with Nisbett and Wilson's seminal article (1977), has uncovered a wealth of evidence that many of our beliefs about the thought-processes that cause our own behavior are actually *confabulated*. Far from having direct access to our own reasoning and decision-making processes, what we actually do in many cases is interpret our own behavior, ascribing mental states to ourselves in much the same sort of way that we might ascribe them to another person. And where the true causes of behavior are obscure to common-sense psychology, such self-attributions will frequently be false. But we aren't aware that what we are doing is confabulating. We tend to operate with a simplified model of the mind, according to which our own thought processes are transparent to us; and so we tend to think, too, that the higher-order awareness that we report is intrinsic to the process reported on.

Consider one of the examples of confabulation described by Gazzaniga (1998). A split-brain patient gets up and begins to walk across the room because the instruction, 'Walk!' is flashed on a screen in his left visual field (hence being available only to the right hemisphere). But when asked what he is doing, the left hemisphere responds, 'I want to get a drink from the fridge.' (In most people the left hemisphere houses both the language centers, which answer the question, and the main elements of the theory of mind faculty, which generates the self-interpretation.) Although the explanation is plainly confabulated, the patient isn't aware that this is so. On the contrary, he takes himself to be acting as he does *because* he is *aware* of a desire for a drink (i.e. as a result of a meta-cognitive state). Yet the causes of his action were actually first-order ones: he got up to walk because he comprehended a written instruction to do so, delivered by a person of some authority (the experimenter).

I don't mean to be claiming, of course, that our meta-cognitive processes are entirely epiphenomenal, and have no effect on our behavior whatsoever. On the contrary, the higher-order interpretative narratives that we weave for ourselves can constrain us and guide us in various ways.[13] One constraint is provided by the desire to act consistently with the self-image that we have constructed. I would be prepared to bet, for example, that having formulated his confabulated explanation, Gazzaniga's patient did indeed go to the fridge to get a drink. Since he thinks that this is what he wants, this is what he would probably do; and the explanation becomes self-fulfilling. My point is just that much *less* of our behavior may actually be caused by conscious thought-processes than we are intuitively inclined to believe.

The moral of the discussion is as follows. Even if a higher-order thought theory of phenomenal consciousness is accepted, and in consequence phenomenally conscious experiences and conscious thought-processes are denied to most species of animal, it can still be true that there are vast swathes of behavior common to humans and other animals that can receive identical psychological explanations. The fact that humans are strongly inclined to explain their own behavior by self-ascribing *awareness* of their own perceptions or *awareness* of their own decision-making should not be allowed to mislead us. For much of this behavior will have a cognitive explanation that is purely first-order, of the sort that we can share with other animals. And once again, the overall moral is that a higher-order thought theory of phenomenal consciousness turns out to have many fewer implications for comparative psychology than you might initially have been inclined to think.

## 6. TWO MODELS OF THE HOT FACULTY

It might be objected that we have moved too hastily from the evidence that humans *sometimes* confabulate when explaining their own behavior to the claim that human reasoning and decision-making processes will *generally* be inaccessible to, and uninfluenced by, higher-order thought. And indeed, such a move is too hasty. There are two different models of the way in which our higher-order thought faculty is embedded into the architecture of our cognition, and connected with other systems, which carry different implications on just this point. It is worth briefly sketching these models, and articulating some reasons for preferring one to the other of them. For on this question will turn the extent of the cognitive differences that we should expect to find between ourselves and those animals that lack a capacity for higher-order thought.

On one model—that has been implicitly assumed up to now, and is the one represented in Figure 11.2—the higher-order thought faculty only has direct access to perceptual (and to quasi-perceptual, e.g. to imagistic or emotional) states.

---

[13] This is one of the insights that is developed by 'dual-process' models of human reasoning and decision-making processes, discussed briefly in fn. 11 above.

The explanation is the standard one given in the cognitive science literature, namely, that the faculty in question evolved for purposes of predicting and explaining (and hence also manipulating) the behavior of other people (Byrne and Whiten, 1988, 1998). This required it to have access to perceptual input. The directing of this faculty upon oneself to explain one's own behavior, in contrast, is a secondary phenomenon, not under independent selection. Hence, while the higher-order thought faculty might have access to stored information (e.g. about someone's previous actions) when constructing its representations, it has no access to the inferential *processes* that generate that information. Call this model, 'the mind-reading model', since it conceives the function of the higher-order thought faculty to be that of attributing mental states to others (and only derivatively to oneself).

The mind-reading model needn't claim that the higher-order thought faculty has *no* access to the inferential processes that take place within the subject, of course. But that access will be limited to processes that in one way or another implicate sensory representations. For example, if some of our thinking is conducted consciously in imaged natural-language sentences, in 'inner speech', as Carruthers (1996) claims, then those processes of thinking will be both phenomenally conscious and available to higher-order thought. Indeed, the mind-reading model can mesh successfully with 'dual process' theories of human cognition (already mentioned in fn. 11), and with accounts like that of Dennett (1991), according to which there is a level of language-dependent mentality (the 'Joycean machine') which is imbued with higher-order thinking. For these processes, involving states that are quasi-perceptual in character, can be made available to higher-order thought in just the same way that perceptual contents are.

The alternative model—that might as well be called 'the self-monitoring model'—claims that at least one of the functions of the higher-order thought faculty is to monitor, to intervene in, and to correct where necessary, the subject's own reasoning processes. This then requires, of course, that the faculty should have *access to* those processes, as depicted in Figure 11.3. The model might be framed in terms of one of two distinct evolutionary explanations. On the one hand it might be claimed that self-monitoring is the *primary* evolutionary function of a higher-order thought faculty—in which case we could expect to find higher-order thought in creatures that as yet lack any capacity to attribute mental states to others (this seems to be the position of Smith *et al.*, 2003). Or it might only be claimed, in contrast, that self-monitoring is an *additional* function of the higher-order thought faculty, that either evolved on the back of a prior mind-reading ability, or that co-evolved simultaneously with it (this seems to be the position of Shallice, 1988).[14]

---

[14] A third alternative is also possible. This is that there are really two distinct higher-order thought faculties, one for mind-reading and one for self-monitoring. This is the position of Nichols and Stich (2003).

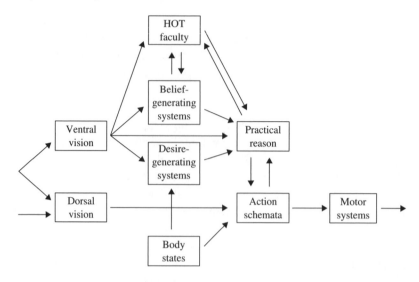

FIG 11.3 A mind with a self-monitoring HOT faculty.

The self-monitoring model needn't claim that the higher-order thought faculty has complete and infallible access to the inferential processes of the subject, of course. So the model is consistent with the confabulation evidence reviewed in section 5. (Although we are still owed a story about *which* reasoning processes are available to the self-monitoring system and which aren't.) But it will claim that *much more* of human cognition will implicate higher-order thought than would be allowed by the mind-reading model. And then one would expect to find, in consequence, *much greater* cognitive differences between humans and those animals that lack a capacity for higher-order thought than the mind-reading model would predict.

If the self-monitoring model is correct, then the thought-processes that are available to it for monitoring will be conscious ones, because they are available to higher-order thought (assuming the correctness of a dispositional higher-order thought account of consciousness, of course). But it still doesn't follow that those processes occur as they do *because of* their conscious status. For here, too, we might be subject to the 'in virtue of' illusion. It may be that many of the first-order processes that are available to higher-order thought take place in accordance with first-order laws or nomic generalizations, shared with many species of non-human animal. And general considerations having to do with the conservation of mechanisms in the process of evolution suggest that this is very likely to be so. In which case the explanations for the resulting behavior can be the same, even though the human behavior is caused by processes that are conscious while the animal behavior isn't.

It is likely that the self-monitoring model will predict *greater* differences between humans and animals in respect of their psychologies than does the mind-reading model, however. (This is why it will be worthwhile to sketch the case supporting the latter, as I shall do in a moment.) For if the access-relations between the higher-order thought faculty and the systems that generate new beliefs and new decisions evolved for purposes of trouble-shooting and improving the operations of the latter, then one might expect that rather more of the activity of those systems in the human case now implicates higher-order thought. But it will remain the case that *many* of the processes in question might be shared amongst humans and non-human animals, despite the absence (I am assuming) of higher-order thoughts from the mental lives of the latter.

The contrast between the mind-reading and self-monitoring models is a large issue for cognitive science to address, of course, and it cannot be discussed adequately here. But it is worth articulating briefly why the mind-reading model is much the more plausible of the two. For if this model is correct, then we should expect the basic psychological differences between ourselves and other animals to be fairly small.[15] But let me stress that even if it is wrong (and some version of the self-monitoring model is correct), those differences will still be far less than one might intuitively have been inclined to think. Certainly the absence of higher-order thought (and hence phenomenal consciousness, given a higher-order account of the latter) from non-human animals needn't represent any sort of radical 'Cartesian divide' between our minds and theirs.

The fundamental point is this: in the case of mind-reading, we have a highly developed competence with obvious adaptive significance. Human beings are quite remarkably good at attributing mental states to others (and to themselves), and hence at engaging in the sorts of manipulative and/or co-operative behavior whose success depends upon those attributions being accurate. And everyone agrees that this competence is part of the natural endowment of any normally developing human being. In contrast, it is far from clear that we possess any very useful competence in the domain of self-monitoring. Of course we are good at *attributing* mental states to ourselves (absent the confabulation cases), but for a mind-reading theorist this is just a matter of our turning our mind-reading abilities upon ourselves. What is in question is whether we have the sort of highly-developed capacity to monitor, trouble-shoot, intervene in, and improve

---

[15] Note that this isn't to claim that there will only be minor cognitive differences between humans and other animals *overall*. On the contrary, if some version of 'dual reasoning process' theory or Dennett's 'Joycean machine' is correct, then the overall differences might be quite large. But on these views, the higher-level processes will be *realized in* the operations of the lower-level systems that we mostly share with other animals (Frankish, 2004). The two main differences, that make the higher-level reasoning system possible, would consist in our possession of a higher-order thought faculty together with a language faculty.

upon our own reasoning processes on-line, in the way that the self-monitoring model requires.

There is little reason to think that we possess any such natural competence. Indeed, naïve subjects are quite remarkably poor at distinguishing good sequences of reasoning from bad ones, or at fixing up the latter to make them better. This isn't to say that naïve subjects are bad *at reasoning*, of course. For each of our first-order information-generating systems will have been under selection pressure for speed and reliability. And moreover, some of the heuristic reasoning processes that people employ turn out to be quite remarkably successful (Gigerenzer *et al.*, 1999). Rather, it is to say that naïve subjects are bad at reasoning *about reasoning*—at identifying mistakes in reasoning, at theorizing about standards of good reasoning, and at improving their own and others' reasoning. Yet this is precisely the competence that the self-monitoring model predicts we should have.

One of the defining features of human civilizations, in fact, is that they contain socially-transmitted bodies of belief about the ways in which one *should* reason. And these bodies of belief (such as the canons of good scientific method, developed piecemeal over the last five centuries or so) have to be laboriously acquired through processes of formal education. Insofar as we have any competence in evaluating and improving reasoning, therefore, this isn't a *natural* competence, but a socially transmitted one. Hence we have no reason to think that the architecture of our cognition is as the self-monitoring model claims, or as Figure 11.3 depicts.

## 7. CONCLUSION

I have been concerned to argue that the question of animal consciousness probably doesn't matter very much, except for those of us who are interested in the strengths and weaknesses of competing theories of consciousness. I have argued elsewhere that whether or not non-human animals are phenomenally conscious, sympathy and concern for animal suffering can still be just as appropriate (see Chapters 9 and 10 of this volume). And I have argued in the present chapter that whether or not non-human animals are phenomenally conscious, the behavior that humans and animals share can (and should) receive just the same kinds of (first-order) psychological explanation. So the question of animal consciousness matters little for psychology. As folk-psychologists, we merely need to adjust our beliefs about the properties of our mental states that carry the true explanatory burden. And scientific/comparative psychology, too, should continue to expect that many of the mental processes that are responsible for animal behavior are also responsible for our own.

# CHAPTER 12

# On Being Simple-Minded

The question 'Do fishes think?' does not exist among our applications of language, *it is not raised*. (Wittgenstein.)

The present chapter isn't directly about consciousness (neither *phenomenal* nor *state*—at least, not if any sort of higher-order account of these properties is correct). But it *is* about mindedness, and it *is* about both first-order access consciousness and creature consciousness/perceptual consciousness. (See Chapters 1 and 3, where this terminology is introduced and discussed.) I shall argue that ants and bees exemplify a simple form of belief/desire/perception psychology, sharing the same fundamental cognitive architecture as ourselves. This essay is included here partly to reinforce the arguments of Chapter 11, and partly to illustrate just how great is the distance between mindedness, on the one hand, and phenomenal consciousness, on the other. Many philosophers have assumed that they are the same thing, or are intimately connected. But phylogenetically, at least, they couldn't be further apart.

## 1. ON HAVING A MIND

How simple-minded can you be? Many philosophers would answer: no more simple than a language-using human being. Many other philosophers, and most cognitive scientists, would allow that mammals, and perhaps birds, possess minds. But few have gone to the extreme of believing that very simple organisms, such as insects, can be genuinely minded.[1] This is the ground that I propose to

---

[1] One notable philosophical exception is Tye, 1997. (Exceptions amongst cognitive scientists will be mentioned later in the chapter.) While I share some of Tye's conclusions (specifically, that honey bees have beliefs and desires), I offer different arguments. And the main focus of Tye's paper is on the question whether insects have phenomenally conscious experiences. This is quite another question from mine. Whether bees are belief/desire reasoners is one thing; whether they are phenomenally conscious is quite another. For a negative verdict on the latter issue, see Carruthers, 2000. It should also be stressed that the main question before us in this paper is quite different from the ones that formed the focus of Bennett's famous discussion of honey bee behavior (Bennett, 1964). Bennett argued that bee signaling systems aren't a genuine language, and that honey bees aren't genuinely rational in the fully-fledged sense of 'rationality' that is distinctive of human beings. (His purpose was to build towards an analysis of the latter notion.) Our concern, rather, is just with the question whether bees have beliefs and desires. (On this question, Bennett expressed no clear opinion.)

occupy and defend in the present chapter. I will argue that ants and bees, in particular, possess minds. So I will be claiming that minds can be very simple indeed.

What does it take to be a minded organism? Davidson (1975) says: you need to be an interpreter of the speech and behavior of another minded organism. Only creatures that speak, and that both interpret and are subject to interpretation, count as genuinely thinking anything at all. McDowell (1994) says: you need to exist in a space of reasons. Only creatures capable of appreciating the normative force of a reason for belief, or a reason for action, can count as *possessing* beliefs or engaging in intentional action. And Searle (1992) says: you need consciousness. Only creatures that have *conscious* beliefs and *conscious* desires can count as having beliefs or desires at all.

Such views seem to me to be ill-motivated. Granted, *humans* speak and interpret the speech of others. And granted, *humans* weigh up and evaluate reasons for belief and for action. And granted, too, humans engage in forms of thinking that have all of the hallmarks of consciousness. But there are no good reasons for insisting that these features of the human mind are necessary conditions of mindedness as such. Or so, at least, I will briefly argue now, and then take for granted as an assumption in what follows.

Common sense has little difficulty with the idea that there can be beliefs and desires that fail to meet these demanding conditions. This suggests, at least, that those conditions aren't conceptually necessary ones. Most people feel pretty comfortable in ascribing simple beliefs and desires to non-language-using creatures. They will say, for example, that a particular ape acts as she does because she *believes* that the mound contains termites and *wants* to eat them. And our willingness to entertain such thoughts seems unaffected by the extent to which we think that the animal in question can appreciate the normative implications of its own states of belief and desire. Moreover, most of us are now (post-Freud and the cognitive turn in cognitive science) entirely willing to countenance the existence of beliefs and desires that aren't conscious ones.

It isn't only ordinary folk who think that beliefs and desires can exist in the absence of the stringent requirements laid down by some philosophers. Many cognitive scientists and comparative psychologists would agree. (Although sometimes, admittedly, the *language* of 'belief' and 'desire' gets omitted in deference to the sensibilities of some philosophical audiences.) There is now a rich and extensive body of literature on the cognitive states and processes of non-human animals (e.g. Walker, 1983; Gallistel, 1990; Gould and Gould, 1994). And this literature is replete with talk of information-bearing conceptualized states that guide planning and action-selection (beliefs), as well as states that set the ends planned for and that motivate action (desires).

True enough, it can often be difficult to say quite *what* an animal believes or desires. And many of us can, on reflection, rightly be made to feel uncomfortable when using a that-clause constructed out of our human concepts to describe the thoughts of an animal. If we say of an ape that she believes *that the mound contains termites*, for example, then we can easily be made to feel awkward about so doing. For how likely is it that the ape will have the concept *termite*? Does the ape distinguish between termites and ants, for instance, while also believing that both kinds belong to the same super-ordinate category (insects)? Does the ape really believe that termites are living things which excrete and reproduce? And so on.

These considerations give rise to an argument against the very possibility of non-linguistic thought, which was initially presented by Davidson (1975). The argument claims first, that beliefs and desires are content-bearing states whose contents must be expressible in a sentential complement (a that-clause). Then second, the argument points out that it must always be inappropriate to use sentential complements that embed *our* concepts when describing the thoughts of an animal (given the absence of linguistic behavior of the appropriate sorts). In which case (putting these two premises together) it follows that animals cannot be said to have thoughts at all.

The error in this argument lies in its assumption that thought contents *must* be specifiable by means of that-clauses, however. For this amounts to the imposition of a *co-thinking constraint* on genuine thoughthood. In order for another creature (whether human or animal) to be thinking a particular thought, it would have to be the case that someone *else* should also be capable of entertaining that very thought, in such a way that it can be formulated into a that-clause. But why should we believe this? For we know that there are many thoughts— e.g. some of Einstein's thoughts, or some of the thoughts of Chomsky—that *we* may be incapable of entertaining. And why should we nevertheless think that the real existence of those thoughts is contingent upon the capacity of someone *else* to co-think them? Perhaps Einstein had some thoughts so sophisticated that there is no one else who is capable of entertaining their content.

The common-sense position is that (in addition to being formulated and co-thought from the inside, through a that-clause) thoughts can equally well be characterized *from the outside*, by means of an indirect description. In the case of the ape dipping for termites, for example, most of us would, on reflection, say something like this: we don't know how much the ape knows about termites, nor how exactly she conceptualizes them, but we do know that she believes *of* the termites in that mound that they are there, and we know that she wants to eat them. And on this matter common sense and cognitive science agree. Through careful experimentation scientists can map the boundaries of a creature's concepts, and can explore the extent of its knowledge of the things with which it deals (Bermúdez, 2003). These discoveries can then be used to provide an external characterization of the creature's beliefs and goals, even if the concepts in question are so alien to us that we couldn't co-think them with the creature in the content of a that-clause.

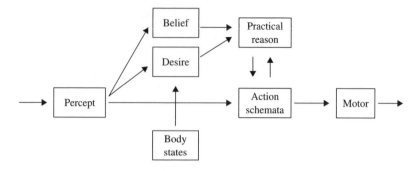

FIG 12.1 The core architecture of a mind.

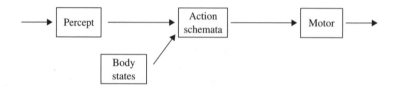

FIG 12.2 An unminded behavioral architecture.

What does it take to be a minded organism, then? We should say instead: you need to possess a certain core cognitive architecture. Having a mind means being a subject of perceptual states, where those states are used to inform a set of belief states that guide behavior,[2] and where the belief states in turn interact with a set of desire states in ways that depend upon their contents, to select from amongst an array of action schemata so as to determine the form of the behavior. This sort of belief/desire architecture is one that humans share. It is represented diagrammatically in Figure 12.1.

The crucial components of this account are the beliefs and desires. For it is unlikely that possession of perceptual states alone, where those states are used to guide a suite of innate behavioral programs or fixed-action schemata, could be sufficient for a creature to count as possessing a mind. Consider the architecture represented in Figure 12.2. The innate behavior of many mammals, birds, reptiles, and insects can be explained in such terms. The releasing factors for an innate behavior will often include both bodily states (e.g. pregnancy) and perceptual information, with the perceptual states serving to guide the

---

[2] Note that, by virtue of their availability to belief-formation and decision-making, the perceptual states in question are therefore first-order access conscious. This is the basis for Tye's (1997) claim that the perceptual states of bees are phenomenally conscious, by virtue of being so available.

detailed performance of the behavior in question, too.[3] (Consider a butterfly landing neatly on a leaf to lay her eggs.) But engaging in a suite of innately coded action patterns isn't enough to count as having a mind, even if the detailed performance of those patterns is guided by perceptual information. And nor, surely, is the situation any different if the action patterns aren't innate ones, but are, rather, acquired habits, learned through some form of conditioning.

I shall assume that it isn't enough for an organism to count as having a mind, either, that the animal in question should be merely *interpretable as* possessing beliefs and desires. For as Dennett (1987) has taught us, we can adopt what he calls 'the intentional stance' in respect of even the most rigidly pre-programmed behavior. No, the architecture represented in Figure 12.1 needs to be construed *realistically*. There needs to be a real distinction between the belief-states and the desire-states, in virtue of which they possess their distinctive causal roles (guiding and motivating action, respectively). And these states must, in addition, be both discrete, and structured in a way that reflects their semantic contents. And their detailed causal roles, too (the ways in which particular belief states and particular desire states interact) must be sensitive to those structural features.

Dennett (1991) thinks that only natural language can provide these properties. It is only with the first appearance of the *Joycean machine*—the stream of inner verbalization that occupies so much of our waking lives—that humans come to have discrete structured semantically-evaluable states, where the interactions of those states are sensitive to their structures. So although Dennett might *say* that many animals possess simple minds, all he really means is that their behavior is rich enough to make it worth our while to adopt the intentional stance towards them. But he denies that non-human animals possess minds *realistically construed*, in the way that the present chapter proposes to construe them.

To be minded means to be a thinker, then. And that means (it will hereafter be assumed) having distinct belief states and desire states that are discrete, structured, and causally efficacious in virtue of their structural properties. These are demanding conditions on mindedness. The question is: how simple can an organism be while still having states with these features?

---

[3]  Do informational states that don't interact with beliefs and desires deserve to be counted as genuine *perceptions*? Common sense suggests that they do. Ask someone whether they think that the fish *sees* the net sweeping towards it through the water and they will answer, 'Of course, because it swims deftly in such a way as to avoid it.' But ask whether the fish has *thoughts* about the net or its own impending capture, and many will express skepticism. Moreover, the 'dual systems' theory of vision (Milner and Goodale, 1995; Clark, 2002) suggests that the perceptual states that guide our own movements on-line aren't available for belief or desire formation, either. Yet we wouldn't deny, even so, that our detailed movements occur as they do because we *see* the shapes and orientations of the objects surrounding us.

## 2. MEANS/ENDS REASONING IN RATS

Dickinson and colleagues have conducted an elegant series of experiments, reported in a number of influential papers, providing evidence for the view that rats, at least, are genuine means/ends reasoners (Dickinson and Balleine, 1994, 2000; Dickinson and Shanks, 1995). They argue that rats engage in goal-directed behavior, guided by beliefs about causal contingencies, and by goals that are only linked to basic forms of motivation via learning. (We, too, have to monitor our own reactions to learn what we want; Damasio, 1994.) These arguments are convincing. But at the same time Dickinson advances a particular conception of what it takes to be a truly minded creature. The latter will need to be resisted if the position that insects have minds is to be defensible.

Here are some of the data (Dickinson and Balleine, 2000). Rats don't press a lever for food any more when hungry than when nearly satiated, *unless* they have had experience of *eating* that food when hungry. While the reward-value of the food is something that they know, the increased value that attaches to food when hungry is something that they have to learn. Similarly, rats caused to have an aversion to one food rather than another (via the injection of an emetic shortly after eating the one food but not the other) will thereafter stop performing a trained action causally paired with just that food, in the absence of feedback resulting from its actions (i.e. without receiving any rewards). However, they will do so *only* if they have been re-presented with the relevant food in the interval. They have to *learn* that they now have an aversion to the food in question. But once learned, they make appropriate decisions about which of two previously learned actions to perform—they know which action will make them sick, and choose accordingly.

Dickinson thinks that the data warrant ascribing to rats a two-tier motivational system much like our own. There is a basic level of biological drives, which fixes the reward value of experiences received. And there is an intentional level of represented goals (e.g. to eat *this* stuff rather than *that* stuff), which has to be linked up to the basic level via learning to achieve its motivating status. Others have made similar proposals to explain aspects of the human motivational system (Damasio, 1994; Rolls, 1999).

In other experiments Dickinson and colleagues have shown that rats are sensitive to the degree of causal efficacy of their actions (Dickinson and Charnock, 1985; Dickinson and Shanks, 1995). In particular, the rat's rate of action drops as the causal connection between act and outcome falls. It even turns out that rats display exactly the same *illusions* of causality as do humans. The set-up in these experiments is that the probability of an event occurring (e.g. a figure appearing on a TV monitor, for the humans) or a reward being delivered (for the rats) is actually made independent of the action to be performed (pressing the space-bar, pressing a lever), while sometimes occurring in a way that happens to be temporally paired with that action. If (but only if) the unpaired outcomes are signaled in some way (by a coincident sound, say), then both rats and humans continue to believe (and to behave) as if the connection between act and outcome were a causal one.

The conclusion drawn from these and similar studies, then, is that rats are genuine means/ends reasoners. They possess learned representations of the goals they are trying to achieve (e.g. to receive a particular type of food). And they have acquired representations of the relative causal efficacy of the actions open to them. Taken together, these representations will lead them (normally, when not fooled by cunning experimenters) to act appropriately. However, Dickinson and colleagues claim that *only* creatures with these abilities can count as being genuinely minded, or as possessing a belief/desire cognitive architecture of the sort depicted in Figure 12.1 (Heyes and Dickinson, 1990; Dickinson and Balleine, 2000). Their reasoning is that otherwise the animal's behavior will be explicable in terms of mere innate motor-programs or learned habits created through some form of associative conditioning. These further claims are unwarranted, however, as we shall see.

## 3. NON-ASSOCIATIVE LEARNING AND NON-CAUSAL INSTRUMENTAL REASONING

Dickinson assumes that if behavior isn't caused by means/ends reasoning in the above sense, then it must either be innate or the product of associative conditioning. But this assumption is false. The animal world is *rife* with non-associative forms of learning (Gallistel, 1990). Many animals (including the Tunisian desert ant) can navigate by dead reckoning, for example. This requires the animal to compute the value of a variable each time it turns—integrating the direction in which it has just been traveling (as calculated from the polarization of the sun's light in the sky; Wehner, 1994), with an estimate of the distance traveled in that direction, to produce a representation of current position in relation to a point of origin (home base, say). This plainly isn't conditioned behavior of any sort; and nor can it be explained in terms of associative mechanisms, unless those mechanisms are organized into an architecture that is then tantamount to algorithmic symbol processing (Marcus, 2001).

Similarly, many kinds of animal will construct mental maps of their environment which they use when navigating; and they update the properties of the map through observation without conditioning (Gould and Gould, 1994).[4] Many

---

[4] Other animals navigate by the stars, or by using the Earth's magnetic field. Night-migrating birds study the sky at night when they are chicks in the nest, thereby extracting a representation of the center of rotation of the stars in the night sky. When they later leave the nest, they use this information to

animals can adopt the shortest route to a target (e.g. a source of food), guided by landmarks and covering ground never before traveled. This warrants ascribing to the animals a mental map of their environment. But they will also update the properties of the map on an on-going basis.

Food-caching birds, for example, can recall the positions of many hundreds or thousands of hidden seeds after some months; but they generally won't return to a cache location that they have previously emptied. Similarly, rats can be allowed to explore a maze on one day, finding a food reward in both a small dark room and a large white one. Next day they are given food in a (distinct) large white room, and shocked in a small dark one. When replaced back in the maze a day later they go straight to the white room and avoid the dark one (Gould and Gould, 1994). Having learned that dark rooms might deliver a shock, they have updated their representation of the properties of the maze accordingly.[5]

Many animals make swift calculations of relative reward abundance, too, in a way that isn't explicable via conditioning. For example, a flock of ducks will distribute 1:1 or 1:2 in front of two feeders throwing food at rates of 1:1 or 1:2 within one minute of the onset of feeding, during which time many ducks get no food at all, and very few of them experience rewards from both sources (Harper, 1982). Similarly, both pigeons and rats on a variable reward schedule from two different alcoves will match their behavior to the changing rates of reward. They respond *very* rapidly, closely tracking random variations in the immediately preceding rates (Dreyfus, 1991; Mark and Gallistel, 1994). They certainly aren't averaging over previous reinforcements, as associationist models would predict.

Gallistel and colleagues have argued, indeed, that even behavioral conditioning—the very heartland of associationist general-purpose learning models—is better explained in terms of the computational operations of a specialized rate-estimating foraging system (Gallistel, 1990, 2000; Gallistel and Gibbon, 2001). One simple point they make is that animals on a delayed reinforcement schedule in which the rewards only become available once the conditioned stimulus (e.g. an illuminated panel) has been present for a certain amount of time, will only respond on each occasion after a fixed proportion of the interval has elapsed. This is hard to explain if the animals are merely building an association between the illuminated panel and the reward. It seems to require, in fact, that they should construct a representation of the reinforcement intervals, and act accordingly.

guide them when flying south (in fall in the northern hemisphere) and again when flying north (in spring in the northern hemisphere). The representations in question are learned, not innate, as can be demonstrated by rearing chicks in a planetarium where they observe an artificially generated center of night-sky rotation.

[5] Similarly, western scrub jays will update the representations on their map of cached foods, and behave accordingly, once they learn independently of the different decay rates of different types of food. Thereafter they access the faster-decaying caches first. See Clayton *et al.*, 2004.

Moreover, there are many well-established facts about conditioning behavior that are hard to explain on associationist models, but that are readily explicable within a computational framework. For example, *delay* of reinforcement has no effect on rate of acquisition so long as the intervals between trials are increased by the same proportions. And the number of reinforcements required for acquisition of a new behavior isn't affected by interspersing a significant number of unreinforced trials. This is hard to explain if the animals are supposed to be building associations, since the unreinforced trials should surely *weaken* those associations. But it can be predicted if what the animals are doing is estimating relative rates of return. For the rate of reinforcement per stimulus presentation *relative to* the rate of reinforcement in background conditions remains the same, whether or not significant numbers of stimulus presentations remain unreinforced.

There are many forms of learning in animals that aren't simply acquired associations, then. And consequently there is much animal behavior that isn't mere habit, but that doesn't involve representations of causality, either. A bird who navigates to a previously established food cache, using landmarks and a mental map on which the location of the cache is represented, certainly isn't acting out of habit. But then nor does the action involve any explicit representation of the causality of the bird's own behavior. The bird doesn't have to think, 'Flying in that direction will *cause* me to be in that place.' It just has to integrate its perception of the relevant landmarks with the representations on its mental map, then keying into action the flying-in-that-direction action schema. The causation can be (and surely is) left implicit in the bird's action schemata and behavior, not explicitly represented in the bird's reasoning.[6]

But for all that, why shouldn't such animals count as exemplifying the belief/ desire architecture depicted in Figure 12.1? If the animal can put together a variety of goals with the representations on a mental map, say, and act accordingly, then why shouldn't we say that the animal behaves as it does because it *wants* something and *believes* that the desired thing can be found at a certain represented location on the map? There seems to be no good reason why we shouldn't. (And nor is there any good reason to insist that an animal only has genuine desires if its goals are acquired through learning.) Dickinson is surely misled in thinking that means/ends reasoning has to involve representations of causal, rather than merely spatial, 'means'.[7]

[6] The same is surely true of humans. When I want a beer and recall that there is a beer in the fridge, and then set out for the kitchen, I don't explicitly represent my walking as the *cause of* my getting the beer. Rather, once I know the location, I just start to walk.

[7] Bermúdez (2003), too, claims that there can be no genuine decision-making (and so no real belief/ desire psychology) in the absence of representations of instrumental causality. And this seems to be because he, too, assumes that there are no kinds of learning between associative forms of conditioning and genuine causal belief. But given the reality of a variety of kinds of spatial learning (reviewed briefly above), it seems unmotivated to insist that sophisticated navigation behaviors aren't really guided by decision-making, merely on the grounds that there are no causal beliefs involved.

The difference between rats and many other animals is just that rats (like humans) are generalist foragers and problem solvers. For this reason they have to learn the value of different foods, and they are especially good at learning what acts will cause rewards to be delivered. But unlearned values can still steer intentional behavior, guided by maps and other learned representations of location and direction. And so there can, surely, be minds that are simpler than the mind of a rat.

## 4. INSECTS (1): INFLEXIBLE FIXED-ACTION PATTERNS

How simple-minded can you be? Do insects, in particular, have beliefs and desires? Few seem inclined to answer, 'Yes.' In part this derives from a tradition of thought (traceable back at least to Descartes) of doubting whether even higher mammals such as apes and monkeys have minds. And in part it derives from the manifest rigidity of much insect behavior. The tradition I shall ignore. (Some aspects of it have been discussed briefly in section 1 above.) But the rigidity requires some comment.

We are all familiar with examples of the behavioral rigidity of insects. Consider the tick, which sits immobile on its perch until it detects butyric acid vapor, whereupon it releases its hold (often enough falling onto the bodies of mammals passing below, whose skins emit such a vapor); and then when it detects warmth, it burrows. Or there are the caterpillars who follow the light to climb trees to find food, in whom the mechanism that enables them to do this is an extremely simple one: when more light enters one eye than the other, the legs on that side of its body move slower, causing the animal to turn towards the source of the light. When artificial lighting is provided at the bottom of the trees, the caterpillars climb downwards and subsequently starve to death. And when blinded in one eye, these animals will move constantly in circles. How dumb can you be! Right?

Even apparently sophisticated and intelligent sequences of behavior can turn out, on closer investigation, to be surprisingly rigid. There is the well-known example of the Sphex wasp, that leaves a paralyzed cricket in a burrow with its eggs, so that its offspring will have something to feed on when they hatch. When it captures a cricket, it drags it to the entrance of the burrow, then leaves it outside for a moment while it enters, seemingly to check for intruders. However, if an interfering experimenter moves the cricket back a few inches while the wasp is inside, she repeats the sequence: dragging the insect to the burrow's entrance, then entering briefly once more alone. And this sequence can be made to 'loop' indefinitely many times over.

Or consider the Australian digger wasp that builds an elaborate tower-and-bell structure over the entrance of the burrow in which she lays her eggs (Gould and Gould, 1994). (The purpose of the structure is to prevent a smaller species of parasitic wasp from laying *her* eggs in the same burrow. The bell is of such a size and hung at such an angle, and worked so smooth on the inside, that the smaller wasp cannot either reach far enough in, nor gain enough purchase, to enter.) She builds the tower three of her own body-lengths high. If the tower is progressively buried while she builds, she will keep on building. But once she has finished the tower and started on the bell, the tower can be buried without her noticing—with disastrous results, since the bell will then be half on the ground, and consequently quite useless. Similarly, if a small hole is drilled in the neck of the tower, she seems to lack the resources to cope with a minor repair. Instead she builds *another* tower and bell structure, constructed on top of the hole.

In order to explain such behavior, we don't need to advance beyond the architecture of Figure 12.2. The digger wasp would seem to have an innately represented series of nested behavioral sub-routines, with the whole sequence being triggered by its own bodily state (pregnancy). Each sub-routine is guided by perceptual input, and is finished by a simple stopping-rule. But once any given stage is completed, there is no going back to make corrections or repairs. The wasp appears to have no conception of the overall goal of the sequence, nor any beliefs about the respective contributions made by the different elements. If this were the full extent of the flexibility of insect behavior, then there would be no warrant for believing that insects have minds at all.

It turns out that even flexibility of behavioral strategy isn't really sufficient for a creature to count as having a mind, indeed. For innate behavioral programs can have a conditional format. It used to be thought, for example, that all male crickets sing to attract mates. But this isn't so; and for good reason. For singing exposes crickets to predation, and also makes them targets for parasitic flies who drop their eggs on them. Many male crickets adopt the alternative strategy of waiting silently as a satellite of a singing male, and intercepting and attempting to mate with any females attracted by the song. But the two different strategies aren't fixed. A previously silent male may begin to sing if one or more of the singing males is removed (Gould and Gould, 1994).

Admittedly, such examples suggest that something *like* a decision process must be built into the structure of the behavioral program. There must be some mechanism that takes information about, for example, the cricket's own size and condition, the ratio of singing to non-singing males in the vicinity, and the loudness and vigor of their songs, and then triggers into action one behavioral strategy or the other. But computational complexity of this sort, in the mechanism that triggers innate behavior, isn't the same as saying that the insect acts from its beliefs and desires. And the latter is what mindedness requires, I am assuming.

## 5. INSECTS (2): A SIMPLE BELIEF/DESIRE PSYCHOLOGY

From the fact that *much* insect behavior results from triggering of innately represented sequences of perceptually guided activity, however, it doesn't follow that *all* does. And it is surely no requirement on mindedness that *all* the behavior of a minded creature should result from interactions of belief states with desire states. Indeed, some of our own behavior consists in fixed-action sequences— think of sneezing or coughing, for example, or of the universal human disgust reaction, which involves fixed movements of the lips and tongue seemingly designed to expel noxious substances from the mouth. So it remains a possibility that insects might have simple minds *as well as* a set of triggerable innately represented action sequences.

In effect, it remains a possibility that insects might exemplify the cognitive architecture depicted in Figure 12.1, only with an arrow added between 'body states' and 'action schemata' to subserve a dual causal route to behavior (see Figure 12.3).[8] In what follows I shall be arguing that this is indeed the case, focusing on the minds of honey bees in particular. While I won't make any attempt to demonstrate this, it seems likely that the conclusion we reach in the case of honey bees will generalize to all navigating insects. In which case belief/desire cognitive architectures are of very ancient ancestry indeed.

Like many other insects, bees use a variety of navigation systems. One is dead reckoning (integrating a sequence of directions of motion with the velocity traveled in each direction, to produce a representation of one's current location in relation to the point of origin). This in turn requires that bees can learn the expected position of the sun in the sky at any given time of day, as measured by an internal clock of some sort. Another mechanism permits bees to recognize and navigate from landmarks, either distant or local (Collett and Collett, 2002). And some researchers have claimed that bees will, in addition, construct crude mental maps of their environment from which they can navigate. (The maps have to be crude because of the poor resolution of bee eyesight. But they may still contain the relative locations of salient landmarks, such as a large free-standing tree, a forest edge, or a lake shore.)

Gould (1986) reports, for example, that when trained to a particular food source, and then carried from the hive in a dark box to new release point, the bees will fly *directly* to the food, but only if there is a significant landmark in their vicinity when they are released. (Otherwise they fly off on the compass bearing

---

[8] Note that if the 'dual visual systems' hypothesis of Milner and Goodale (1995) generalizes to other perceptual modalities and to other species, then there should really be two distinct 'percept boxes' in Fig. 12.3, one feeding into conceptual thought and decision-making, and another feeding into the action schemata so as to provide fine-grained on-line guidance of movement. See Fig. 11.1.

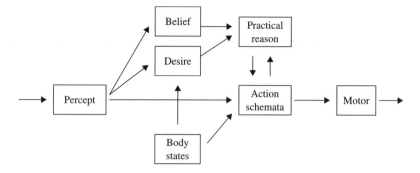

FIG 12.3 A mind with dual routes to action.

that would previously have led from the hive to the food.) While other scientists have been unable to replicate these experiments directly, Menzel *et al.* (2000) found that bees that had never foraged more than a few meters from the nest, but who were released at random points much further from it, were able to return home swiftly. They argue that this either indicates the existence of a map-like structure, built during the bees' initial orientation flights before they had begun foraging, or else the learned association of vectors-to-home with local land-marks. But either way, they claim, the spatial representations in question are allocentric rather than egocentric in character.

As is well known, honey bees dance to communicate information of various sorts to other bees. The main elements of the code have now been uncovered through patient investigation (Gould and Gould, 1988). They generally dance in a figure-of-eight pattern on a vertical surface in the dark inside the hive. The angle of movement through the center of the figure of eight, as measured from the vertical, corresponds to the angle from the expected direction of the sun for the time of day. (e.g. a dance angled at 30° to the right of vertical at midday would represent 30° west of south, in the northern hemisphere.) And the num-ber of 'waggles' made through the center of the figure of eight provides a measure of distance. (Different bee species use different innately fixed measures of waggles-to-distance.)

Honey bees have a number of innately structured learning mechanisms, in fact. They have one such mechanism for learning the position of the sun in the sky for the time of day. (This mechanism—like the human language faculty—appears to have an innate 'universal grammar'. All bees in the northern hemi-sphere are born knowing that the sun is in the east in the morning, and in the west in the afternoon; Dyer and Dickinson, 1994.) And they have another such mechanism for learning, by dead reckoning, where things are in relation to the hive. (Here it is 'visual flow' that seems to be used as the measure of distance traveled; Srinivasan *et al.*, 2000.) They *may* have yet another mechanism for constructing a mental map from a combination of landmark and directional information. (At the very least they have the capacity for learning to associate landmarks with vectors pointing to the hive; Menzel *et al.*, 2000.) And they have yet another mechanism again for decoding the dances of other bees, extracting a representation of the distance and direction of a target (generally nectar, but also pollen, water, tree sap, or the location of a potential nest site; Seeley, 1995).

Although basic bee motivations are, no doubt, innately fixed, the goals they adopt on particular occasions (e.g. whether or not to move from one foraging patch to another, whether to finish foraging and return to the hive, and whether or not to dance on reaching it) would appear to be influenced by a number of factors (Seeley, 1995). Bees are less likely to dance for dilute sources of food, for example; they are less likely to dance for the more distant of two sites of fixed value; and they are less likely to dance in the evening or when there is an approaching storm, when there is a significant chance that other bees might not be capable of completing a return trip. And careful experimentation has shown that bees scouting for a new nest site will weigh up a number of factors, including cavity volume, shape, size and direction of entrance, height above ground, dampness, draftiness, and distance away. Moreover, dancing scouts will sometimes take time out to observe the dances of others and check out their discoveries, making a comparative assessment and then dancing accordingly (Gould and Gould, 1988).

Bees don't just accept and act on any information that they are offered, either. On the contrary, they evaluate it along a number of dimensions. They check the nature and quality of the goal being offered (normally by sampling it, in the case of food). And they factor in the distance to the indicated site before deciding whether or not to fly out to it. Most strikingly, indeed, it has been claimed that bees will also integrate communicated information with the representations on their mental map, rejecting even rich sources of food that are being indicated to exist in the middle of a lake, for example.[9]

How should these bee capacities be explained? Plainly the processes in question can't be associative ones, and these forms of bee learning aren't conditioned responses to stimuli. Might the bee behavior be explained through the existence of some sort of 'subsumption architecture' (Brooks, 1986)? That is, instead of having a central belief/desire system of the sort depicted in Figure 12.3, might bees have a suite of input-to-output modular systems, one

---

[9] In these experiments two groups of bees were trained to fly to weak sugar solutions equidistant from the hive, one on a boat in the middle of a lake, and one on the lake shore. When both sugar solutions were increased dramatically, both sets of bees danced on returning to the hive. None of the receiving bees flew out across the lake. But this wasn't just a reluctance to fly over water. In experiments where the boat was moved progressively closer and closer to the far lake shore, more and more receiving bees were prepared to fly to it. See Gould and Gould, 1988.

for each different type of behavior? This suggestion is wildly implausible. For (depending on how one individuates behavior) there would have to be at least five of these input-to-output modules (perhaps dozens, if each different 'goal' amounts to a different behavior), each of which would have to duplicate many of the costly computational processes undertaken by the others. There would have to be a scouting-from-the-hive module, a returning-to-the-hive module, a deciding-to-dance-and-dancing module, a returning-to-food-source module, and a perception-of-dance-and-flying-to-food-source module. Within each of these systems essentially the same computations of direction and distance information would have to be undertaken.

The only remotely plausible interpretation of the data is that honey bees have a suite of information-generating systems that construct representations of the relative directions and distances between a variety of substances and properties and the hive,[10] as well as a number of goal-generating systems taking as inputs body-states and a variety of kinds of contextual information, and generating a current goal as output. Any one of these goal states can then in principle interact with any one of the information states to create potentially unique behavior, never before seen in the life of that particular bee. It appears, indeed, that bees exemplify the architecture depicted in Figure 12.3. In which case, there can be minds that are capable of just a few dozen types of desire, and that are capable of just a few thousand types of belief.[11] How simple-minded can you be? Pretty simple.

## 6. STRUCTURE-DEPENDENT INFERENCE

Recall, however, that the conditions on genuine mindedness that we laid down in section 1 included not just a distinction between information states and goal states, but also that these states should interact with one another to determine behavior in ways that are sensitive to their compositional structures. Now, on the face of it this condition is satisfied. For if one and the same item of directional information can be drawn on both to guide a bee in search of nectar and to guide the same bee returning to the hive, then it would seem that the bee must be capable of something resembling the following pair of practical inferences (using BEL to represent belief, DES to represent desire, MOVE to represent

---

[10] Note that this satisfies the two criteria laid down by Bennett (1964, §4) for a languageless creature to possess beliefs. One is that the creature should be capable of learning. And the other is that the belief-states should be sensitive to a variety of different kinds of evidence.

[11] The bee's capacity for representing spatial relations is by no means unlimited. There is probably an upper limit on distances that can be represented. And discriminations of direction are relatively crude (at least, by comparison with the almost pin-point accuracy of the Tunisian desert ant; see Wehner and Srinivasan, 1981). However, bees are also capable of forming a limited range of other sorts of belief, too. They come to believe that certain odors and colors signal nectar or pollen, for example (Gould and Gould, 1988).

action—normally flight, but also walking for short distances—and square brackets to represent contents).

(1)  BEL [nectar is 200 meters north of hive]

BEL [here is at hive]

DES [nectar]

MOVE [200 meters north]

(2)  BEL [nectar is 200 meters north of hive]

BEL [here is at nectar]

DES [hive]

MOVE [200 meters south]

These are inferences in which the conclusions depend upon structural relations amongst the premises.[12]

It might be suggested that we have moved too swiftly, however. For perhaps there needn't be a representation of the goal substance built explicitly into the structure of the directional information-state. To see why this might be so, notice that bees don't represent what it is that lies in the direction indicated as part of the content of their dance; and nor do observers acquire that information from the dance itself. Rather, dancing bees *display* the value on offer by carrying it; and observing bees know what is on offer by sampling some of what the dancing bee is carrying.

It might be claimed, then, that what really happens is this. An observing bee samples some of the dancing bee's load, and discovers that it is nectar, say. This keys the observer into its fly-in-the-direction-indicated sub-routine. The bee computes the necessary information from the details of the dance, and flies off towards the indicated spot. If it is lucky, it then discovers nectar-bearing flowers when it gets there and begins to forage. But at no point do the contents of goal-states and the contents of the information-states need to interact with one another.

This idea won't wash, however. Although the presence of nectar isn't explicitly represented in the content of the dance, it *does* need to be represented in the content of both the dancer's and the observer's belief-states. For recall that bees don't dance even for a rich source of nectar that is too far away (Gould and Gould, 1988). The distance information therefore needs to be integrated with the substance-information in determining the decision to dance. Equally, observers ignore dances indicating even rich sources of nectar if the indicated distances are too great. So again, the distance information derived from the dance needs to be

---

[12] Is there some way of specifying in general terms the practical inference rule that is at work here? Indeed there is. The rule might be something like the following: BEL [here is at $x$, $F$ is $m$ meters and $n°$ from $x$], DES [$F$] → MOVE [$m$ meters at $n°$]. This would require the insertion of an extra premise into argument (2) above, transforming the first premise into the form, BEL [hive is 200 meters south of nectar].

integrated with the value information before a decision can be reached. So we can conclude that not only do bees have distinct information states and goal states, but that such states interact with one other in ways that are sensitive to their contents in determining behavior. In which case bees really do exemplify the belief/desire architecture depicted in Figure 12.3, construed realistically.

One final worry remains, however. Do the belief and desire states in question satisfy what Evans (1983) calls 'the Generality Constraint'? This is a very plausible constraint on genuine (i.e. compositionally structured) concept possession. It tells us that any concept possessed by a thinker must be capable of combining appropriately with any other concept possessed by the same thinker. If you can think that *a is F* and you can think that *b is G*, then you must also be capable of thinking that *a is G* and that *b is F*. For these latter thoughts are built out of the very same components as the former ones, only combined together with one another differently.

Now, bees can represent the spatial relationships between nectar and hive, and between pollen and hive; but are they capable of representing the spatial relationships between nectar and pollen? Are bees capable of thoughts of the following form?

BEL [nectar is 200 meters north of pollen]

If not, it may be said, then bees can't be counted as genuine concept-users; and so they can't count as genuine believer/desirers, either.

It is possible that this particular example isn't a problem. Foragers returning to a nectar site to find it almost depleted might fly directly to any previously discovered foraging site that is near by; including one containing pollen rather than nectar if pollen is in sufficient demand back at the hive. But there will, almost certainly, be other relationships that are never explicitly represented. It is doubtful, for example, that any scout will ever explicitly represent the relations between one potential nest site and another (as opposed to some such belief being implicit in the information contained in a mental map). So it is doubtful whether any bee will ever form an explicit thought of the form:

BEL [cavity A is 200 meters north of cavity B]

Rather, the bees will form beliefs about the relations between each site and the colony.

Such examples aren't really a problem for the Generality Constraint, however. From the fact that bees never form beliefs of a certain kind, it doesn't follow that they *can't*. (Or at least, this doesn't follow in such a way as to undermine the claim that their beliefs are compositionally structured.) Suppose, first, that bees do construct genuine mental maps of their environment. Then it might just be that bees are only ever *interested in* the relationships amongst potential new nest sites and the existing colony, and not between the nest sites themselves. But the same sort of thing is equally true of human beings. Just as there are some spatial relationships that might be implicit in a bee's mental map, but never explicitly believed; so there are some things implicit in our beliefs about the world, but never explicitly entertained, either, because they are of no interest. My beliefs, for example, collectively entail that *mountains are less easy to eat than rocks*. (I could at least pound a rock up into powder, which I might have some chance of swallowing.) But until finding myself in need of a philosophical example, this isn't something I would ever have bothered to think. Likewise with the bees. The difference is just that bees don't do philosophy.

Suppose, on the other hand, that bees *don't* construct mental maps; rather they learn a variety of kinds of vector information linking food sources (or nest sites) and the hive, and linking landmarks and the hive. Then the reason why no bee will ever come to believe that one nest-cavity stands in a certain relation to another will have nothing to do with the alleged absence of genuine compositional structure from the bees' belief states, but will rather result from the mechanisms that give rise to new bee beliefs, combined with the bees' limited inferential abilities.

For here once again, part of the explanation is just that bees are only interested in a small sub-set of the spatial relations available to them. They only ever compute and encode the spatial relationships between desired substances and the hive, or between landmarks and the hive, not amongst the locations of those substances or those landmarks themselves. And nor do they have the inferential abilities needed to work out the vector and distance relations amongst landmarks from their existing spatial beliefs. But these facts give us no reason to claim that bees don't really employ compositionally structured belief states, which they integrate with a variety of kinds of desire state in such a way as to select appropriate behavior. And in particular, the fact that the bees lack the ability to draw inferences freely and promiscuously amongst their belief states shouldn't exclude them from having any belief states at all. Which is to say: these facts about the bees' limitations give us no reason for denying that bees possess simple minds.[13]

How simple-minded can you be, then? Pretty simple; and a good deal more simple than most philosophers seem prepared to allow.

---

[13] Having concluded that bees have minds, and so are sometimes perceptually conscious of their environment (i.e. that they are both *creature*-conscious, and have perceptual states that are first-order *access*-conscious, in the language introduced in Chs. 1 and 3 of this volume), can we also conclude that their struggles and sufferings are appropriate objects of sympathy and moral concern? If bees are belief/desire reasoners, then they will be capable of simple forms of frustration of desire. And then if the arguments of Ch. 10 are sound, their frustrations will be appropriate objects of sympathy. But whether sympathy for their *sufferings* is apposite—along the lines argued in Ch. 11—isn't quite so simple. (Tye, 1997, leaps to this conclusion too swiftly.) For that will depend upon whether their pain perceptions feed into belief-formation and/or their practical reasoning system, on the one hand, or whether those percepts serve merely to guide a set of innate fixed-action patterns, on the other. So it will depend, in effect, on whether pain perceptions are made available to the upper (cognitive) pathway in the Fig. 12.3 architecture, or only to the lower (non-cognitive) one. And we can't read this straight off the behavior itself.

# BIBLIOGRAPHY

Achinstein, P. 1983. *The Nature of Explanation*. Oxford University Press.

Armstrong, D. 1968. *A Materialist Theory of the Mind*. Routledge.

—— 1984. Consciousness and causality. In D. Armstrong and N. Malcolm, *Consciousness and Causality*. Blackwell.

Aydede, M., and Güzeldere, G. 2005. Cognitive architecture, concepts, and introspection. *Noûs* 39.

Baars, B. 1988. *A Cognitive Theory of Consciousness*. Cambridge University Press.

—— 1997. *In the Theatre of Consciousness: The workspace of the mind*. Oxford University Press.

Bach-y-Rita, P. 1995. *Non-Synaptic Diffusion Neurotransmission and Late Brain Reorganization*. Demos Press.

—— and Kercel, S. 2003. Sensory substitution and the human-machine interface. *Trends in Cognitive Sciences* 7: 541–6.

Balog, K. 1999. Conceivability, possibility, and the mind–body problem. *Philosophical Review* 108: 497–528.

Baron-Cohen, S. 1995. *Mindblindness*. MIT Press.

Bennett, J. 1964. *Rationality: An essay towards an analysis*. Routledge.

Bermúdez, J. 1995. Non-conceptual content. *Mind and Language* 10: 333–69.

—— 1998. *The Paradox of Self-Consciousness*. MIT Press.

—— 2003. *Thinking without Words*. Oxford University Press.

Berry, D., and Broadbent, D. 1984. On the relationship between task performance and associated verbalizable knowledge. *Quarterly Journal of Experimental Psychology* 36A: 209–31.

—— 1987. Explanation and verbalization in a computer assisted search task. *Quarterly Journal of Experimental Psychology* 39A: 585–609.

Block, N. 1978. Troubles with functionalism. In C. Savage (ed.), *Minnesota Studies in the Philosophy of Science* 9.

—— 1986. Advertisement for a semantics for psychology. *Midwest Studies in Philosophy* 10: 615–78.

—— 1993. Holism, hyper-analyticity, and hyper-compositionality. *Mind and Language* 8: 1–26.

—— 1995. A confusion about the function of consciousness. *Behavioral and Brain Sciences* 18: 227–47.

—— 2002. The harder problem of consciousness. *Philosophical Review* 99: 391–425.

—— and Stalnaker, R. 1999. Conceptual analysis, dualism and the explanatory gap. *Philosophical Review* 108: 1–46.

Botterill, G., and Carruthers, P. 1999. *The Philosophy of Psychology*. Cambridge University Press.

Brooks, R. 1986. A robust layered control system for a mobile robot. *IEEE Journal of Robotics and Automation* RA-2: 14–23.

Burge, T. 1996. Our entitlement to self-knowledge. *Proceedings of the Aristotelian Society* 96: 91–116.

Byrne, A. 2001. Review of *Phenomenal Consciousness* by Peter Carruthers. *Mind* 110: 440–2.

Byrne, R. 1995. *The Thinking Ape*. Oxford University Press.

—— and Whiten, A. (eds.) 1988. *Machiavellian Intelligence*. Oxford University Press.

—— (eds.) 1998. *Machiavellian Intelligence II: Evaluations and extensions*. Cambridge University Press.

Carruthers, P. 1989. Brute experience. *Journal of Philosophy* 86: 258–69.

—— 1992*a*. Consciousness and concepts. *Aristotelian Society Proceedings*, supp. vol. 66: 41–59.

—— 1992*b*. *The Animals Issue: moral theory in practice*. Cambridge University Press.

—— 1996. *Language, Thought and Consciousness*. Cambridge University Press.

—— 1997. Fragmentary versus reflexive consciousness. *Mind and Language* 12: 180–194.

—— 1998: Thinking in language?: Evolution and a modularist possibility. In P. Carruthers and J. Boucher (eds.), *Language and Thought*. Cambridge University Press.

—— 2000. *Phenomenal Consciousness: a naturalistic theory*. Cambridge University Press.

—— 2002. The cognitive functions of language. & Author's response: Modularity, Language, and the flexibility of thought. *Behavioral and Brain Sciences* 25: 657–719.

—— 2004. Practical reasoning in a modular mind. *Mind and Language* 19, 259–78.

—— and Smith, P. K. (eds.) 1996. *Theories of Theories of Mind*. Cambridge University Press.

Caston, V. 2002. Aristotle on consciousness. *Mind* 111: 751–815.

Chalmers, D. 1996. *The Conscious Mind*. Oxford University Press.

—— 1999. Materialism and the metaphysics of modality. *Philosophy and Phenomenological Research* 59: 473–96.

—— and Jackson, F. 2001. Conceptual analysis and reductive explanation. *Philosophical Review* 110: 315–60.

Chomsky, N. 1988. *Language and Problems of Knowledge*. MIT Press.

—— 1995. *The Minimalist Program*. MIT Press.

Churchland, P. 1981. Eliminative materialism and the propositional attitudes. *Journal of Philosophy* 78: 67–90.

Clark, A. 1998. Magic words: How language augments human computation. In P. Carruthers and J. Boucher (eds.), *Language and Thought*. Cambridge University Press.

—— 2002. Visual experience and motor action: are the bonds too tight? *Philosophical Review* 110, 495–520.

Clayton, N., Emory, N., and Dickinson, A. 2004. The rationality of animal memory: the cognition of caching. In S. Hurley (ed.), *Animal Rationality*. Oxford University Press.

Clegg, S. 2002. Content and infant consciousness. Paper presented at the sixth conference of the Association for the Scientific Study of Consciousness. Barcelona.

Clements, W., and Perner, J. 1994. Implicit understanding of belief. *Cognitive Development* 9: 377–97.

Cohen, L. J. 1993. *An Essay on Belief and Acceptance*. Oxford University Press.

Collett, T., and Collett, M. 2002. Memory use in insect visual navigation. *Nature Reviews: Neuroscience* 3: 542–52.

Cowie, A., and Stoerig, P. 1995. Blind-sight in monkeys. *Nature* 373: 247–9.

Crane, T. 1998. Intentionality as the mark of the mental. In A. O'Hear (ed.), *Current Issues in Philosophy of Mind*. Cambridge University Press.

Crick, F. 1994. *The Astonishing Hypothesis: the scientific search for the soul*. Scribner's Sons.

—— and Koch, C. 1990. Towards a neurobiological theory of consciousness. *Seminars in the Neurosciences* 2: 263–75.

Damasio, A. 1994. *Descartes' Error*. Picador Press.

Davidson, D. 1975. Thought and talk. In S. Guttenplan (ed.), *Mind and Language*. Oxford University Press.

—— 1982. Rational animals. *Dialectica* 36: 317–27.

—— 1987. Knowing one's own mind. *Proceedings and Addresses of the American Philosophical Association* 60: 441–458.

Davies, M. 1993. Introduction: Consciousness in philosophy. In M. Davies and G. Humphreys (eds.), *Consciousness*. Blackwell.

Dennett, D. 1978a. Towards a cognitive theory of consciousness. In his *Brainstorms*. Harvester Press.

—— 1978b. Why you can't make a computer that feels pain. In his *Brainstorms*. Harvester Press.

—— 1978c. How to Change your Mind. In his *Brainstorms*. Harvester Press.

—— 1987. *The Intentional Stance*. MIT Press.

—— 1991. *Consciousness Explained*. Allen Lane.

—— 1995. Consciousness: more like fame than television. Paper delivered at a Munich conference. Published in German as: Bewusstsein hat mehr mit Ruhm als mit Fernsehen zu tun. In C. Maar, E. Pöppel, and T. Christaller (eds.), *Die Technik auf dem Weg zur Seele*. Munich: Rowohlt, 1996.

—— and Kinsbourne, M. 1992. Time and the observer: the where and when of consciousness in the brain. *Behavioral and Brain Sciences* 15: 183–247.

Dickinson, A., and Balleine, B. 1994. Motivational control of goal-directed action. *Animal Learning and Behavior* 22: 1–18.

—— —— 2000. Causal cognition and goal-directed action. In C. Heyes and L. Huber (eds.), *The Evolution of Cognition*. MIT Press.

—— and Charnock, D. 1985. Contingency effects with maintained instrumental reinforcement. *Quarterly Journal of Experimental Psychology* 37B: 397–416.

—— and Shanks, D. 1995. Instrumental action and causal representation. In D. Sperber, D. Premack, and A. Premack (eds.), *Causal Cognition*. Oxford University Press.

Dretske, F. 1993. Conscious experience. *Mind* 102: 263–83.

—— 1995. *Naturalizing the Mind*. MIT Press.

Dreyfus, L. 1991. Local shifts in relative reinforcement rate and time allocation on concurrent schedules. *Journal of Experimental Psychology* 17: 486–502.

Dummett, M. 1981. *The Interpretation of Frege's Philosophy*. Duckworth.

—— 1991. *Frege and Other Philosophers*. Oxford University Press.

Dyer, F., and Dickinson, J. 1994. Development of sun compensation by honeybees. *Proceedings of the National Academy of Science* 91: 4471–4.

Ericsson, A., and Simon, H. 1980. Verbal reports as data. *Psychological Review* 87: 215–51.

—— —— 1993. *Protocol Analysis: Verbal reports as data*. (Revised edition.) MIT Press.

Evans, G. 1982. *The Varieties of Reference*. Oxford University Press.

Evans, J., and Over, D. 1996. *Rationality and Reasoning*. Psychology Press.

Feinberg, J. 1977. Harm and self-interest. In P. Hacker and J. Raz (eds.), *Law, Morality and Society*. Oxford University Press.

Feinberg, J. 1985. Psychological egoism. In his *Reasons and Responsibility*. McGraw Hill.

Flanagan, O. 1992. *Consciousness Reconsidered*. MIT Press.

Fodor, J. 1978. Propositional attitudes. *The Monist* 61: 501–23.

—— 1983. *The Modularity of Mind*. MIT Press.

—— 1987. *Psychosemantics*. MIT Press

—— 1990. *A Theory of Content and Other Essays*. MIT Press.

—— 1998. There are no recognitional concepts, not even RED. In his *In Critical Condition*. MIT Press.

—— and Lepore, E. 1992. *Holism: a shopper's guide*. Blackwell.

Frankish, K. 1998a. A matter of opinion. *Philosophical Psychology* 11: 423–42.

—— 1998b. Natural language and virtual belief. In P. Carruthers and J. Boucher (eds.), *Language and Thought*. Cambridge University Press.

—— 2004. *Mind and Supermind*. Cambridge University Press.

Gallistel, R. 1990. *The Organization of Learning*. MIT Press.

—— 2000. The replacement of general-purpose learning models with adaptively specialized learning modules. In M. Gazzaniga (ed.), *The New Cognitive Neurosciences/ 2nd edn*. MIT Press.

—— and Gibbon, J. 2001. Time, rate and conditioning. *Psychological Review* 108: 289–344.

Gazzaniga, M. 1994. Consciousness and the cerebral hemispheres. In M. Gazzaniga (ed.), *The Cognitive Neurosciences*. MIT Press.

—— 1998. *The Mind's Past*. California University Press.

Gennaro, R. 1996. *Consciousness and Self-Consciousness*. John Benjamins Publishing.

Gigerenzer, G., Todd, P., and the ABC Research Group. 1999. *Simple Heuristics that Make Us Smart*. Oxford University Press.

Gopnik, A. 1993. How we know our minds: the illusion of first-person knowledge of intentionality. *Behavioral and Brain Sciences* 16: 1–14.

Gordon, R. 1986. 'Radical' simulationism. In P. Carruthers and P. Smith (eds.), *Theories of Theories of Mind*. Cambridge University Press.

Gould, J. 1986. The locale map of bees: do insects have cognitive maps? *Science* 232: 861–3.

—— and Gould, C. 1988. *The Honey Bee*. Scientific American Library.

—— 1994. *The Animal Mind*. Scientific American Library.

Grice, P. 1957. Meaning. *Philosophical Review* 66: 377–88.

—— 1969. Utterer's meaning and intention. *Philosophical Review* 78: 147–77.

Harman, G. 1990. The intrinsic quality of experience. In J. Tomberlin (ed.), *Philosophical Perspectives: Action theory and philosophy of mind*. Ridgeview.

Harper, D. 1982. Competitive foraging in mallards. *Animal Behavior* 30: 575–84.

Heal, J. 1994. Moore's paradox: a Wittgensteinian approach. *Mind* 103: 5–24.

Hempel, C. 1965. *Aspects of Scientific Explanation*. Free Press.

Hermer-Vazquez, L., Spelke, E., and Katsnelson, A. 1999. Sources of flexibility in human cognition: Dual-task studies of space and language. *Cognitive Psychology* 39: 3–36.

Heys, C., and Dickinson, A. 1990. The intentionality of animal action. *Mind and Language* 5: 87–104.

Horgan, T., and Woodward, J. 1985. Folk psychology is here to stay. *Philosophical Review* 94: 197–225.

Humphrey, N. 1986. *The Inner Eye*. Faber & Faber.

Hurlburt, R. 1990. *Sampling Normal and Schizophrenic Inner Experience*. Plenum Press.

—— 1993. *Sampling Inner Experience with Disturbed Affect*. Plenum Press.

Hurley, S. 1998. *Consciousness in Action*. Harvard University Press.

Jackson, F. 1982. Epiphenomenal qualia. *Philosophical Quarterly* 32: 127–36.

—— 1986. What Mary didn't know. *Journal of Philosophy* 83: 291–95.

—— 1998. *From Metaphysics to Ethics*. Oxford University Press.

Jacob, P., and Jeannerod, M. 2003. *Ways of Seeing*. Oxford University Press.

Kelly, S. 2001. Demonstrative concepts and experience. *Philosophical Review* 110: 397–420.

Kim, J. 1974. Non-causal connections. *Nous* 8: 41–52.

Kirk, R. 1994. *Raw Feeling*. Oxford University Press.

Kosslyn, S. 1994. *Image and Brain*. MIT Press.

Kriegel, U. 2003. Consciousness as intransitive self-consciousness: two views and an argument. *Canadian Journal of Philosophy* 33: 103–32.

Kripke, S. 1972. Naming and necessity. In G. Harman and D. Davidson (eds.), *Semantics of Natural Language*. Reidel.

Laurence, S., and Margolis, E. 2003. Concepts and conceptual analysis. *Philosophy and Phenomenological Research* 67: 253–82.

Levelt, W. 1989. *Speaking: from intention to articulation*. MIT Press.

Levine, J. 1983. Materialism and qualia: the explanatory gap. *Pacific Philosophical Quarterly* 64: 354–61.

—— 1993. On leaving out what it's like. In M. Davies and G. Humphrey (eds.), *Consciousness*. Blackwell.

—— 2001. *Purple Haze*. Oxford University Press.

Lewis, D. 1966. An argument for the identity theory. *Journal of Philosophy* 63: 17–25.

—— 1969. *Convention*. Blackwell.

—— 1980. Mad pain and Martian pain. In N. Block (ed.), *Readings in Philosophy of Psychology*, vol. I. Harvard University Press.

Lewis, D. 1986. Causal explanation. In his *Philosophical Papers*, vol. 2. Oxford University Press.

Loar, B. 1981. *Mind and Meaning*. Cambridge University Press.

—— 1982. Conceptual role and truth-conditions. *Notre Dame Journal of Formal Logic* 23: 272–83.

—— 1990. Phenomenal states. In J. Tomberlin (ed.), *Philosophical Perspectives: Action theory and philosophy of mind*. Ridgeview.

—— 1997. Phenomenal states. In N. Block, O. Flanagan, and G. Güzeldere (eds.), *The Nature of Consciousness*. MIT Press.

Locke, J. 1690. *An Essay Concerning Human Understanding*. Many editions now available.

Luntley, M. 2003. Non-conceptual content and the sound of music. *Mind and Language* 18: 402–26.

Lurz, R. 2002. Reducing consciousness by making it hot. *Psyche* 8. http://psyche.cs. monash.edu.au/v8/

—— 2005. Conscious beliefs and desires. In U. Kriegel and K. Williford (eds.), *Consciousness and Self-Reference*. MIT Press.

Lycan, W. 1987. *Consciousness*. MIT Press.

—— 1996. *Consciousness and Experience*. MIT Press.

Mackie, J. 1977. *Ethics: Inventing right and wrong*. Penguin Press.

Malcolm, N. 1984. Consciousness and causality. In D. Armstrong and N. Malcolm (eds.), *Consciousness and Causality*. Blackwell.

Marcel, A. 1998. Blindsight and shape perception: deficit of visual consciousness or of visual function? *Brain* 121: 1565–88.

Marcus, G. 2001. *The Algebraic Mind*. MIT Press.

Mark, T., and Gallistel, R. 1994. The kinetics of matching. *Journal of Experimental Psychology* 20: 1–17.

Martin, M. 1995. Bodily awareness: a sense of ownership. In J. Bermúdez, N. Eilan, and A. Marcel (eds.), *The Body and the Self*. MIT Press.

May, R. 1985. *Logical Form*. MIT Press.

McCulloch, G. 1988. What it is like. *Philosophical Quarterly* 38: 1–19.

—— 1993. The very idea of the phenomenological. *Aristotelian Society Proceedings* 93: 39–58.

McDowell, J. 1994. *Mind and World*. MIT Press.

McGinn, C. 1982. The structure of content. In A. Woodfield (ed.), *Thought and Object*. Oxford University Press.

—— 1989. *Mental Content*. Blackwell.

—— 1991. *The Problem of Consciousness*. Blackwell.

Menzel, R., Brandt, R., Gumbert, A., Komischke, B., and Kunze, J. 2000. Two spatial memories for honeybee navigation. *Proceedings of the Royal Society: London B* 267: 961–6.

Millikan, R. 1984. *Language, Thought, and Other Biological Categories*. MIT Press.

—— 1986. Thoughts without laws: Cognitive science with content. *Philosophical Review* 95: 47–80.

—— 1989. Biosemantics. *Journal of Philosophy* 86: 281–97.

Milner, D., and Goodale, M. 1995. *The Visual Brain in Action*. Oxford University Press.

Mumford, S. 1998. *Dispositions*. Oxford University Press.

Nagel, E. 1961. *The Structure of Science*. Routledge.

Nagel, T. 1974. What is it like to be a bat? *Philosophical Review* 82: 435–56.

—— 1979. Death. In his *Mortal Questions*. Cambridge University Press.

—— 1986. *The View from Nowhere*. Oxford University Press.

Nelkin, N. 1996. *Consciousness and the Origins of Thought*. Cambridge University Press.

Nichols, S., and Stich, S. 2003. *Mindreading: an integrated account of pretence, self-awareness, and understanding of other minds*. Oxford University Press.

Nisbett, R., and Ross. L. 1980. *Human Inference*. Prentice-Hall.

—— and Wilson, T. 1977. Telling more than we can know. *Psychological Review* 84: 231–95.

Papineau, D. 1987. *Reality and Representation*. Blackwell.

—— 1993. *Philosophical Naturalism*. Blackwell.

—— 2002. *Thinking about Consciousness*. Oxford University Press.

Parfit, D. 1984. *Reasons and Persons*. Oxford University Press.

Paulescu, E., Frith, D., and Frackowiak, R. 1993. The neural correlates of the verbal component of working memory. *Nature* 362: 342–5.

Peacocke, C. 1986. *Thoughts*. Blackwell.

—— 1992. *A Study of Concepts*. MIT Press.

Pinker, S. 1994. *The Language Instinct*. Penguin Press.

Povinelli, D. 1996. Chimpanzee theory of mind? In P. Carruthers and P. K. Smith (eds.), *Theories of Theories of Mind*. Cambridge University Press.

—— 2000. *Folk Physics for Apes*. Oxford University Press.

Prinz, J. 2004. *Gut Reactions: a perceptual theory of emotions*. Oxford University Press.

Ramachandran, V., and Blakeslee, S. 1998. *Phantoms in the Brain*. Fourth Estate.

—— Rogers-Ramachandran, D., and Cobb, S. 1995. Touching the phantom limb. *Nature* 377: 489–90.

Rolls, E. 1999. *Emotion and the Brain*. Oxford University Press.

Rosenthal, D. 1986. Two concepts of consciousness. *Philosophical Studies* 49: 329–59.

—— 1993. Thinking that one thinks. In M. Davies and G. Humphreys (eds.), *Consciousness*. Blackwell.

—— 1997. A theory of consciousness. In N. Block, O. Flanagan, and G. Güzeldere (eds.), *The Nature of Consciousness*. MIT Press.

Ruben, D-H. 1990. *Explaining Explanation*. Routledge.

Russell, B. 1921. *The Analysis of Mind*. Allen & Unwin.

Salmon, W. 1984. *Scientific Explanation and the Causal Structure of the World*. Princeton University Press.

—— 1989. Four decades of scientific explanation. In P. Kitcher and W. Salmon (eds.), *Minnesota Studies in Philosophy of Science* 13.

Scanlon, T. 1982. Contractualism and utilitarianism. In A. Sen and B. Williams (eds.), *Utilitarianism and beyond*. Cambridge University Press.

Schaffner, K. 1976. Reductionism in biology. In R. Cohen *et al.* (eds.), *Philosophy of Science Association 1974.* Reidel.

Seager, W. 2001. Comments on Carruthers. *SWIF discussion forum.* www.swif. uniba.it/lei/mind/forums/forum2.htm

Searle, J. 1983. *Intentionality.* Cambridge University Press.

—— 1992. *The Rediscovery of the Mind.* MIT Press.

—— 1997. *The Mystery of Consciousness.* A New York Review Book.

Seeley, T. 1995. *The Wisdom of the Hive: the social physiology of honey bee colonies.* Harvard University Press.

Shallice, T. 1988. *From Neuropsychology to Mental Structure.* Cambridge University Press.

Shergill, S., Brammer, M., Fukuda, R., Bullmore, E., Amaro, E., Murray, R., and McGuire, P. 2002. Modulation of activity in temporal cortex during generation of inner speech. *Human Brain Mapping* 16: 219–27.

Shoemaker, S. 1988. On knowing one's own mind. *Philosophical Perspectives* 2: 183–209.

—— 1990. First-person access. *Philosophical Perspectives* 4: 187–214.

Shriver, A., and Allen, C. 2005. Consciousness might matter very much. *Philosophical Psychology* 18.

Siewert, C. 1998. *The Significance of Consciousness.* Princeton University Press.

Singer, P. 1979. *Practical Ethics.* 2nd edn., 1993. Cambridge University Press.

Sklar, L. 1967. Types of inter-theoretic reduction. *British Journal for the Philosophy of Science* 18: 109–24.

Smith, J., Shields, W., and Washburn, D. 2003. The comparative psychology of uncertainty monitoring and meta-cognition. *Behavioral and Brain Sciences* 26: 317–73.

Smith, P. 1996. Language and the evolution of mind-reading. In P. Carruthers and P. Smith (eds.), *Theories of Theories of Mind.* Cambridge University Press.

Stanovich, K. 1999. *Who is Rational? Studies of individual differences in reasoning.* Laurence Erlbaum.

Stich, S. 1983. *From Folk Psychology to Cognitive Science.* MIT Press.

Stoerig, P., and Cowie, A. 1997. Blind-sight in man and monkey. *Brain* 120: 535–59.

Sturgeon, S. 1994. The epistemic view of subjectivity. *Journal of Philosophy* 91: 221–35.

—— 2000. *Matters of Mind.* Routledge.

Tye, M. 1995. *Ten Problems of Consciousness.* MIT Press.

—— 1997. The problem of simple minds. *Philosophical Studies* 88: 289–317.

—— 1999. Phenomenal consciousness: the explanatory gap as a cognitive illusion. *Mind* 108: 705–25.

—— 2000. *Consciousness, Color and Content.* MIT Press.

van Fraassen, B. 1980. *The Scientific Image.* Oxford University Press.

Vygotsky, L. 1934. *Thought and Language* (trans. Kozulin.) MIT Press, 1986.

Walker, S. 1983. *Animal Thought.* Routledge.

Warren, V. 1985. Explaining masochism. *Journal for the Theory of Social Behavior* 15: 103–29.

Wehner, R. 1994. The polarization-vision project. In K. Schildberger and N. Elsner (eds.), *The Neural Basis of Behavioral Adaptations*. Gustav Fischer.

—— and Srinivasan, M. 1981. Searching behavior of desert ants. *Journal of Comparative Physiology* 142: 315–38.

Weiskrantz, L. 1986. *Blindsight*. Oxford University Press.

—— 1997. *Consciousness Lost and Found*. Oxford University Press.

Welch, R. 1978. *Perceptual Modification*. Academic Press.

Whorf, B. 1956. *Language, Thought, and Reality*. Wiley.

Wilson, T. 1985. Strangers to ourselves. In J. Harvey and G. Weary (eds.), *Attribution: basic issues and applications*. Academic Press.

—— 2002. *Strangers to Ourselves*. Harvard University Press.

—— and Stone, J. 1985. Limitations of self-knowledge. In P. Shaver (ed.), *Self, Situations and Social Behavior*. Sage.

—— Hull, J., and Johnson, J. 1981. Awareness and self-perception: verbal reports on internal states. *Journal of Personality and Social Psychology* 40: 53–71.

Wittgenstein, L. 1921. *Tractatus Logico-Philosophicus*. Routledge.

—— 1953. *Philosophical Investigations*. Blackwell.

Young, J. 1986. *Philosophy and the Brain*. Oxford University Press.

# INDEX